Not Recommended for College

Not Recommended for College

Marty Urand

To order additional copies of this book, contact:
Xlibris
1-888-795-4274
www.Xlibris.com
Orders@Xlibris.com
533964

Contents

Quarter One
Growing Up in the city
1943-1961

Quarter Two
College & Basketball
1962-1966

Third Quarter
My Career

1965-2004

The Fourth Quarter
Retirement
2004 - ?

Not Recommended for College

The words on the following pages represent the "dash" between the two dates seen on most grave monuments at cemeteries. The story is a factual chronological order of events that *"God only knows"* why they occurred within Marty's life!

The story begins in the city of New York (Rochester Avenue, Brooklyn) and will end in Texas, hopefully in no less than twenty five years (2035). Since basketball was the ticket for traveling from New York to Texas, the story is told in quarters, like a basketball game.

It is a story of a kid who finds out that there is a fine line between "a leader and someone who is being chased!"

A leader on the streets as well in sports, organizations, and schools, but who was chased all the way to Texas because of education! His lack of education and loss of his four year old brother left him down, but not out. It took caring people to end that chase and hardship by giving him their compassion, love, and most of all high expectations for achieving a better life.

Those who reached out to him through their careers such as school custodians, a singer, N.Y. Police Department (P.A.L.), a college professor, and coaches, blessed him! But best of all, it was a fictitious coach who filled his head as he tried to learn how to read through a non-traditional method.

Marty was able to build a life based on a fictional coach within the Chip Hilton Series. Not only did this series teach Marty the basics of reading, but this series inspired him to enter coaching as a lifelong profession.

Not Recommended for College was an outcome, based on a set of beliefs that a school system with counselors lacking high expectations for their students can often contribute to their students lack of success.

Marty's life took many twists and turns. The "Not Recommended for College" stamp which appeared on his high school transcript haunted him for many years. He was determined to overcome that repelling message and prove not only should he be recommended for college, but he would spend decades teaching and inspiring other students to rise above their "labels" and put forth the effort to achieve greatness.

"Circumstances don't make you, they reveal you!"
Chuck Pagano, Colts Head Coach

QUARTER ONE

Growing Up in the city

1943-1961

East Brooklyn

"Back in the day", the best place to play basketball, or even to learn to play basketball, was in the city of New York. The Knicks had been in New York long before I came into play in 1943, on Rochester Avenue in Brooklyn. My first venue was in our apartment across the street from Tilden High School, where my mother had attended school for two years before going to work for the rest of her life.

Evelyn and Jack Urand (1942)

My Dad was in Panama representing our country in the U.S. Army, but "The City" was too much for him to leave behind. He was discharged because of a busted eardrum, and he returned to New York when I was two years old, living with my mother in East Brooklyn.

I learned many of my eastside traits from my dad, one of which was to fight and scrap for whatever I wanted ... even when I was fighting for things that did not belong to me! My first real physical fight occurred in pre-school as I pushed my way to the front of a block-built truck that several of us had constructed together. I knew there was only one place on this "truck" for a driver, and I decided that no matter what, the driver would be me. All it took was a push here and a shove there before I would end up getting my way. I enjoyed these fast and easy lessons, and the easiest lesson for me to learn was to fight for what I wanted.

In life you are either a passenger
or a pilot, it is your choice.
Author unknown

MARTY URAND

To me, being a leader meant always being the "driver" every day!

I already knew that attending school and studying was going to hamper my "style". Again, like my dad, I liked living on the edge. Even at a young age, it was fun getting away with things that even I knew were wrong!

For example, when I was five or six years old living on Rochester Avenue in a fifth floor apartment with no air conditioning, during the hot city summers I raced downstairs when I saw the iceman coming down the street on a horse drawn wagon filled with blocks of ice. He sold either full blocks or half blocks of ice and even carried them to his customers' apartments. The iceman's customers leaned out of their apartment windows, yelling down to him with their "ice" orders as he pulled the wagon into the curb to keep it from rolling. Then, using his large steel calipers with two extremely sharp pointed claws, he dug into the ice and grabbed an ice block. To keep the ice from melting, he covered the ice blocks with large sheets of rawhide while he delivered the ice blocks to his customers. He could carry several heavy five or ten-cent blocks that rested on a small piece of rawhide lying over his shoulder.

Once the ice was securely on the iceman's shoulder, he entered our apartment building and delivered the ice to his customers. While he was delivering his blocks of ice, I scrambled down the five flights of stairs, grabbed a half block of ice from his wagon, and with "my" block of ice I quickly scrambled back up those five flights of stairs, and ran back into our apartment. I usually heard a mixture of yells from those who saw me, "Hey kid, you're going to hell," or "That a boy, hold it tight!" I never knew how people would react; it was always such a mixed bag on each adventure.

When I finally made it into our apartment, I placed the ice on a large metal pan and set a small fan facing the ice away from the window so the cold air would not escape. Then I got my mom, led her into the kitchen, and sat her down in front of the cold "iced" air. She must have loved it because she never once asked where this ice came from or how I paid for it.

I loved standing behind her, with my arms around her neck and my cheek next to hers as we enjoyed the magnificent cool breeze together.

I would have to say that the ice stint was one of many "wrong doings" that occurred during my youth. The excitement was a great thrill for me! I remember my friends always telling stories of how they did this and that, but they were always group things. I took great pride in accomplishing this ice caper by myself, and I never shared this achievement with others. Keeping this to myself made it special. I had a satisfied smugness, a self-dignity in knowing what I had done. I felt more grown up because I did something I thought was great, and I was able to keep it special and secret from the others.

P.S. 208

My parents, Evelyn and Jack, had an ongoing battle on where to live within the city. My dad of course wanted to bring our family to the Seward Park High School area (the Eastside) where he had attended two years of high school. Moreover, my mother, having had enough of Rochester Avenue, wanted to establish residency in a more respectable area of Brooklyn. And as usual, she won that argument, and Ebbets Field, Empire Boulevard, Carroll Street, and Utica Avenue; here we came.

My first elementary school, PS. 208, was directly across the street from Bellevue Hospital. I did not know what kind of hospital Bellevue was, but whenever my mom disagreed with my dad, he always told my mom that someday she would land up at Bellevue. It wasn't until I was older that I realized Bellevue hospital was a mental institution... and I do believe my dad really thought my mother was crazy for wanting a different life. My dad thought the eastside area was good enough for him, so he believed it should be good enough for our family.

My elementary years were super! School was coloring, counting, adding, and of course, recess and P.E. – they were great. My personality was coming around as fast as my running speed, and let's not forget my fighting ability and my quick temper.

My first sport to play was baseball, or stickball to be exact. For stickball, all we needed was a broomstick and a Spalding ball (Pennsylvania Pinkie). Then we would draw a box on a wall, add a pitcher, and we were ready to play the beginning version of stickball. I was not yet allowed in the streets like the older boys who played the regular version of stickball: hitting for sewers, which were circular drainage covers located in the middle of the street. Stickball became a way of life for me and "learning on the streets" was a heck of a lot more fun and exciting than going to school.

It got worse at school when I began having trouble with spelling and reading. It just was not coming to me, and I became embarrassed when forced to read aloud in front of my classmates. Their laughing was getting to me, and there was no way I could dodge their snickering or use my speed to run from it. Therefore, I used my next best skill, which was to fight and hit those who laughed at me. Then a bell went off in my head, it was so revolutionary! I finally figured it out. I used the maneuver of fighting to stop the other kids from laughing at me for the remainder of elementary and middle school: it was that good!

Mom certainly wanted me to stand out!
The only boy wearing a bow tie,
front row on the right!

This is how my plan worked: when the teacher called my name to read a paragraph in class, all I had to do was get angry with a classmate. If the teacher let that slide, I quickly slapped the closest kid near me. The teacher always reacted to that and would immediately send me to the principal's office. For several weeks, each day around mid-morning, I intentionally got in trouble and again "found" myself in the principal's office. I quietly waited there until I was forgotten. Then I would sneak out, walk down to the cafeteria for lunch, and after lunch, I would sneak back in and rejoin my regular class as if nothing had ever happened. My daily trips to the front office continued until the teachers caught on and my parents were let in on the scheme of things.

My father was furious and had only one method of dealing with things that "pissed" him off. He would slap first and ask questions later. He was mainly upset because he did not know how to handle me and the problems I kept getting myself into. My dad had never had a father who watched over his activities, and subsequently, my dad had run wild on the Eastside with no parental involvement. It was several years later when I realized that not having had guidance from his father, or any other positive role models on parenting, my dad used his own father's discipline tactics of yelling and becoming physically aggressive.

But in reality, my mother was the real disciplinarian in our family. She had a way of screaming that sounded like she could fit right in with the "best" on Delancey Street, a street in New York where sidewalk sellers of all kinds screamed, screeched, and yelled while trying to get the pedestrians' attention in order to sell their "stuff".

Moreover, my mom knew the type of punishments that could really get to a seven-year-old boy. The worst punishment my mother ever dealt me was to force me to practice reading with my dad. If I mispronounced several words, he would grumble, then yell, and finally jump up screaming. I ran, crying, knowing that if he caught me he would kick the "crap" out of me for not remembering what he had just explained to me.

Although neither of my parents were recreational readers, my dad had an amazingly advanced vocabulary and was a master at solving crossword puzzles. He solved crossword puzzles quickly and more accurately than all of those who continually challenged him. He "never let a crossword puzzle" get the best of him".

Unfortunately, none of his high-level vocabulary was reflected in anything else he did. He was a whiz in efficiently solving his crossword puzzles in record time, but he never transferred this knowledge to an interest in reading. (Unless it was a paper involving betting at the horse track.)

My First Bonus

At nine years of age, I found a unique way to make some extra money. I always carried a new Spalding in my back pocket, and having this ball gave me a feeling of independence or for nothing else, I became a good friend to those who could not afford their own Spalding.

My first bonus (money earned for services provided) came at Ebbets Field, where the old Brooklyn Dodgers played their home games. However, there was a small problem for me to get to the ballpark... the field was about five miles away from my home. However, this problem was quickly resolved when I saw two kids around 12 years old holding onto the back of a trolley as it rolled along the tracks.

The trolleys had wires extending from two large vertical arms, which were attached to the two suspended wire tracks eight feet above the trolley. As long as we were heading in a straight line, I really did not have a problem holding on. It did pass through my mind, however, that I could get my fingers cut off and never be able to play sports again; but at nine, my thinking was that if it was easier, faster, and more fun- it was a no brainer.

There were often some "clowns" driving behind the trolley, beeping or seeing how close they could get their hood ornaments to my butt while I was in my crouched position. I learned to live with the ribbing I received because of their "fun-filled" activity; unless of course, I turned around and looked straight into the windshield of a police car. When this occurred, I jumped off the moving trolley to the curbside so I would not be run over by the cops and continued my trip home on foot!

On reaching Ebbet's field, the fun really began. It was not anticipation of watching a "Bums" (nickname for the Dodger's) game, but the location or position we were going to snag in the parking lot during the game. You see, there were about a dozen thirteen to sixteen year olds who spread out in the parking lots, beyond the seats or stands. This was our turf, our place of business for our "bonuses". These bonuses did not come easily. I would check out which of the lots had the least or youngest guys "playing" that area because I knew that if a ball was hit for a home run, I had to be quick enough to recover this ball first, and then of course I could keep it. There were no negotiations: no rock, paper, scissors, or shooting it out (odds and evens). It was like a Johnny Cash song, where he sang about fighting in the streets with the "mud, blood, and the beer!"

We were rolling under and over cars during the games, fighting to keep any/all home run balls. There were always two or three of us in the lot who left our positions to watch any fights. Although, to be honest, we really just wanted to pick up any baseballs that might roll loose from the other boys during these fights. Since the boys who were fighting could not get up fast enough, or were just too tired, I could usually grab or pick up many of those balls that came loose during the fights.

When the "Bums" played the Yanks
in the World Series, it was like
A National Holiday!

After grabbing a ball, I hid it in an unlocked car to maintain my mobility and to keep both of my hands free to catch the next over the fence ball, or to be ready for the next altercation. I returned to this unlocked car with each ball I caught and threw it in with my previous baseball treasures. In those days, the car radios worked even with the cars' ignitions off, so we also searched for any unlocked cars to turn on their car radios. We turned the volume up as loud as it would go so we could hear the game and better anticipate where the next home run ball might drop. When we heard the announcer screaming, we went to work looking and listening for the thud a baseball makes as it hits the roof or hood of one of the cars. If I did not hear the thud, I knew the baseball either had hit the concrete or had gone through a convertible top. Either way, I had to search and recover before the next batter stepped to the plate.

My best day was snagging "three over the fence balls"! Since I usually liked to play the area with the least amount of "players", right field was the area where I usually liked to "compete". Although many of the home run hitters were right-handed hitters, a good percentage of balls were hit over the left field fence. In addition, I had "The Duke" Snyder, a great left-handed home run hitter to keep me busy.

At the end of the games, I cashed in my "catches" by standing outside the main gate yelling, "Hey, get your Duke Snyder's 6th inning home run ball right here, one dollar!" I continued repeating that until I sold out of my inventory. No one knew if it was or wasn't Duke's ball, so I got the money, and they got the thrill of thinking they had the ball that Duke hit. So we all went home happy.

With the money rolling in, I found great satisfaction in paying for the trolley to ride back home. It was "Uptown" passing the other "players" as they were walking or hanging on to the back of a trolley for dear life!

Happy Felton's Knothole Gang

After a year of shagging balls in the parking lot, the fights were getting to me. Between my dad whacking me for something I had done, and me having those parking lot fights, I realized I needed to give up my "ball shagging occupation". However, I still attended games whenever I could save enough Borden milk coupons to sit in the Schaffer Beer Bleachers and become probably the youngest Brooklyn "Bum", a nickname for those sitting in the Schaffer Beer bleachers.

I attended one game really early to see if I could catch a couple of batting practice balls: kind of doing it the legal way, but still selling these practice balls as if they were game balls and pocketing the cash. But one day, after arriving early, I saw some boys my age playing in the infield, and realized Campy (Roy Campanella) was hitting ground balls to a kid at shortstop who was standing in front of Pee Wee Reese. Other kids were fielding the ground balls the best they could and then throwing them to first base where a boy was playing first in front of Hodges. "As I watched in awe, I thought, "Holy crap, what the hell is this?" I immediately ran down from the bleachers to the section behind home plate and asked one of the seat cops (ticket checkers) how I could get down on the field like those other kids.

He explained that before each home game boys were selected for the "Happy Felton's Knothole Gang" by trying out and being chosen as one of the best players in the group. However, no one was allowed to try out for the Knothole gang more than once in a season. In addition, for their efforts, the winners received a glove, a bat, and a ball signed by the Dodgers. "Oh, by the way, kid", the seat cop added, "the winner also sits with the team in the dugout the entire game". I was all over that! "You got to be kidding me, how do I meet this Happy" guy?"

Well, in three weeks I had a tryout but did not win. I had been so nervous that I kept making one error after another. However, the next month, I did try out again, but this time I signed up using the name Dave. I was picked to try out again, and came a bit closer to winning, but I still wasn't chosen.

Since they selected their participants by name only, all I had to do for each tryout was register under a different name each time, so I kept trying. My chance finally came at the end of the season while using the name "Tony" when I signed up.

At that point and time, it was the highlight of my life. Moreover, this time I won and received all the goodies I had been wanting. The game was televised and my friends all watched it on television and they just assumed Tony was my middle name. Therefore, going to school on Monday was the best school day I ever had. The teachers were even nice to me. I guess it was my first encounter with the mystique of sports, performing, and being placed on a pedestal for being an athlete. I eventually sold the ball with all of the Dodgers' autographs about a year later. It meant nothing to me, since the ball had "Best wishes" with the name "Tony" written on it!

Team Roster Increases

At home, we had to clear room on the bench for a new member of our "family" team, my baby sister, Ilene. All was good as far as I was concerned. My coaches (parents) gave me more playing time on the streets since much of the focus was now off me. They now had to take time to teach baby Ilene the plays of life. The only real "play" that I had at this point was to bring the ball home and then to eat dinner with the family at 6:30 pm.

My father was beginning to work more hours at his family-owned *Famous Malts* shop. He and his brothers owned, managed, and worked at their malt shop in New York City on 42nd street. I guess my dad was feeling the financial pressure of another "player" in our apartment, or maybe he just needed to get some mental relaxation of his own, away from my mother. It was about this time in my life that the coaching assignments were beginning to shift. My mother was starting to take over the head-coaching job in our family home! Because of his many hours at work, my dad was not around very much at all.

The highlight of my fun was after dinner, around nightfall at so-called homework sessions at a friend's house. However, instead of going to my friend's house, ten of us met at Crown Heights Hospital and ran the grounds. This was the only area for miles that had grass... gorgeous, soft grass, and best of all: no dog crap.

We chased each other and hid behind bushes, another rarity in Brooklyn, until the hospital police came after us. The real goal or objective had been to get the attention of the hospital police and then out run them and hide. They certainly motivated us to improve our speed! Though we out-manned them 5-1, the real excitement occurred when one of the guards focused on chasing only one of us and not the others. That was the highlight: ducking into bushes and holding our breaths while the guards ran right by us going after one of our friends as he ran off the grounds causing the guards to stop. We took it as winning a great challenge.

I was about fun: whether it was joking, laughing, playing pranks, or making someone else look stupid, but I could not handle anyone having fun at my expense. Again, Johnny Cash sang about a *Boy Named Sue.* "Some gal would giggle, and I'd get red; then some guy would laugh, and I'd bust his head!"

It seemed that I used the word "fun" as an excuse for any occasion when things did not go my way. Not liking someone's plays (rules), being forced to study, seeing a friendship going sour, or a few years later telling my female counterparts that things were over by using the excuse, "because it just isn't 'fun' any more".

As for school, it was still not any fun either. Going to class, singing, doing artwork, and sitting in the principal's office were definitely not cool. It was not as if I were failing all of my subjects; it was just the same one - "reading". Possibly, if the teachers had been just a bit more understanding, things could have worked out. They had not needed to make a fool of me by asking me to read aloud in front of my classmates! Surely, they could have figured out that I did not do well under these circumstances!

The teachers and classmates said I had a good, likeable, fun loving personality, but for some reason, my reading teacher, as well as my past reading teachers, just had a case of the hates! Maybe part of it was because I *could* be such a jerk and that slapping other students was not acceptable. However, the teachers never realized that much of my poor behavior was to take the pressure off my reading difficulties by diverting my teachers' attention to my poor behavior.

My days on Carroll Street were now coming to an end. Although we stayed in Brooklyn, we were on the move once again. At the age of nine, I moved with my family a few miles away to an apartment on Kings Highway. It was a nice place and just off Ocean Avenue. We lived there before the big King Plaza Mall was built years later.

The new school I was now attending was on the very end of our street and close to our apartment, so I did not have to rely on my dad to drive me to school. However, the main reason I liked living so close to this new school was that the schoolyard stayed open all of the time. At night, the schoolyard was loaded with talented athletes, mainly junior high kids, and a few high schoolers from the neighborhood. I always enjoyed playing with older kids; they were just more fun! They were "better" than I was in several ways: they had more fights, used more cursing, and usually they were better at sports than I was, and more importantly, many of them did not read much better than I did.

One of those boys from the junior high was Lester Yellen, who was named after a great ball player. He befriended me and helped me improve my ball playing skills, and he treated me as if I were his little brother. Lester took me everywhere to play sports, to let me watch him and his friends play for the PAL (Police Athletic League), or he would take me to the Garden to watch the ECAC basketball tourney. We watched game after game of college basketball teams playing from all over the country. I never realized that there was a level after high school other than the Knicks and the Pros! "What is this college level all about? When do you go? What do you do there?" I wondered. "Did they just play ball?" I wasn't sure, but I liked what I had seen so far.

It was at the ECAC Tournament when I fell in love with the "Redmen" basketball team from St. Johns

University! It was a great team. Although, after watching Oscar Robertson from the University of Cincinnati score 52 points, I thought Robertson's team ran a close second to St. John's! All I knew after leaving "The Garden" was that I wanted to find out more about this college basketball thing! I was hooked! My friend Lester knew I had very few coins, so he paid for almost everything. Tickets to *Madison Square Garden*, food, and travel were often taken care of by Lester. Under his influence, I was really improving in all of my sports.

In addition to basketball, I also loved baseball; however, the timing of our move to Brooklyn really caused problems with me joining any teams or clubs. It was too late to register and this prevented me from joining any organized sports. I was anxious to get a chance to be in game situations like my storybook hero, Chip Hilton from the *Chip Hilton Sports Series*. I was turned on by reading about Chip's coach (Hank Rockwell) who could motivate his players to excel, and I wanted to be a player like them.... I wanted to be Chip! But, most of all, I wanted to have a "Coach"... I wanted to be on a real team."

Lester was concerned about my education and was pleased to see me reading the "Chip Hilton" books. He also gave me other books to read such as *The Jinx, The Dugout,* and *The Pitcher's Duel.* All were baseball novels, since Lester enjoyed baseball more than basketball. I did not care which sport; I just loved reading any of the books about Chip Hilton.

Two other major things happened during my family's "stop over" on Kings Highway. First, our family had a new member who joined our team, my new baby sister, Enid. I was now outmanned, two girls against me!

The second happening was a scare from hell. My friends and I were always looking for excitement, kind of like we did at the hospital grounds. Only this time the stakes were higher... much higher!

The task or challenge was to be able to press the apartment building's garage button that caused a massive double door to electronically descend and finally close. Our goal was to scramble under the door before it closed and hit any of us in the head, or worse, trapped one of us beneath the rubber on the bottom of the door. We felt we were invincible, so it seemed all great fun.

My five-year-old sister, Ilene, was a big daredevil and fit right in with us on this challenge. Unfortunately, one day she took too much of a risk and did not make it! Although not hit, she was trapped under the garage door and could not good out, which had never happened to any of us before. We had no idea that the door would not come back up by simply pressing the up button. Seeing her trapped, I was afraid Ilene was going to be slowly choked right in front of our eyes! The door had stopped just inches from my sister's neck.

When pressing the up button did not solve the door problem, I got down on the ground where the door had her trapped and tried to "bench press" like Lester did all of the time, but it was just impossible. I was able to get the garage door to move up about two inches more before the motor locked and would not allow the door to move upward any more than those two inches. Fortunately, Ilene did stop crying when she felt the pressure around her neck lessen, which calmed me down a little.

My friends were pretty smart, and found some blocks of wood and some semi-large rocks to place under the garage door to prop it up more securely, which let me stop pushing up on the door as a safety backup. We remained in that position until the fire department came to release the garage door and free my sister.

My friends never told their parents they were involved in this fear packed adventure, and I deserved all the blame my parents heaped on me. As far as they knew, it was just Ilene and me there. It did not matter about the others anyway because it was my responsibility to take care of Ilene. I was her older brother, after all. My dad never said anything more after that night, but I could tell he thought I had not been alone and that I was covering up for my friends. However, other than a bad scare and a rough looking scrape around Ilene's neck, it was soon business as usual, and my friends and I were back playing in the garage a few days later; after things had cooled down with the building superintendent. And we did not repeat our mistake of playing with the garage door.

That same year, my sister Ilene made the cover of the New York Daily News for being the first schoolchild to be vaccinated with the Salk vaccine! At the time, this was a major medical breakthrough against Polio.

In those days, polio was a topic that came up often by mothers talking amongst themselves. I was afraid of this disease because I never understood what it was or how it affected people. We just knew it was something horrible. We heard much less about cancer during that period... people focused on polio as "the deadly disease" of the time!

1901 - 1985

Rockaway Beach provided summer fun!

Each summer our family, along with my mother's parents, went to Rockaway, Queens. Rockaway Beach is a neighborhood on the Rockaway Peninsula in the New York City borough of Queens. It is located on the South Shore of Long Island.

We rented a bungalow one block from the beach. There were ten rows of bungalows and they were filled to capacity, each housing its share of children!

Going to Rockaway was the highlight of the year and we each looked forward to the end of June, when school was out. I was eight when we first began taking our vacations in Rockaway. Each of us had our daily routines set up. My grandparents had their friends who they met at the shuffleboard courts, my mother looked forward to her traveling Mahjong games while Ilene and Enid played around the bungalows with their friends.

As for me, I was driven to doing my "Sand Sifting" each morning at dawn! Sand sifting is an activity that utilizes a wooden coke box with the bottom taken out. The bottom is replaced with chicken wire (small quarter inch boxes) attached to the three sides of the box. The one side that is removed, is placed on top of the sand and pulled by two long handles, one attached to each side of the sand sifter. The handles provide leverage to pull through the sand, and when I shake the box, the sand funnels out leaving anything larger than a quarter of an inch inside the box. Whatever was left in the box was my "treasure".

Although it was quite tiring, I had a hard time sleeping each night due to my high expectations for each morning's "search for gold!" I would head out the door as soon as I saw sunlight, but I was not alone on these treasure hunts! There were literally hundreds who sifted, but not on a daily basis. The driven ones were "under the Boardwalk" each morning at the crack of dawn!

Our beach number was on 54th street and I worked the boardwalk to 75th. Although some days were better than others, there was always something valuable or at least interesting. The reason so many people liked sand sifting under the boardwalk was because so many people dropped coins, bills, rings, wallets, etc. through the cracks between the wooden planks.

I would not miss a day because I was so motivated by the mysterious findings that were possible with each pull of my sifter! I averaged at least two to three dollars an outing. During my years, I came across rings that brought good rewards, and on one lucky pull, I even found a ten-dollar bill.

The best area for sifting was on 98th Street at Rockaway's "Playland". I spent many evenings at Playland, and the amount of my sifting earnings during the day dictated the length of time that I would be able to stay at Playland at night.

I was often up at dawn to sift as the nightly winds still howled through the pilings that supported the boardwalk all the way through to 1st Street. The real trick to successful sifting was to beat the sanitation department there. The sanitation workers were not particularly fond of the sifters arriving first on the scene because the workers liked to scour/sift the area for themselves each morning as they cleared out the garbage underneath the boardwalks.

MARTY URAND

*Yesterday's endings are seeds
for today's beginnings.*

LEWIS LOSONCY

A New Borough: Queens

Well, my mom finally got to my dad, and we left dear old Brooklyn for the greener pastures of Queens, NY. Our new home was a garden apartment located in a large complex between Flushing N.Y and Jamaica, N.Y. just one block from Jewel Avenue. We were actually about three miles from where the old New York State Fair had been located several years before. After the State Fair closed, these grounds were turned into an amazing swimming facility called the Aquacade, which had huge diving boards and a pool that was at least a city block long. It was also a great place to ride our bikes during the summers. There were no trolley cars in Queens, just regular buses, the Q-44 to be exact! The Q-44 ran between Forest Hills to the Astoria. There was a bridge between Kew Garden Hills and Forest Hills with a small body of water that separated the two areas. This was a very scenic area.

The bicycle played a major role in my life when I was ten and a half years old. The *Schwinn Phantom bicycle* was considered the "Beast of the East!" Naturally, every kid wanted one of these black, red, and chrome bikes. The coolest thing was that it had a single shock absorber in the middle, not like the Mercury, which had two scrawny shocks below the handlebars, just above the front chrome fender. This Schwinn had great white walls and fat tires, which classified it as a truck bike! I was no different from the others; I wanted one of those bikes, big time. However, my father was still working all kind of hours on Times Square trying to make things work out for our new and improved venue. Therefore, unfortunately for me, my "dream bike" was unaffordable for us.

Therefore, instead of the Schwinn, my first bike was a used bike bought through the newspaper, but it was ok: an English Racer (skinny, thin tires) with hand brakes. My Dad knew a lot about bikes and he always looked for the different and unusual designs. However, my mother never wanted him to be a part of any selection process. Frankly, she despised his taste in everything! Their biggest arguments came when we went out to eat on Sundays and he dressed like Ed Norton on the old television show *"The Honeymooners"* with Jackie Gleason. She would scream at him, and we would all have to wait for him to change clothes and get dressed again. Dad never got respect from Mom, but I never knew if it bothered him or not: he was so quiet at home. He was certainly different around the ya-whos he hung out with at the racetracks.

At the horse track, all of his friends yelled out, "Hey Jackie!", when he walked in, and they greeted him with the respect that mattered to him. I noticed that his pace slowed down and his chest filled up as he acknowledged the riff-raff who hung around the track. It was his time to shine! He had no brothers to tell him what to do, and no wife nagging at him. He became a different person once he entered the horse track!

As kids, we were excited when our father came home from *Famous Malts* because he usually came home with a bargain he'd found in the city. Often the products were black market, or he found a "great deal" that he happened to fall into. He would rather buy something from the black market than purchase anything of value considered to be "above board". He loved the challenge of shopping and bargaining for great deals.

My dad stored everything of value in the trunk of his car. These items ranged from cash, a pistol, small appliances that he would give away to family members or friends, plus stamps, stocks, bonds, and even toilet paper. He never let anyone look in his trunk! The people he knew asked him, "Jack, do you have a body in there?" Although they were half joking, that had even passed through my mind. Dad was no Tony Soprano by any means, don't get me wrong, but he would have loved that character!

Famous Malts, Inc.

Famous Malts, Inc. was the money cow for my dad and his "brothers". My father had three brothers, Irving the oldest, Ben, and then Phil. My dad was the youngest of his brothers and sisters.

Uncle Phil (left), Dad (back corner),
and Leo (by the door),
Times Square (1956)

Each one of the brothers was a character unto himself. Each in his own way had a vice, or an unusual or bad habit of some kind. It was by luck alone that none of them were serving time. In fact, they probably would have been safer in jail than on the streets. To get in a fistfight was not something out of the ordinary for them. They each had tempers and very different ways of thinking. None of the brothers attended high school for any length of time, but each possessed, "in a manner of speaking" a psychology degree earned from their living on the streets on the New York's "East Side"

Between the brothers and their employees, *Famous Malts* was just short of a "nut house". The store was open 24/7, and had no doors or walls on the side facing the subway or on the front facing 42nd Street just off of Times Square. I was amazed and to some degree infatuated with the street.

For one thing, there were 35 movie theatres on the block and a half between 8th and 6th Avenues. There was every kind of movie known to man showing on this block and a half. These theaters were never crowded; I would seldom really see people go in and what is worse, I seldom saw anyone come out! My father had two rules for me when I first began working at the "store". First, never go into one of these so-called theaters, and second, never eat any of the food that we served in "our schlock house!" There were times when my dad had left the shop, and I would eat a hot dog from our store. However, if he came back and caught me, he would grab the food out of my hands and usually throw it straight into the garbage. Then he would give me money and send me across the street to eat "some decent food"!

The store was built for speed with a large U-shaped counter and no chairs. My dad figured if our customers ate standing up at the counters, they would eat faster and leave sooner.

My dad had a philosophy for everything to make transactions go smoothly but most of all to go quickly. We sold three flavors of malts, and he told us never to ask customers what flavor they wanted because that would slow the service down. His rule of thumb was simple: vanilla for African Americans, chocolate for white people, and strawberry for Orientals. How he came up with that distribution, I don't know, but I would have to say he was correct most of the time, or the customers were just afraid to argue with him about it.

New Yorkers were constantly searching for spectacular attractions, whether it was singers, dancers, athletes, horses, or any other allure on the streets. Times Square and Broadway were known for these side acts and made the light filled streets fantastic! Pockets of crowds formed in the street whenever an attraction broke out its acts, merchandise, etc. We were one of those attractions that people loved to watch!

"Our malt shop was on 42ⁿᵈ and Times Square."

The store sold hamburgers and hot dogs, but it was best known for its fabulous malts. Not only were the malts delicious, but the customers came for the fun of watching the techniques, the speed, and the flair we used in preparing our malts and in serving them.

It took no more than four to six seconds to whip out malt on our high speed Hamilton mixers. Our wooden floor, which we called the "planks", kept us from getting shocked or electrocuted by the milk and electricity that merged around us as we whipped our malts.

As malt finished mixing in our automated malt can, I could reach behind me with my left hand and grab an empty glass, while simultaneously using my right hand to pull the malt can from the mixer, throw the malt through the air just in time for me to catch the malt in the glass in my left hand. Our New York malts were thin, and were easily sucked through straws. In comparison, malts in the South were usually thicker, and because of the thickness, the malts in the South were often eaten with spoons. My coaches said I had good hands for athletics, and I attribute the store and my technique in making malts for some of those skills.

On the workers' side of the counter was a large chrome table filled with empty, clean glasses. At the end of the table was the dishwasher. One person washed dishes and glasses for 45 minutes out of every hour just to stay up with the volume of business. Each plate and glass was hand washed and then put into a steamer and pushed out to replenish the glass stock continuously.

One day the *New York Times* newspaper ran a special event giving out wooden tokens, each worth one nickel, to people on Times Square to see how many malts we could make in a one-hour period. The brothers added two machines to the four that were there on a daily basis. The milk was cooled at a lower temperature to insure that the milk would become a bit thicker and consequently last longer, assuring us that we would not have to spend too much time changing out the milk sleeves during this "malt" marathon!

At noon, the event *kicked* off, and it was a spectacular event at that! The customers were no less than three deep behind the u-shaped counter at any given time, yelling their flavors, which we usually did not abide by, and then they were passing their "nickel" wooden tokens to us. The brothers also helped in collecting the tokens while the workers just made malts, one after another and another, etc. etc., speedily slamming them down for the brothers to pick up and distribute. We were certainly moving faster than we were accustomed to and consequently many glasses were broken on both sides of the counter. At the end of that hour, the brothers counted over 500 tokens!

I liked working at the store each weekend. It made me feel older and more responsible. I always enjoyed showing off my athleticism and performing in front of others..... as long as it wasn't reading. Throughout the day, pockets of people gathered and watched us performing our "Make the Malt Show". It did not take long to realize that the customers were "creatures of habit". Many of them came into the store at the same time daily, asked for "the usual", paid, and then left without saying another word. Over time, I prepared the "usual" orders for our regular customers as soon as I saw them walking up from the subway toward our store. The customers usually gave me insincere smiles, not the kind that were very appreciative; it was more of a courteous movement of the lips. I began thinking that maybe our customers felt deprived by not being able to order using their best "short order cook" tones of voice.

Most customers placed whatever they were carrying onto the counter. My dad always busted their chops, yelling at them to get their crap off the counters. He yelled so he could make room for more customers and their money! The only time they rebelled was if he told them to remove or trash their newspapers. They just ignored that part of his "demands". Most New Yorkers carry and read their newspapers at lunch, on the can, on the train, and any other moments they have free, only throwing the paper away as they arrive near their homes. At the counter in our store, they ignored my dad's demands and placed their beloved papers close to their bodies. Once their newspapers were "safe" they proceeded to place their orders by using phrases such as, "Two long ... hold the kraut", and "gimmie a malted". It was always funny to me that they used short slang words for the food but would always say "malted" instead of malt.

I enjoyed serving and working fast, even if only getting a tip maybe every 20th customer. I did not expect much in tips except on New Year's Eve. Everyone left tips that night. All of the windows on the other stores in our area of Times Square were boarded up so the large crowds could not be pushed through the glass front windows. However, when they came to our store we had no problem since *Famous Malts* had no glass, and people were just pushed or shoved in by the large crowds. Once in, they usually decided to eat and have something to drink! This was great for us!

On New Year's Eve, I'd have to say that due to their alcohol consumption, 90% of the customers were feeling no pain. The workers all wanted to work that evening because the so-called "tips" were outrageous! I use the word "tips" very loosely; it was more like robbery. When we received a bill larger than a dollar, we placed the change on the counter and the dollars under their plates. We hoped the customer might pick up the change and forget the dollars under those plates, which helped each of us make two hundred dollars plus in tips on New Year's Eve.

As I think back, every day in New York City seemed to resemble New Year's Eve. On the streets in the area of our store, we could always count on vendors selling everything from hats, gloves, ties, paintings (done with spray cans), performing magic tricks, and of course there were the portable food stands! The entertainment that always had captured my attention were the vendors who set up small stands or tables with three cups and they'd then place a nut under one cup, moving the cups quickly. People would pay to win bucks by guessing which of the cups had the nut under it. Crowds loved to try to "beat the odds" and choose the correct cup. However, as soon as the police saw the venders, the venders folded their boards, grabbed their objects, and sprinted down the street: to eventually stop and start another "Shill" game elsewhere!

People and the festivities were always interesting to watch. On my lunch hour I would go across the street to Nedick's or grab a slice of pizza (15 cents!) and sit around the corner on the concrete, leaning against a storefront, just eating and watching what amounted to a "carnival" of people and activities. I knew most of the storeowners and workers up and down Broadway and 42nd.... They were all "schlock" houses in that area! Not that they sold food, but whatever they were selling was either cheap, rejects, or just fronts to what was "really" going on in the back!

I often sat in front of a camera store and watched the most amazing billboard: It was the Camel cigarette sign! It has a man blowing smoke rings out over Times Square. Every 46 seconds the man "exhales" a new ring perfectly over the traffic and people. Many of the city people did not even look up; they just took this for granted, I guess. The camel billboard was one of my two favorite animated signs.

The other sign that fascinated me had a Coca-Cola glass that filled up and tipped forward as if someone were drinking out of it. It took only 30 seconds and then repeated itself over and over.

I just loved the city, but I had no use for the schools or of course for reading. My thinking was that this was my future, my life... helping my dad, working in the store, and waiting each year for the excitement of New Year's Eve to return once again.

My most remembered customers

I served several interesting customers each weekend at our shop. Every weekend morning at precisely 8:10 AM, George, "Horsey", came in, headed to my side at the back side of the store, where an additional 90 degree counter split off of the end of the main counter toward the back of the store. My dad called him "Horsey" and he came in to speak "horses" with my dad. The papers he carried were not ones I was familiar with at the time. They were called the *Telegraph* (the "bible" for horse bettors).

The Telegraph gives the entire scoop about horses and their races. It probably could even report when the horses took their last crap; it was so thorough and complete. When Horsey wasn't talking horses, he was talking stocks and even stamps since he and my dad both collected stamps. Horsey was a poorly dressed man with very few teeth, but he knew the horses! He never called me by my name, he just said, "Hey Jackie's kid, where is your old man?" He was polite enough, but I could hardly understand him with his very thick New York accent, and his vowels seemed to get lost somewhere in the large spaces between his teeth. I just knew to serve him coffee and a piece of Drake's pound cake whenever he came in. He must have been special because my dad admonished me never to ask him to pay. My first thought was that he might be either a cop or a health inspector, but I realized after he came around a few times, that he could not be either one of those. In the summer, when I worked during the week, I would always see either a cop or a health inspector receiving the "good ole handshake" with money sticking out from under their hands from one business or the other, including ours.

"Horsey" (George) and My Dad (1957)

During the week, different deliveries were being made each day. One day it was Sabbath bread/rolls, and the next it was hamburgers and frankfurters, etc. The drivers would come into the back of the store, and when it was my turn to wash dishes, I could hear them talking behind my dad's office door. They talked about horseracing, who should win, etc, which I later found out were called "tips". Several large companies owned horse stables, and their deliverymen usually gave us tips about which of their horses they thought had a good chance of winning in the daily races!

My Dad said that the workers from the garbage company always had the best tips. My Dad was very different on "The Street". He knew everyone and vice versa! This was his world, the world that he loved. He was sought after for his ability to give "genuine" tips, as well as being the head of his class for being the best reader of the Telegraph newspaper!

When George (Horsey) came in on Sundays, he and my dad often talked, argued, and debated about which horses had the best chances of winning that weeks' races. Horsey would give my dad envelopes filled with cash to use to place bets for Horsey. During the week, *Horsey* stayed low-keyed and out of sight. My dad told me that he had heard Horsey was wanted for theft and grand larceny in over twenty states! We just accepted him for how he was with us and enjoyed his knowledge and his "uniqueness"

My Dad would place the bets for Horsey and then on the following Sundays he would give Horsey back the envelope with any and all of Horsey's winnings. Their conversations reminded me of school as they would talk about one subject and then without a bell, jump and talk about the next subject, ect. Again, their subjects were very limited: horses, stocks, and stamps in that order for years.

About seven years later, my dad told me Horsey was ill, and Horsey was afraid he was getting closer to being caught for some of his activities. Horsey was keeping all of his money in some nasty downtown hotel, and since Horsey had no other relatives, he gave my Dad a large amount of money to hold for him in the store safe and told my dad to keep it for himself if something ever happened to him. Horsey had also asked my dad to go to Horsey's hotel and pick up Horsey's stamp collection in case of his death.

Then one Sunday came and there was no Horsey! No questions were asked by either my Dad or me. We had a great Christmas, said a short prayer in Horsey's name, and later my dad went to grieve by himself for a while. The next day my Dad went to Horsey's apartment and I was told never to mention the stamps to anyone! Evidently, Horsey thought the stamps could be worth plenty of money someday. He had several of the high priced "stick-ons" but we would later find out these stamps were stolen property and could not be sold.

Another person of interest was also one of my dad's regular customers. This man knew a great deal about sports, and he and I talked forever. My dad would come from the back and look at us talking and yell at me at the top of his lungs, "What in the hell do you two have in common?" This guy was a piece of work!

He was extremely obese, and dressed as if he was heading to a resort or maybe Fire Island. He always wore starched Bermuda shorts, a triple X Hawaiian shirt, and sandals.

He was educated, with a degree from NYU, very polite, and followed the NY Knicks, NY Yankees, and NY Giants. Every other team in existence was "full of crapola" in his opinion. I guess he did not like the Dodgers because they did not have an N.Y. in front of their name. He would take twenty to thirty minutes to convince me of this each and every time he came into the store. In the meantime, I was a nervous wreck waiting for my Dad to resurface with vulgarity that would embarrass me in front of Woody. I called him Woody. He never told me his name, but when he walked in his highly starched pants, his pants always stuck out in the crotch area! This person was as straight as they come, believe me, but he had no class!

Some of the cruel bastards I worked with called him Quasimodo or "the tongue". He had a very large, nasty tongue that flopped around outside his mouth because it seemed to be too large to fit inside of his mouth. I became used to it and didn't even notice after awhile, but the dumb asses that I worked with had no mercy! When Woody would leave, I'd always tell the workers not to say things about him because he could hear them. I was very sensitive about hurting Woody's feelings. However, when he left the store, I did throw away his drinking glass! All those years my dad never knew about that. I probably had thrown *away* over ten glasses a month for four or five years!

Finally, the third person of interest to me was a girl who passed the store every Saturday and Sunday at precisely 8:45 am and at again at 5:10 pm. I would watch the clock and wait so I could see her. In the mornings, I could see her through the one window we had that was facing the stairs to the subway station. She would walk up the stairs next to the window and glance in at me, never saying anything or showing any emotions whatsoever. I would then go to the front of the store, standing behind rows and rows of franks on a grill, and greet her with, "Good morning, Beautiful". Again, she did not acknowledge me. This went on for some time, until I eventually gained the courage to make a move. This time when she came up from the train station, I met her and walked with her to the corner. She seemed nervous as we reached the corner in front of the hat store, as if she did not want me to know where she went from there. I sensed this and never went past that corner. I did find out her name was Margret and I assumed it was short for Margareta. I asked her out on several occasions, but she never said yes. I really looked forward to seeing her when I worked on the weekends. During the summer, she never worked during the week, so I looked forward to the weekends even more!

Margret, I guess, was my first "dream" girlfriend. I never put my arm around her, and I never kissed her, but she was the girl that I dreamed of every night.

Scraping up Friends

After a swift and speedy move one weekend, it was off to another new school for that dreaded first day. The move would not have been so difficult if we could have made the move in the summer and I could have started school with everyone else. However the move came in November, and I have no clue why November was the lucky month. When my mother makes up her mind, things happen! She could move into a new apartment and have all the boxes unpacked, gone to the store, have groceries and refrigerator items bought, and pictures hanging on the wall by the time we woke up in the morning!

Once I was deposited at the new elementary school at the beginning of the school day, it was not business as usual; it was a nightmare. Moving became even more traumatic as I got older. At age eleven, even I could tell that this was much worse than my previous moves: Not to say that the earlier moves were an easy task, but this one had "do-do" written all over it.

My teachers were nice enough and so were the kids in my fifth grade class. It was the awkwardness of everyone staring at me and checking out my clothes, the type of sneakers I had on, etc. However, it was always the pronunciation of my last name that set off the giggling among the students. I am sure that my sisters were even more embarrassed than I was. Mispronouncing the name of Urand, kind of sounds like urine! I would always have to correct the teacher and that meant talking out in front of the whole class of strangers. Thank God this move was in elementary school. If it had been in secondary school, I would have had to go through this process for each of my classes!

Recess did not come soon enough! I was ready to get out and away from the teachers and kids. It was also a relief to get up from my desk before everyone found out what kind of student I was. I guess this was the reason that I always felt like I was being chased! What was after me... chasing me? ...It was reading. I knew the day was coming when the teacher would ask, "Marty, would you mind reading the second paragraph?" In the beginning, I tried to take a teacher's help and criticism. It was the "flock", my classmates, who got under my skin and then I would begin sweating as I began to show my anger. I had the greatest role models for anger: my mom and my dad! They both had unusually volatile tempers. Although having a "short" temper may just have been a New York characteristic, a prerequisite for living in New York!

As I aged, my temper seemed to reach new heights. However, the mad person in me still showed up during reading. All the other times I was the picture of a well-rounded student. I found out that personality could go a long way, and I was a charmer when I wanted to be. The girls would flirt and giggle, and the boys wanted to test me. It was always a boy who would bring up "smack" about my poor reading ability. So we would get into it with words, pushing, or by me going "Ali" on them!

After lunch, we all rushed outside to the schoolyard for recess. Everyone did their own things: chasing each other, screwing around on the seesaw, climbing monkey bars, or playing punch ball on the asphalt softball diamond. I sat against the fence taking everything in. It was almost time to go back to class, when I saw two guys getting ready to race. It was neat that each of these boys stood on either side of the painted home plate and took off racing in opposite directions. One runner headed up the first base line as the other ran up the third base side, passing each other at second base and then racing the baselines back to their own side of home plate. In this case, Ronnie, who was coming around second base heading for third, was in the lead. He beat Dennis by two steps.

I had assumed it was over, but then, "Big Dog"- Speedy Brennan, came up to home base to race against Ronnie, the winner of the earlier race. I realized that the first race had just been to win the chance to complete against "Big Dog".

As Dennis and Speedy both counted to three, *I* took off from just watching, and sprinted toward the home plate. God only knows why, but I sprinted through home base toward first just a few seconds after the race started and joined the race against Ronnie and Speedy. Everyone was cheering and screaming for Speedy to beat Ronnie, and initially paid no attention to me.

So here I was, joining the race and now just five or six steps away from reaching first base. Speedy touched first and was heading for second, as I steadily pulled closer to him. Both of us were ahead of Ronnie in running past second base. As Speedy and I neared third base, I sprinted on the inside of the third base, stretched, and really turned it on, approaching home plate, when Speedy suddenly pushed me from behind. Speedy could not handle me kicking his butt in our race and embarrassing him in front of all the fifth graders!

As it was, I was the one who was embarrassed. When I slid, I skinned everything there was to skin! *My knees, forearms, elbows, and worst of all my forehead and face were also scraped.* Going to school the next day was a nightmare! I had puss coming out from the band-aids my mother had slapped all over me. Nevertheless, when I arrived at school the next morning, I was pleasantly surprised, because suddenly everyone knew my name, and I was told that I had actually won yesterday's race. The girls flirted, and I guess the guys were feeling like there was a new sheriff in town. I could not have been treated any better.

I felt like a winner until two things happened. First, I got word that Speedy was going to wait for me after school to kick my ass! That's always "nice" to live with when trying to keep my mind on school. It was back to reality for me. Secondly, the time had come for my class to find out that the "fast runner" was an imbecile when it came to reading!

When my time came to read, I really tried reading aloud and working with the teacher as she was trying to help me. However, it just became unbearable. In one quick motion, I whacked the boy sitting behind me and before I knew it, I was sitting in the principal's office. After several of these incidents of misbehavior reoccurred over the next days, the principal did something that I was not accustomed to. He sent me to sit in the custodian's office (a large broom closet). He claimed that he was tired of me being in his office each day. However, as I thought about it later, the principal may have been trying an innovative "line of attack" to improve and expand my reading abilities.

Reading time was every morning at ten o'clock until I had lunch at 12:00. The custodian told me to join my class for lunch while he completed his jobs around the lunchroom area. After lunch, I headed back to the custodian's office instead of to my next class and let him assume I had been thrown out of class again. He gave me "clean up" responsibilities and afterwards it was time for me to read and talk with him about one of the sport books he had chosen for me. The teachers were just as happy that I wasn't in their classes and

MARTY URAND

assumed the principal was still dealing with me. Therefore, my school day was now as follows: go to class until reading class until the teacher asked if I was ready to stay and read. I would say no, and she would point to the door. I would go straight to the custodian, bypassing the principal, and then I would return to my regular class each day after lunch at two o'clock, just in time for the math class and then off to afternoon recess.

I loved school now... it was *great*. And what really made it great was Mac, the elementary school custodian! He was the real deal. Mac was strong, low keyed, a lover of sports, and he really tried to help me. However, one day he threw a curve into the schedule. He handed me a book and asked me to try to read it. It was the same series of books that Lester had given me to read. The books were small with large type and had very colorful jackets. The first book he brought to me was called *The Buzzer Beater*. Mac told me it was from the Chip Hilton Series about a coach and his teams. The coach always made the right calls, perfect substitutions, and instinctively pumped the players up to go wild and win the game!

I was hooked on this book, but in the beginning, Mac pretty much read it to me each day. He loved these books as well. Since I was no longer allowed in the library, Mac checked out books for me to read with him. It took me about two weeks to finish a book and he would always show up with another one; this time it was *A Pass and a Prayer*. Great jacket, same old coach, and to no surprise, their team kept winning. This time he allowed me to take the book home to read.

For me to read a book was very unusual, especially to take it *home* and read! It naturally got my father's attention, and this I knew was not going to turn out good. I always tried to stay under his radar.

He would see me with a book and then begin his questioning! He would say, "Martin, let me hear you read". He was curious on whether or not I could read. He was not at all trying to see me fail. It was just a sudden response, since in the past, I never would utter a word and he would go ballistic on me.

The Beginning of Athletics

At the age of 12, and now living a supposedly better life in Queens, I became even more interested in sports. The first team I played on was the Kew Garden Hills Little League "Royals" baseball team. I did relatively well in both hitting and playing the infield. I was fast, with quick hands, and a good head for learning the concepts and rules of the game.

Kew Garden Hills Little League, "Royals."
Sisters Ilene and Enid were my biggest fans!

I played for two years making real improvements in all aspects of the game, and I met some good people playing ball, both on the dirt field at Kew Gardens and on the streets. Queens was no different from Brooklyn as far as stickball and school were concerned. The differences were that there was more grass and far fewer high-rise apartments in Queens. The area I lived in had blocks after blocks of two story, "two-family", Garden Apartments.

The best part of my new neighborhood were the kids I met and played with. There were some neat guys and a couple of very cute girls here. Girls were beginning to appeal to me more and more, but athletics still came first. Although the neighborhood athletes were pretty much the guys I hung with, the "hoods" were still a part of my life. The "hoods" were my friends who I hung with after the park shut down at 5 PM.

I really liked sports, but I was beginning to realize that I was shorter than many of my friends. Dennis Petrone was a good three inches taller, Johnny Curcio was close to my size, but was built really well; Ronnie, from across the street, was a monster. He was huge, had a square chin, and very broad shoulders. Johnny was always pitching with his father, and he became a big star player in Little League. However, my friend who really helped me with my insecurities because of my lack of height was my friend, Paul. He was already 13 and only one inch taller than I was.

Paul was a great athlete as well as a super guitar player. He went to a different school than I did and played several different sports. One sport we both played was hockey on roller skates in front of his house on 70th Road. He lived in a brick house across from a section of the Garden Apartments. Paul mainly hung around with a very tall friend of his, Artie, who was not as athletic, but who, like Paul, also played a guitar well. Both of them practiced their music regularly, and then when finished, they would come out and organize some games on the streets. They were both mature, *driven*, and leaders!

The New York City Parks Department started a softball league that was hosted by the Daily Mirror Newspaper. Each borough in New York had a tournament and the winners played to see whose team would become the "City Champion". Paul naturally organized our team since there was one rule that eliminated most of our friends; players had to be "under five feet tall" to participate. I was 4'11", and Paul made it just under the wire when we went to sign up with others from our neighborhood.

We practiced and played a game a week. We kept winning and made it through Queens and were waiting for the next brackets to see which borough we were going to play. I looked forward to playing against any of the other four boroughs except the Bronx! I associated the Bronx with the Yankees, and I did not like the Yankees because they usually beat up on my Dodgers.

One week before the brackets hit the Daily Mirror, I got hurt during baseball practice. I was playing first base in that same school yard where I had planted my face into the blacktop in the "big race". That day Artie was on the first base sideline while I played first base, and we were talking during batting practice. Paul was up at bat next, and being a lefty, he pulled the ball down the first base line where I was talking to Artie and the ball from Paul's line drive slammed into the side of my head. I went down in a hurry, and I was knocked cold for several minutes! It took me awhile before I could remember a damn thing. Since my mother did not know how to drive, and we could not get in touch with my father, Marty Silverman rode me home on his bike.

I was so out of it that it took me awhile to remember things. I was groggy, and my mind remained "foggy" for several more days. As I became more aware, I realized our team was playing against Brooklyn at Prospect Park at the end of that week, and I had to get myself together so my parents would let me play. This was big time since AAA baseball played their games at Prospect Park. Manhattan was to play the Bronx with Staten Island having a bye. It was going to be old home week for me!

My father and I out-voted my mother, who had not wanted me to play. She felt it was too soon for me to be back playing baseball after having been knocked out. Nevertheless, after a lot of begging, she gave in and we all headed out to the game in our parents' car, and I felt ok...normal. Our team played well, I got a couple of hits, Paul jerked one out of the park, and we won! Thank Heavens Manhattan beat the Bronx, so we had a week to prepare for our next game against Manhattan's team. This game was going to be played at our home field: the field that had come close to doing me in on two occasions! Nevertheless, we *were* *excited* to be hosting the game only a few blocks from *our* homes.

Once again the field was not kind to me or the team, as we lost to Staten Island 5 to 4. We thought they had some older guys playing on their team for them. Not only did several of their baseball players have mustaches, but I think one of them was even married..... I believe he had a young boy in the stands calling him dad. What kind of bull is that? Eventually I got used to the fact that when the "City" ran a tournament, it was like Ali Baba and the Forty Thieves! People used fictitious names, presenting birth certificates of dead people for all I knew. I was in a basketball tournament later in high school where my park team played against half the Knicks who were using fake names. That is the way the city was, take it or leave it!

Anyway, we ended up being the runners-up of the tournament, and that was not too shabby. We were excited as we waited for our trophies to be awarded. Mayor Robert Wagner had a ceremony at City Hall, but to our surprise, he gave each of the players on our team a pair of roller skates instead of the large trophies we had expected. I did not realize it back then, but I sounded just like Allen Iverson when I said, "Skates? We're talking about skates!??" Everyone was bent at the "so called" *trophy* for being runner-up in this big ass city! Give me a break! Skates,?????

Trophies are still the name of the game when it comes to awards. The bigger the better was any kid's mantra. And trophies did not come easily, because in my time, teams had to win and win big in order to receive trophies.

Several of the players on my team threw their skates away while we were coming back home from City Hall: they said they were too embarrassed to use them! One of the players gave his pair to a saxophone player who was playing music in the subway for tips. With the musical case open resting on the floor several coins were scattered on the purple velvet that lined the case when the box of skates were tossed into the open case. It all happened quickly as we were running to catch our train before the doors closed. We all had our faces pressed on the windows trying to see the reaction of the sax player as the train slowly left the station! We didn't know what to expect, but he kept playing his sax! Anything for a laugh was what we were made of!

I was so happy several years later when I learned that the *Daily Mirror Newspaper* went out of business. And I am sure it was not because they went broke spending money on awards!

The Junior High Days

"This is what I am talking about... freedom!" I liked junior high much better than elementary school. We were up and going here and there with only one thing on our minds, and that was to stay far away from those ninth graders. They looked big and nasty, with nothing on their minds besides girls and fighting! We stayed clear of these people; even the girls were tough!

Parsons Junior High
I am the second from the right on the top row.

The start of my basketball career began at Parson Junior High School, located on Parson's Boulevard, close to

Queens Boulevard ("HBO's Entourage"), and it was about six miles from my home on 70th Avenue, a block off Main Street. Parsons was a 7th through ninth grade school, so when we entered high school, we entered as sophomores. This was big time to me and I liked it even more because it was further away from my home.

At Parsons Jr. High there was "everything" running in the halls. It was a miniature Times Square! We certainly had more than our share of weirdoes. I could not believe we were at a school with so many misfits.

My friends and I all had pegged pants with saddle stitching tapered down to our pointy shoes (French toes). I was the only one who did not have pointy shoes, and I wanted these shoes for myself. My parents on the other hand liked neither the bell-bottoms nor the peg pants…, which I favored! What was neat was that my best "teacher", Arthur "the Custodian", gave me "lost/left over" clothes, which he had collected from lockers in the gym and from the hall lockers when students left our school or were being sent to reform school, or just forgot to clean out their lockers at the end of the year. In some cases students had been picked up off the streets, whisked off to detention school and never had the chance to empty the junk from their lockers. Arthur once gave me a neat wool Army jacket that was called an "Eisenhower" jacket. I renamed it a "McArthur" jacket since "Mac" and "Arthur" were my two "best teachers"!

I again had a great situation at school…. I was thrown out of my English Literature class (reading) where we had to read our asses off. Arthur heard about me through Mac, from the elementary school, so Arthur knew the books I had been reading and he picked up right where Mac and I had left off in 6th grade. Arthur brought me more of the *Chip Hilton Sports Series* for us to read together, as well as some for me to take home to read.

By now, I knew not to let my Dad see me trying to read, so I would usually read under the sheets using a flashlight. I slept in the living room on a sofa that made into a bed. It was the next best thing to having my own room! My sisters, Ilene and Enid, shared a room and since my brother Jeffrey had just recently been born, he stayed in my parents' room. He was fun except at night when he cried through most of the night, keeping everyone up. He cried quite a bit! During the day, he was fine, but we all dreaded the evening time when Jeffrey would cry non-stop.

Our extended family was a lot of fun. On the weekends, we went down to the lake and played, or if we wanted an even greater time, we traveled to the Island. My father had two nieces living in Elmont, Long Island. They were the daughters of his oldest sister, Bea. My cousin Ruthie was married to Murray, and they had two children, Mona and Ira, who were fun, personable, and caring people. They lived very close to my other cousin, Delly and her husband, Hy. They had four kids: Alan, a year younger than me, Spencer, Freddie, and an adorable daughter named Jaci. Freddie was Jeffrey's age and everyone had more in common than just being related. Murray and Hy were partners in a very successful liquor store. It was a treat to head out to the island to visit and play in their beautiful, grassy back yards and in streets that were not lined with parked cars! It seemed that most streets were round at the end which I learned later was called cul de sacs. These cul de sacs were a far cry from the parallel streets where I grew up. Moreover, I did not see any sewers in the middle of any of their streets. Each house had a garage and neat mailboxes that we always leaned our bikes on. It seemed like heaven.

Occasionally my father's brother Phil and his wife Rose also made the trek to the island with their two boys, Talbot and Mark. Talbot and I were always in trouble when we got together, and Mark, his little brother, was a cute kid who I tried to take under my wing! When we were all out there, it was sports, eating, and more sports before we headed back to the city.

I liked that kind of living... split-level homes, riding our bikes in the street, beautiful grass lawns in front and in back of each house. We all enjoyed the large family atmosphere and were always asking if we could visit our cousins again.

My dad's family was special in their own ways. His brothers were a bit different, but still good people. The only one of my Dad's brothers I have not mentioned so far is Ben, second oldest. He was a stern, straight up kind of person who always wore white long sleeved shirts. Everyone seemed afraid of him: my dad, his brothers, sisters, etc. I personally liked Ben because he always had money for me. *Not like coins, but more like large bills.* Ben liked to drink, although I couldn't decide if he was an alcoholic or not. I enjoyed watching Ben operate around the store and liked being around him when we got together for social visits. Ben lived in an adjoining house with Aunt Bea (Delly and Ruthie's Mom) and Bea's husband Jack Richmond, the class of the family in my opinion! I was definitely impressed with my dad's side of the family.

With everything seemingly going well with me, the roof fell in! I needed sneakers and my dad told my mother that he would take me for shoes when he came home from work that evening. He usually got home around 7:30 PM, and to get my shoes, we would have a forty-five minute drive to Delancey Street on Manhattan's eastside. Dad was a piece of work, but he had a heart of gold and was sentimental and proud about me playing sports. Through the family stories, I heard all about how well my dad did in sports and my father was especially successful in basketball. He always wanted the best for me, especially when it came to athletics. That seemed like the only thing we really had in common. I hated stamps because he spent so much time with his stamp collection, and had very little time for me or the rest of the family. The stock market was over my head, but I was enjoying the horses, although he was very reluctant to educate me on them.

Therefore, sports became the common ground for sharing time together. When I wanted to go watch a sporting event, my dad would make time to get me to an event or give me the money for just about anything..., which included Knicks tickets!

We were heading to "his" neighborhood to buy sneakers from the same place he bought his shoes when he was a kid. The storeowners were just shutting down the outside part of their businesses when they saw my dad. They were always happy to see him and they would wrestle around as if they were 15 years old. It did not take long to pick out and buy the sneakers I wanted, and we were heading to the car when I saw a shoe store across the street and asked if he was up to buying me one more pair of shoes. He said he would. My dad liked the idea that I was supportive of his old neighborhood since my mother would not even drive down there with him. She did not mind me going with him but warned him never to take the girls down to that "hole-in-the wall" of a neighborhood.

While there, I certainly could tell a major difference in his personality, demeanor, and his good-natured attitude. He was in heaven on the streets of the Eastside! I knew that he was a "major" fan of buying food at the corner hot dog vendors, and he had an even greater appreciation for the vendors in his stomping ground. We naturally purchased a couple of "dogs" and drinks, and with each bite he would ask, "Can you tell the difference? Isn't this food better?" He had so much pride in supporting these people who were trying, but struggling, to make a living! It was as if, the true law of the streets supports the underdog whenever possible!

I know it was then that I gained my appreciation for the vendors of New York. My mother of course hated the thought of eating in the streets! She always said that it was too unhealthy. As I have grown older, I have come to agree with her on that point but....

But, as I learned from my dad, it was not only a treat to eat from the vendors, but in the winter it was a way to stay warm being near the steam coming from the boiling of water and from the roasting of chestnuts that surrounded the vendor's stand. When I visit New York in the winter, I still love stopping and buying some of the roasting chestnuts. It was the place to be to show support for New York City!

My dad and I walked across the street and I showed him the French toed shoes I wanted. His first response to me was, "I don't think your mom will be ok with those." I answered that she doesn't care what shoes I wear, even though I knew she did. Therefore, he bought the pointed "French" toed shoes and I was thrilled. However, I was becoming nervous as we neared the apartments. I was wearing the new sneakers and I put my French toed shoes into the sneaker box so my mom would assume my old tennis shoes were in the box. Then she wouldn't know anything about the French toed shoes. As I was trying to "sneak" into the house, my mom came out and asked to see how bad my old sneakers were. She wanted to see why I had "needed" to buy a new pair. She had been in a pissy mood before we left because Dad was so willing to take me in the first place. The last thing we had heard when we were walking back to the car was my Mom yelling at him, "Sure, your kids need something and you run to buy things, but when I need something you tell me that we are broke!"

Finally, I had to open the shoebox with the French toed shoes inside. She took one look and hit the fan! Looking at my dad, she said, "What are you a schmuck? How could you buy your son shoes that a juvenile delinquent would wear?" The fight continued into the night, and I went to sleep without hearing the verdict. However, in the morning when I awoke, my new shoes were not there. My mom told me that dad returned them. I knew he was going to be upset when he got home because there were no such things as "returns" on the Eastside. However, he did not mention that to my mother.

My dad came home at 8:00 PM with no refund, but with the new shoes, he had exchanged my French toed shoes for. When I saw them, I was shocked! They were black loafers, the kind you put a penny in, but they had square toes. No kidding, they were square! I asked my parents if they really expected me to wear them. And that is when I found out how upset my dad was due to the previous night's argument with my mom. He jerked me up by my throat and said, "Never lie to me again about the need for shoes or I will kick your ass all over this street".

It seemed that the pace of my parent's arguments picked up as I finished my first semester at Parsons

Junior High. My grades for that semester were surprisingly better (not good, but better) since I had actually studied some. My parents were happy that I finally understood the importance of settling down to study at home. However, the real reason I stayed in to study was that I did not want anyone to see me on the streets wearing my new "squared shoes!" Although there was something positive going on, I was proud of my grades even though I had just squeaked by. I was good to go for another semester!

I had just finished the book *Championship Ball* and was starting on *The Hard Court Upset* when I learned of basketball tryouts at my school. Therefore, it was an easy decision to start practicing more and putting my schoolbooks on the shelf. Arthur was upset with me; he kept saying that in order to be an athlete, I have to pass my courses—all of them! So I had a crash course on "No Pass, No Play" at this time in my life. What a rude awakening that was! "Who in the hell ever thought that dumb rule up?" I fumed. What in the hell does playing basketball have to do with reading and doing math?" However, I did study some so that I could become eligible to participate in sports.

When tryouts were being held, it was unfortunate that I was en route to jail! I had lost my bus pass several days prior to tryouts, and I needed thirteen more cents to get home on the Q-44 bus. I was in the process of trying to borrow money from anyone I bumped into after school. I had collected eleven cents but still needed two more cents, when I saw a younger kid pick up a deposit bottle off the street, which was coincidently worth a 2-cent refund: the same amount I needed to get home. I asked him to give me the empty bottle, but he wouldn't so I just grabbed for the bottle, figuring I needed it more than him. When he did not let go, I popped him in his mouth. He cried and bled a little, while I ran with the bottle. I cashed in the bottle for the two cents and I was able pay my fare home.

Before school started in the mornings was always one of the most enjoyable parts of the day. It was where we were in a holding "tank" (the schoolyard) until the homeroom bell signaled. The custodian always made sure there were two basketballs and two Spaldings available before school started in the mornings. From the outside, I thought the school grounds were pretty close to resembling the "yard" in a prison!

On the day of basketball tryouts, the police came to the school for a shake down because there had been multiple related instances of harassing and bullying students for money at lunch, before school, and after school.

During my class, an office monitor came to my classroom with a note for my teacher. Her eyes looked up and to the back of the room where I always camped out. She said "Martin!" and before she could finish, I knew I had a problem.

When I arrived at the principal's office, the first face I saw was that of my dad, almost foaming from his mouth, shouting, "You make me take off from work for this?" Thank God, that by the time he reached me two cops grabbed him and calmed him down. Others who had already been called in were sitting on the benches. Among them sat the biggest hood of all, William "Billy" Moss, the one person we all knew to try to stay on his good side at all times. He was an older boy, but more like 15 going on 25. Although no one ever saw him in a fight, he had that look that said, "Screw-off, you piece of crap". And we did! There were several others lining the benches, and a wooden chair with the wooden bars on the back was awaiting my arrival.

When I sat down I tried not looking at my parents, but with my head down, I could still hear my mother crying. She was the only mother crying. There were several mothers there, but only one other father besides mine--which irked my dad even more!

Finally, they called my parents and me into the office and explained to them what I was being accused of doing. Then, the kid that I "borrowed" the bus fare from entered the room. Before he finished his side of the story, my father was once again foaming, cussing, and biting his knuckles on his right hand, staring at me with pure fury in his eyes.

The police "escorted" me off campus to the police station with my parents watching me get into the back of the squad car. They watched: rather my mother watched as my dad was shoving her in the direction of their car.

The "Punch"

When I was driven home in a police car several hours later, my friends Ronnie, Dennis, Gloria, and Johnny were sitting on the stoop waiting to hear the details. When the police car stopped, my dad stood at the door waiting. As I stepped out, my dad just stood there, glaring at me. I was trying to think of something to say to show how sorry I was when a punch from hell arrived, knocking out my two front teeth! I really don't remember anything else other than my mother yelling, "Jack, Jack", and I was out.

It felt like six years later when I finally awoke from the punch, but life went on.

Basketball tryouts came and went, but they did not include me. I asked the coach when I returned to school if I could get a tryout, and he basically told me to kiss off! Here I was in the 7th grade and I had a terrible reputation already as a hoodlum and a dumb butt to boot. Arthur was upset with me because I didn't come to him for the money, but I told him the school had been locked tighter than hell, and I could not get to him.

However, I was passing my courses by the skin of my teeth, since luckily there was not a grade given in reading. Arthur was the only one at that school who was giving me any academic assistance with my reading. The teachers were down on me because I was a problem, always in fights and hanging with the wrong crowd. I felt that if I hadn't lost my bus pass, I might have been ok! It was kind of a turning point, and I had just failed. It was three strikes and I was out! Gonzo, gone!

I was truly circling the drain when I met my first real girlfriend, Barbara Unowitz. It was the middle of the 7th grade and I spent a lot of time with her since I was not in basketball, and did not want to continue hanging with the troublemakers. Barbara lived up Jewel Avenue in a big house, and her dad owned a steel corporation. She had some brothers who I liked playing with also. They were younger, but enjoyed sports so we had a common ground.

Barbara and I dated from the time I was twelve and a half, until I was almost fourteen years old. One of the neat things we did was to go to Coney Island in the family Cadillac driven by their chauffeur. The chauffeur picked me up first and brought me to her house. I then went in and got "my boundaries from her dad". After listening to him for about ten minutes, he gave me fifty bucks for the afternoon and told me, "Take care of my daughter and don't come back with any money, spend it all on her!"

We had a great time together, but we broke up when my family and I moved back to Brooklyn, a few months after I graduated from Parsons Junior High.

The Birthday Gift

On the weekend of April 20, 1956, I turned thirteen! My father often treated me as if I were older than I really was. He even taught me how to drive when I was only eleven, and I always had money in my pocket because he thought carrying cash was very important in life.

When my 13th birthday came my dad was his usual non-emotional self, but he had a different "air" around him, like he was proud of me. The only other time I had seen this from him was at the trotters (Yonkers) when he gave me thirty dollars to go with him to the horse track. The money was for nine races and I was to bet two dollars on each race, and then use two more dollars to get into the track and buy a program. The remaining ten dollars was for me to keep my mouth shut as to anything I saw or heard at the track.

My dad hung with degenerates, lifelong gamblers who were sprawled all over concrete flooring next to the track railing. They all knew my dad. That also included some of the jockeys. If a jockey winked at my dad as the jockey walked his horse around the track during their warm up, my dad would then give me a hundred dollar bill and tell me to place a ten dollar bet on that jockey's horse!

The minute that these guys sitting around the track saw my dad after looking up from their Telegrams (betting guide for the night's races), they began chanting, "Jackie, Jackie!" Or they would start asking; "Hey Jackie, how does number 4 in the fifth look to you?" My dad helped them win plenty of cash throughout the years with his knowledge of the horses, jockeys, and more importantly, the owners.

Dad was in heaven picking horses at the track!
He was considered one of the best
handicappers in N.Y.C.!

My dad always covered his *Telegraph* with his notes on the horses, jockeys and he also listed all tips he had heard on each page of his *Telegram*. Using all this information, he had a master sheet with the places for each of the top five finishers in each race. He was never too far off in any given race!

My very first race to bet on was a 50-1 shot. "Adios" something was the horse's name. At the trotters, the track is a half mile and the horses have to run around the track twice to make the mile distance. Around they came for the first time and my horse was so far back in last place that the announcer never even mentioned my horse's name! Needless to say, my dad was rolling on the ground laughing at me. As they approached the back turn coming toward the finish line, a very weird thing happened. The horse that was leading by three lengths, "broke", which means that its hind leg got out of stride and hit the carriage. This caused the horse to get out of rhythm and pull to the right, which triggered each of the other horses to "break" as well. It was a funny sight... seeing eleven horses jumping around trying to regain their strides and rhythm to regain their trot and finish the race!

Adios was so far back that "the break" never even affected him, and he trotted in as the winner at a pace of 2:17. The race should have finished at least in a time of 2:04. Anyway, I went and collected one hundred and two dollars for the first two-dollar bet of my life! My dad just said he felt sorry for me because he believed now I would be "hooked!" And he was right!

During my birthday week, my dad decided to be the hero and give me something that he thought every boy wanted. It was a Sunday and the store was busy. I was on the side of the store facing the subway, busily taking orders one after another. I could not see my father when he came in from the other side of the store, but I could tell when my father was around because the workers acted differently and treated the customers much nicer. Dad rushed onto the planks and yelled to me, "Give me your apron, and take lunch". While I was taking off my apron, I heard him say, "I have a birthday gift on the desk." I opened the white flimsy (White Castle looking) door only to see a familiar girl sitting on the desk, with her feet on the chair. As I got closer, I about freaked out! I immediately looked around to see if any of the clowns that were working were peeking around the door! I was at a loss for words, which was not a common thing for me! She tried to make it easy for me by saying "Hi Marty" and I must have gone deaf, because I never heard a word other than my name! I about fainted; it was Margret!

I was so shocked, but most of all disappointed that it was the girl of my dreams. Looking back it reminded me of the movie "10", when Dudley Moore falls in love with Bo Derrick only to find out that she had such a foul mouth that it turned him off!

I was embarrassed, to say the least, and I left the store while my dad was serving customers, and I never looked at Margret again! All those times walking her to the corner, never realizing the line of work she was in... Who is the schmuck now!?

My 9th grade year was more of the same, but my reading did improve and I still loved my stories about Chip Hilton and his coach Hank Rockwell. The coach was so cool. He was tough as a boot, but he had a warm-hearted personality, even to those who did not play for him. I was a true fan of Coach Rockwell and wanted to play on a team so I could get better and be a hero like William "Chip" Hilton! However, I had no one helping me improve as an athlete. If it had not been for Paul asking me to go to the park and play basketball or baseball, I would have just hung out with the "gavonnes" who were searching for girls or looking for trouble.

Gloria Goldhammer was a bright girl who I liked being around. She helped me with my homework as well as my reading. I also liked going to her house because she had a drop dead gorgeous older sister. She was so attractive that she had even had a date with the movie star, Tony Curtis. Gloria invited me over to her house because she knew that I liked him in all of his movies. I was excited to meet this movie star and see how he acted around the "knockout" sister. Gloria introduced me and his response turned me off so badly that I dropped him from my fan club status. I said, "Hi, my name is Marty, how're you doin?" He said, "My name is Crash Helmet!" What in the hell was that? The look on my face was like the kid who played basketball for Bobby Knight and was hit in the face with Knight's head while in the huddle. That ball player looked up in disbelief, that the coach would purposely hit him with his damn head! I immediately turned and left without saying "ougotz" to him. Gloria followed me out and said she knew where I was coming from. Gloria told me later that her sister disliked her date with him as well.

My first semester at Forest Hills High School was not good. Once again, along with Paul, I tried out for the basketball team. However, we both were unsuccessful, and we were cut on the first day. That took some of the thrill out of being in high school. However, the semester flew by quickly as my family was busy packing, getting ready to move again to a less expensive apartment but with three bedrooms.

Heading Back to Brooklyn

Before we hit the road, saying goodbye to my friends and the suburbs of Queens did not come easy.

My dress code fit in well at Lafayette
High School. Many hoods and Italians
that looked like the mafia!

My friends could not believe that I was leaving this wonderful area for the concrete jungle of Brooklyn.

I saw it in a different light though. I visualized the beaches and rides at Coney Island, Nathan's hot dogs, and most of all, getting a fresh slate to start over. It was my chance to "start over"... to try to recreate myself.

We moved to the Marlboro Projects, a low-income city housing project. Before the projects were built, there had been a beautiful lake where the retired mafia had lived and played Bocce along the lakeside. Then within a two-year period, there were 15 high-rise buildings between West 8th Street and Stillwell Avenue and Bay 50th. Some of the apartment houses had only six floors and some of the larger complexes had 16 floors with long terraces that served as walkways to each apartment. The walkways were also used as small playgrounds for the young children living in these apartments to ride their tricycles and pull their wagons.

In the middle of the projects were four full court fenced-in basketball courts. Each basket had a chain net and a silver perforated backboards. People packed the park all day until nightfall. Even during school hours, the park was still crowded with young men who were out of work or who were cutting classes. My high school, Lafayette, was right across the street from Marlboro Park.

Lafayette High School is an old school built in the 30's. The school was used in a scene from the movie, "The French Connection" with Gene Hackman (Popeye) as the detective who was on a mad pursuit chasing a drug dealer throughout the city, the projects, and under the Stillwell train tracks, (the El). Other trivia about Lafayette H.S. is that Sandy Koufax, Bobby Aspromonte, and other big name baseball players went to school there before going into professional baseball careers. Larry King was another graduate of Lafayette H.S. as was Gary David Goldberg TV producer (Family Ties, Brooklyn Bridge, etc.).

My buddies in Queens told me they thought I would be in trouble the minute I went to Lafayette High School, and they were right! I was in three fights during my first week. Two of my fights during that week were on the basketball court and one was as I was walking home from school. So much for having a second chance in life! It seemed like Brooklyn was filled with gangs and people who were constantly looking for "pissing contests!"

The big incident occurred during my second week of school at Lafayette. During lunch, I was showing off to my new friends when I looked down and saw a rubber band lying on the floor. Without thinking at all, I picked it up with my pencil, pulled it back like a sling shot, and let it fly. We all cracked up, as this "object" landed smack in the middle of a girl's Boston cream pie! She was not amused, but god did we laugh. Everyone was laughing so hard that we did not pay much attention to the girl, except noting she had the worst mouth we had ever heard. She came over holding the rubber band in a napkin and growled something to the effect of, "Which one of you $*@ suckers threw this?" When the other guys saw who the girl was, they scattered and I was left there standing by myself!

It did not take long for her boyfriend and about ten others from his gang to find me dressing after my P.E. class. It really was not a fight; they just held me off the ground with a knife under my chin. Lots of screaming and cussing, but all I could hear through my crying was them yelling, "You "tink" you a big man? Ya "tink" we wouldn't find ya?" This must have gone on for several minutes, although it seemed like hours, before a warm voice from the back of this gang said, "Let him go, he is my new neighbor!" Two seconds later I was left bleeding as one of the guys had already knocked out the two new caps from my front teeth. So embarrassed, and with blood flowing, I was just happy to still be alive! As the gang walked away, a deep rhythmic voice yelled, "All right boys, break it up. No fighting in the locker room." It was Coach Frank Rabinowitz, Lafayette High School's Varsity basketball coach. He asked if I was alright, and I was just happy he had come along, but I didn't admit to that. However, out of embarrassment, I just "bragged" that I was used to getting into big brawls and taking on entire gangs at one time. I thought the coach might have been impressed, but eventually I realized he was giving me a chance by just overlooking my attitude. He ignored my comment and asked me if I played basketball. I replied yes, and surprisingly enough, he invited me to try out in one week, which would be right after I got my front teeth capped... again!

The next week there must have been sixty boys trying out after school for the basketball team. I looked around at the other kids shooting balls. Some looked good and some did not. I tried to measure myself up to all of them, but I couldn't really tell. I then tried to identify the players who were on the team already, but no one was wearing any school colors or uniforms to identify them as current basketball players. Finally, I heard Coach Rabinowitz's distinctive voice say, "Alright boys, line up here". He then introduced this year's team who had just finished the season 15-11. I felt funny, like I did not belong. The movie "Grease", which came out many years later, expressed my feelings to a "T." It was when John Travolta tried out for basketball and all he really knew how to do was to fight. I had the same greased hair as he had in the film, but I had stashed my black leather jacket and motorcycle boots in my locker. If I made this team, I would have to get myself cleaned up, that was for sure!

God only knows how I made the team. I knew I impressed coach with my jumping ability and driving. I was also faster than most, but I did not quite measure up with shooting from the outside. However, thankfully, Coach Rabinowitz found "something" he liked, because the next day my name was written on the "team roster", which had been posted on the gym wall. His decision to place my name on that roster provided the vehicle that helped me move forward toward my conscious and subconscious goals through sports. It was the platform for obtaining an identity!

I tried to move away from my past, began dressing differently, and most of all I attempted to behave a bit more civilized. Lafayette was the first "real" basketball team I had ever played on. The players on the basketball team were focused, committed, and good role models for me. During my junior year, I especially looked up to the seniors on our basketball team: Rosen, Berger, Wagner, and Mazzeria.

Our team was in a very tough city league, and we played against great players like Billy Gallanti from Madison and Billy Cunningham (76ers) from Erasmus HS. New Utrecht HS had Stanky and Erdos, while Ft. Hamilton HS had Barnett. Lincoln HS had just lost their All-City scorer in Larry Brown (Future NBA Coach and player), Wingate had Roger Brown, (great ABA player), and then there was the player who never reached the plateau that he deserved, Connie Hawkins from Boys High. This division was considered the "suicide" league within New York City.

Bob Barnett from Fort Hamilton H.S.

My 1960-year book had this team photo of the seniors on Lafayette's basketball team. We had a scrappy team during my final year. I was on the team with Izzy, Ditto, Axelrod, Diamondstein, Fabrican, Iarrussi, and Sherman (Whose dad was the doctor who had once given me shots in my ankle so I could play). Bobby was true to his word though; he never told anyone that I actually believed his dad when he told me that his needles were made out of rubber!

They were all very close because they had been playing together at Sethlow Junior High, and at the "J" (Jewish Community House of Bensonhurst) before they came to Lafayette HS. They all lived about three miles from the school and traveled together on the bus after practice. The star senior Eddie Mazzaria and I were the only members of the basketball team who lived in the projects. Even the cheerleaders were from "the other" area of Bay Parkway and 86th Street. I really wanted to be a part of that group and be able to take the bus with them. They all had such fun together, and I was very jealous!

Therefore, wanting to be part of the "group", I started taking their bus and I traveled away from my home to Bay Parkway with them. At that time, the cost for bus fare was only fifteen cents to Bay Parkway so I ate less for lunch and kept the extra money for the one-way trip. This meant of course, that I would then have to walk back from Bay Parkway to the projects at seven o'clock in the evening, five nights a week. I carried my gym bag filled with three textbooks along with my sweaty clothes. Don't get the idea that I was carrying the textbooks for studying purposes. The reason for the books was to have enough weight in my bag to protect myself if a dog decided to chase my ass; I could take meaningful swings at the growling mongrel with my heavy bag. This went on for my entire junior season. Was it worth it? Yes, without a doubt!

Before my sophomore year ended, the Athletic Director, Dave Halpburn, asked Ronnie Axelrod, Kenny Gershon and me to come into his office. He told us that during the summers he was an Activity Director at a camp in Honesdale, Pennsylvania. He said it was a camp for wealthy Long Island kids attending for a two-month period and the activities were boating, theatre, tennis, and golf.

He went on to say that the owner, Sid King, wanted to add one more sport to compete with the other camps in the area, and basketball was the sport he wanted to add. So the bottom line was, did we want to work at the camp? He admitted there were a couple of drawbacks to the job. We would be dishwashers, and involved with creating a basketball program. And, although the pay would be very little, he felt the experience of doing this would be beneficial for us.

He explained that we would form a team using the best basketball players from the counselors at our camp. Our camp counselor team would be playing against other camps in the area. He added that we would be teaching basketball classes to the campers in between meal times. This was part of our camp chores. We all jumped on this opportunity!

Camp Cherokee

June came and we were off to Camp Cherokee. We left by bus from the Port Authority which was just down the street from my dad's store. Speaking about the store, my mom was happy I was getting a chance to get out of the city, but my dad was not as excited. He said that I would make twenty times more at the store. He claimed that I was looking to play around and not take responsibility for earning money. However, I looked at it as a chance of a lifetime!

The only time I had traveled to the mountains was when I was a cub scout. The highlight of each year in the scouts was to travel by bus to Bear Mountain and visit West Point! On our bus ride to camp, we passed through the Adirondacks, Bear Mountain, and of course the Big Apple restaurant; I was seeing New York in a different light. I had never seen so many trees before.

At camp, life was much different as well. First, I was eating three meals a day for the first time in my life. I actually put on ten pounds because of all the food I was eating.

The three of us enjoyed this life and felt comfortable around the "Islanders". There was one rule we were not too fond of though, we were asked, in a very diplomatic way, not to socialize with the campers, especially the girls! I guess they felt like we were inner-city trash, and I think they were afraid that the parents who were paying big bucks for their kids to have a good summer experience, did not want that experience to include socializing with three jocks from the inner city of Brooklyn!

Nevertheless, the good part of camp outweighed the bad in this policy of not socializing with the campers, and the three of us came to grips with it. Besides, the socializing ban never lasted too long anyway, by the second week after we had gotten to know some of the older female counselors, all was forgotten!

Competing in basketball against counselors at the other camps was so much fun that it helped us not to think of the funky policy or living conditions. The campers and counselors really cheered for us as we joined Bruce Paltrow, Mitchell Finklestein, Jerry Stein, Larry Frank, and a few other counselors who rounded out our team. We did well for this being our first year playing against the surrounding camps, and we won more games than we lost. We kept saying that it would be great if Ditto and Izzy were here because our counselor basketball team would have really cleaned up!

Carl "Pahoo" Evangelista was the Head
Counselor who everyone looked up to!
Pictured: Me, Babs Kusel, and Pahoo

Socially, it was great! Meeting our camp counselor
girlfriends at midnight on the tennis courts, dancing
to Johnny Mathis, panty raids, and me playing the
part of Bernardo in *West Side Story,* which was our
camp play.

However, the highlight of camp was "Color War!" The
entire camp (counselors and campers) were divided
into two teams, a green team and a white team. The
two teams competed against each other in everything,
earning points as we went. It was spectacular in every
sense. The entire camp was decorated in the two

colors. The excitement hit a deafening pitch at every encounter. It was something I will never forget.

I came back the next summer with younger teammates from Lafayette's team. Kenny Gershon and Phil Roth joined me as dishwashers, and once again, we all had a fantastic time. I was a fancy ball handler who drove to the basket well. Everyone at camp had a good time intentionally mispronouncing my last name as "Urine". Well, one thing lead to another and before the summer was over, I was nicknamed "Pisswater Urand" during my last year at Camp Cherokee and went by the initials, "P.W."

"Pisswater" came about because of two factors. First, my basketball idol was Bob Cousey of the Celtics, and in those days, he was considered fancy with his ball handling and passing skills. Another factor was the Knicks had a player who was also crafty, and he was a big guy who did plays in the air that were considered great body control. His name was Sweetwater Clifton. Consequently, urine took the place of Sweetwater's first name. And with a little imagination, "P.W." was derived!

An amazing thing happened at summer camp that came to fruition about twenty years later! On the days when it rained, I would head into counselor Bruce Paltrow's bunks which was usually also filled with the other Lafayette players, and we shared stories about ourselves: where we were from, inner-city games, the girls we were with, and Bruce was always taking notes while eating apples as we talked. Bruce was a health nut even at the age of 16 and his parents sent him a supply of apples each week. We all shared stories of playing in the city, while he would down several apples. In fact, Bruce had a net filled with apples hanging from his bunk bed so he could reach over and pull out one after another to eat. There were times when I had to ask him to take the apple out of his mouth because I could not understand him when he talked or asked a question. He not only shared his thoughts, but he also wanted to know everything the team's adventures and about us.

I did not see Bruce again after that summer. However, years later I made the connection while watching reruns on TV. *The White Shadow* was a show that caught my attention as I watched it. It was all about an inner city team coached by a person who looked and acted just like Kenny Gershon.

Some of the stories that we shared with Bruce and some that Bruce shared with us during those rainy days at camp were played out in *The White Shadow* television series. The name of the producer of that series was Bruce Paltrow.

Unfortunately, Bruce passed away in 2002. However, I had called and talked with Bruce to congratulate him on the 1993 series of The White Shadow. Bruce always comes to mind when I see Pete Caroll (Coach of the Seattle Seahawks, an NFL team) on T.V. because Bruce and Pete both look so much alike! Bruce had a very famous daughter also; her name is Gwyneth Paltrow. I have always wanted to get in touch with her and share some of the camp stories about her dad, to discuss his love for apples, and if she named her child "Apple" because of his love of apples? Maybe one day I will contact her so I could find out for sure.

During that second year of summer camp, our basketball team won the Camp Division. It was great playing with Kenny and non-basketball players who really held their own against the teams from the other camps.

By having added basketball to the camp sports of golf and tennis, the camp took on an all-new dimension that lifted the camp's enrollment.

Jerry "Cherokee" Stein
Best camp swimmer 1959
Addition by Jerry Stein
(Many, many years later!)

Camp Cherokee was a place where we all learned lessons which shaped our lives. We were always kept busy by the planned activities, whether they were sports or arts oriented. If there was no scheduled activity, we embarked on our own adventures that included sports such as basketball, tennis, swimming, waterskiing, baseball, volleyball and non-sports oriented projects in which we had an opportunity to participate.

Cherokee and the older campers had "socials" almost every night. Many of us met our first loves at these get-togethers. There were also the unsanctioned activities. It was a thrill to sneak down to the lake when it was especially hot to go skinny-dipping. There were of course the panty raids and soirees on the tennis courts when there was no moon or in the woods when the moon was bright.

In the end it did not mean much, but the beginning was very different. I do recall that there was resentment that we were going to have real basketball players who were brought in just for that particular purpose. It was the first time that we had seen recruitment in action. There was some discussion among the "regular" campers because we thought that we would not have the chance to play and if we did play with you, we would never see the ball.

Here we were a group of upper middle class kids from Long Island and Westchester, trying to do our best and we would be usurped by a group of basketball *jocks from Brooklyn. During previous inter camp competitions we had done well in most of the other sports but our basketball record was abysmal and we were the laughing stock of all the other competing camps when it came to this sport. At the start of the camp season we got a kick out of making fun of your Brooklyn accent.*

The season progressed and we all did get to play with the Lafayette High School elite basketball team, the outsiders.

Not only that, we beat the pants off the other camp's basketball teams. We now had a real basketball team. We were not only good, we were undefeated, and we were proud. I remember one game during which there was one play - feed the ball to PW. You scored 100 points that day!

We learned a great deal about playing and sportsmanship from the group. The jocks from Lafayette stopped being the jocks and became our friends.

Those two summers were the best summers of my life!

My Next to Last summer in New York!

After coming home from camp, I went right back to work at our malt shop and tried to make up for the cash lost while I was away having fun. It was as if I had never been gone. All the derelicts were still there, in and out of the store, it was just the same as always! Nothing ever changes on the "Street"!

All the usual characters were still coming in, except now Woody was gone. Most of our customers were just customers, as we never really knew anything about their personal lives. When they were gone, they were gone; seldom leaving a clue as to what happened to them. Nevertheless, I missed seeing some of our long-term customers like Woody and hearing his philosophies, his biases, and his "tips".

I think each New Yorker has his own philosophy of life. And for the most part, they are very opinionated! While working in the store, if I took the time to talk to a customer during a slow spell, they would always begin by saying, "You know, kid, I believe that....." and I was stuck listening exclusively to their side of the story, and their opinion on the way they see things.

There were two cops, Sal, an Italian and Kelly, an Irishman who often patrolled *Times Square*. They were both absolutely great guys who came by for a couple of "dogs" and a malt most days. I shared with them my PAL (Police Athletic League) experiences including the fact that I thought I might want to become a police officer if I did not get a scholarship to attend college. Unfortunately, I also told them a joke that I had overheard another cop telling Officer McPhearson at the 62nd Precinct.

I began by looking at Sal and told him about these two cops who saw a kid playing in the gutter with horse manure. When the Italian cop asked the boy what he was doing, the boy replied, "I was building an Irish cop". Sal began laughing while looking at Kelly. Kelly, the Irish cop, did not laugh as I continued telling the joke. The Irish cop then asked the kid, "Why are you building an Irish cop?" The boy looked at both cops and said, "Because I don't have enough shit to build an Italian cop!" Sal looked at me and I could tell that he was not really mad, but he had the look like; "You really don't know me well enough to let one of those slammers fly!" In the meantime, Kelly had a great laugh and every time they came in, Kelly would ask me if I had any more "good" jokes?

It was a week before school started, and my senior year was approaching, which meant there would be some major decisions and outcomes ahead for me. I was working at the store every day, trying to earn as much money as I could, when a glass of malt was thrown at my head. I had waited on a customer in the traditional sense, which meant very little conversation and a lot of pointing. When this white person pointed at the franks with two fingers and said, "Make me malt". I did what I have always done utilizing my dad's theory of "Cultural Cravings" and made chocolate malt for him. I served the malt and waited to be paid when he said, "I didn't order chocolate malt!" "What kind did you order?" was my reply, and I started toward the back to get my dad. I knew this was going to be a problem bigger than my customary everyday fracases. When I was almost to the back, one of the customers yelled, "Watch out, kid". When I whirled around, the glass with the malt was heading toward my head! My arm came up and the glass hit my forearm, splashing the malt all over the walls and me. My temper kicked in and I put one foot on two or three rows of hot dogs that were on the grill, placed my other foot on the glass casing that covered the dogs, which smashed in hundreds of pieces. The glass landed on the rest of the twenty rows of dogs. It wasn't two seconds before I launched myself over the counter pushing and shoving this jerk-off into the street. The blows were coming at that point and I landed two magnificent shots before I was down on the ground with him and he was now on top of me kicking my ass! Trying to avoid each punch and keeping my arms in front of my face, I never saw the cops come. Thank God, they arrived. I could hear Sal saying to Kelly as they were pulling this load off me, "Let's see if this little prick has any more funny Italian jokes to tell?"

"Shirley" was a Big Hit!

Getting my ass kicked was not a good way to end the summer! Several cuts on my face, a black eye, and ribs that were so sore I could not even sit on the commode! My ego was hurt, but nobody would really know who won the fight if I was telling the story. Therefore, I decided to a have a beer bash after I had my two front teeth replaced again! The party was set for one night while my parents were going out for the night. I figured that I could get a group of my friends together and I would tell my side of the story about the fight and surprise them with a stag movie.

By mid-August, the event was set. My parents were heading to the mountains for the weekend. Word hit the street and our apartment was mobbed! Mostly my friends from the park and a few of their girlfriends came. The big attraction for the evening was drinking beer and the showing of an 8mm "stag" film that I named "Shirley". It was an "X" rated film that was unique at the time (1960) and featured a blonde-haired woman wearing nothing but a black velvet necklace and heels. The man was wearing a mask, and black ankle high socks. One of the people who worked in the store loaned the film to me.

With my sisters and brother asleep, the guests began to arrive. By ten p.m. "Shirley" made history! The projector was on the kitchen table just in front of the pyramid of empty beer cans that now reached five rows high. The film was only eighteen minutes in length and the crowd was silent as the reels began to turn and the projector lamp made its way across the smoke filled room onto a white sheet hanging on the window. Ten minutes into the film, laughter and jokes and catcalls were flying with each movement, while we "took in" every educational second"! As the film played, I periodically glanced from the entrance of the hall to the bedrooms, looking or listening for my sisters or brother to wake up to use the restroom that was in the hall by the kitchen..

However, within the next two minutes, all hell broke loose! A familiar loud noise came from the front door as the door hit the safety chain after a key had unlocked the door. My first thought was that it was the police, and then I realized that police would not have a key to our apartment door. Sure enough, it was my parents coming back to get something they had forgotten. They had just finished eating Chinese food at their favorite restaurant and were heading thirty-five minutes up the Belt Parkway when they realized that they had forgotten "the projector" to show home movies to their friends.

I immediately turned off the projector, turned on the lights and slowly walked to the chained door. We were throwing all kinds of our crap out of the rollout windows (housing project designed windows). Slowly walking to remove the chain from the door were the longest few steps I ever had to take. No words were said as my parents walked into the apartment. They looked around and asked where the kids were? After I halfheartedly said, they're asleep", the focal point then became the projector! As my mother started to talk, my father sensed what we were up to and went over to the projector and rewound the film with the lamp off so as not to see or "show" anything!

My mom forcefully said to clear the place and that we would talk later! As I look back, it could have really been an embarrassing scene for me if they had chosen to react in their normal ways. I was happy to not have been punched, cursed at, or anything else I knew I truly deserved! Not to say that it didn't come close to that when they came home the next day!

The house cleared in a heartbeat! All through the evening, I was receiving calls from my friends who had been in the apartment, letting me know how sorry they were for me; but each finished their conversation by saying, "Do you think we will ever get to see the end of the movie?" We never did!

Anything for a laugh!

There were always fights happening, either in the store, with the staff, the brothers, or on the street. When all seemed calm, we might have a continuous flow of major looking mobsters seeking to get a payment from my Uncle Irv! We all knew the drill. When the shylocks asked for Irv, we were instructed to say that they had just missed him. I doubt they believed that, but they always replied, "Well, be sure to tell Irv when you see him, that his friends are looking for him." I really think they knew Uncle Irv was in the back all along, but they just really did not want to beat the old guy up! We of course, thought that there was a contract out on him!

However, Irv was smooth as silk! His eyes moved from side to side without him ever turning his head. All the brothers seem to have a similar walk, which was hunched over as if they were constantly looking for money on the ground. Phil was the only one who was not hunched over, but he did focus on the ground when he walked. Through the years, I got to see all of the brothers engaged in a fight or two. The only one that I never saw fight was Irv. He had kind of an "Ali shuffle" to his walk and never was forced into fighting.

Although, once I did see him swinging a pipe as he chased a person out of the store. His cigar never left his mouth, and with one eyebrow up, he kept mumbling something that sounded like, "Nobody messes with me, I am too smart for these jackasses on the street!" I heard him clearer when he was in the back, still ranting and screaming that the guy would need a "proctologist" to retrieve the pipe!

Irv was a prankster supreme! He really was not as much on telling jokes as he was on playing tricks to make others look silly or stupid. Once, we were attending a wedding, and Irv had a bunch of my cousins gathered together for one of his famous pranks. I think most of the younger family enjoyed these get-togethers so they could see Irv in action. He always made us laugh and brought us together since we all lived so far apart. My cousin Mark loved Irv and was the "runner", the person who would round up the others for the "show". When I finally got there, my cousin Alan was sitting on the floor in his suit and tie, and his legs were open in a straddle position. A fifty-dollar bill lay in a small puddle of water. Irv was telling Alan that he could clean up that water and get the fifty-dollar bill before Alan could stab his hand with the knife Alan was holding. Alan was in a hell of a predicament, probably wondering if he should really try to stab his uncle. Nervously, Alan played along with Irv, and was halfheartedly using a stabbing motion into the puddle. And in the process, Irv was wiping up the water with Alan's butt. Everyone roared, even Alan, who now had pants, which were soaked! Irv was a character to say the least. But again, each of the other brothers had their "MO's" as well.

I guess if I had to say the one thing the brothers all had in common was the fact that even though they had a business there, they hated the "street". Forty-Second Street, Times Square area was filth to them. I guess City Hall felt the same way because ten years later, in an effort to clean up "the street", their store was one of the first to be shut down! Most of the theaters that ran semi-porn were closed down, and the police force added more police to help Sal and Kelly keep 42nd Street cleaned up. The city was looking for more tourism so it beefed up the security and was closing down the "schlock" businesses.

My Senior Year

I will never forget my senior year of high school. There were such great events that occurred. Basketball was the highlight of my life along with my brother (4 yrs. old) becoming the mascot of the team. He was just learning how to dribble and move with the ball. He was special to our entire family, but for some uncanny reason, we each had a fear that something bad was brewing. When my brother was playing all was wonderful. But there were times that we all worried because he would sometimes hold his breath and then pass out, falling hard onto the floor!

In addition, as fate would have it, our deepest thoughts and fears transpired! We were having a typical night with Jeffrey playing in the living room and we were all laughing as he made us do on many occasions. We would laugh and he would do something else to capture our attention so we would laugh some more. But that night, as we sat on the couch, we noticed that something was not exactly right with him, that his movements looked unusual and awkward. But Jeffery soon returned to normal, and we thought nothing more about it.

We all went to sleep without a thought that this night would never be forgotten. That morning, my four-year-old brother died. It was discovered too late that he had a brain tumor, and within twenty-four hours, he was taken from us! He had cried most of the night like he sometimes did, but this time it was different. He was obviously in pain and then he just laid down as if in a deep sleep!

Jeffrey and I had slept in the same bedroom with our beds next to each other, and there were many nights that I watched him tossing, and letting out little cries in his sleep. I worried, having terrible thoughts about his health, and his behavior worried my mother and father as well. I was always so happy when he woke me in the mornings, and I would hold him on top of my stomach for a few minutes before taking him to the bathroom. However, that particular night, when he cried, I had a terrible feeling that he might be sicker than we thought. But he had done this before, and I shook my fears away, and I assumed he would be better in the morning, like usual.

Over the years, my sisters and I have discussed what could have happened. Were there serious signs that were evident, but our family just didn't notice? He was the love of our lives! God only knows why he was taken away!

MARTY URAND

After he was gone,
Laughter became a thing of the past.

After Jeffery's death, my family went to pieces and the fighting between my parents became unbearable. Neither of my parents could handle the tragedy and they blamed each other. My sisters and I could not endure their fighting and deal with our own sadness in the middle of their anger and rage. Neither my sisters nor I were comfortable in that environment. We were also grieving and could not deal with the anger and blame my parents were throwing at one another. After Jeffrey's death, my parents moved us to the other end of the project in an attempt to get away from the memories of that apartment, but the fighting between my parents continued even more.

It was at this point that my younger sisters followed my path and wanted to get away from the family situation! This once happy, loving family experienced the worst setback a family can endure. Textbooks report that the highest level of stress one can encounter is when parents experience a death of one of their children! Unfortunately, my sisters and I can each attest to that.

For me, I knew I needed to get out of the house, and I had only two methods to accomplish this. The first was to enlist in the armed forces and the other was to try to go to college away from N.Y.

One dilemma was that I had a bum ankle and very poor grades. When I was playing well, college scouts took me out to eat and inquired about my feelings toward leaving the city to play ball. However, when the scouts saw my grades, I never heard from them again. It took me several episodes of meeting with coaches excited about me joining their teams and then not hearing back from them to find out why. Finally, I was told it was not my basketball ability that was lacking, but I did not have the grades for their school to be able to offer me a basketball scholarship.

On my transcript, it was marked with a stamp "Not Recommended for College".

When I moved from Queens, I was on a college track (Academic Degree), but when my high school grades began to fall, I switched to Commercial courses. Then when the coaches were concerned I would become ineligible to play basketball, they suggested I be moved to the lowest degree plan, "General". That meant that all my subjects would be identified with an "M" in each of my course grades, indicating that the courses were modified! No one explained the future consequence of this "non-educational" plan.

After 11 years, for the first time in education, I felt cheated! I had not received the same education the others were receiving during the same time we spent in school. Between my mom and dad and what little they knew about school, they never questioned why I never had homework, why I worked in the cafeteria so long, or why I had shop two periods a day. My parents never spoke to a counselor or questioned the decision to move me from one degree plan to another.

In addition, no one made the effort to speak with my teachers during open house.

I thought my living in New York would give me a "head start" in basketball, the Mecca of the basketball world! I thought basketball would take precedence in getting to the next level of playing basketball—college!

But to my surprise, basketball was not the key; it was only when all the smoke cleared that I found out what really counted! Academics were the prize for playing ball at a high level! I certainly did not come to that realization then. At that time, I was limited by my parents' lack of educational knowledge and experiences, and therefore still accepted their low educational expectations for me. It certainly was not their intention to not do what was best for me; they did everything they could for my sisters and me. But education was the one thing that could not be bought or attained without effort! I was not mature enough to understand it. And again, my parents did not know any better. It would have to have been someone at one of my schools to educate me, guide me, and counsel my parents on the importance of my education.

At school, when I got in trouble with grades, I was sent out of the class, or down to the basement where there was a classroom with a pool table and it was called 3G-1, The "Boog". We could play softball against the PE classes, shoot pool, or play cards. Of course, we could always choose to read, which several did: comic books that is. On occasion, I would bring a Chip Hilton book to read, hoping that it would not draw any attention whatsoever! They just had us "serving time", keeping us "out of the way". This was not much different from my elementary and middle schools' treatment.

I had a great set of friends, intelligent as well as being good athletes. One of my best friends, Stuie, used to call me "Hoople" and I thought that was because I played so much basketball. I think he was referring to my ignorance about school as well! My guess is that Lafayette was so poor that it needed all the ADA (Average Daily Attendance) it could get. They never expelled anyone unless there was blood involved Therefore, they did all they could to keep their students in school regardless of the disciplinary factors that arose on a daily basis.

Back Seat: Howie Pashinsky (Football),
Johnny Cianjulli (City Champ in Handball)
Front Seat: Cousin Talbot (New Utrecht) and
Me (Coney Island 1959)

However, it pissed me off that I was never told the reasons my name was removed from their list of available graduating players given to college coaches. All my friends were getting scholarship offers and my self-esteem was not very high on or off the court. I had a growing anger for the people that had played "God" with my life! Talk about a setback and being depressed, not knowing what I was going to do next. Having had no one to talk to about these issues, or a school administrator to help my parents and me understand why education is so important. I had been scamming to get away with as much as I could in school, and it was now kicking me in the ass.

I took a couple of days off, claimed that I was sick, stayed in bed, and just day dreamed for hours. I kept asking myself, "What in the hell am I going to do?" I felt like I was being chased out of everything because of my lack of education. I had made bad choices, but school hiding me away rather than explaining to me and my parents how I was damaging my future was their responsibility! I was really mixed up. On one hand, I was a leader, but on the other hand, I was being chased! Some people tried but they had no real Pull. "Mac, Arthur, where are you?" They had tried the most to get me on the right track, and I needed them back in my life.

In the yearbook, I wrote, ***"To be half as good as my father and to play at St. Johns!"***

What a joke!

On the Move-Again!

JCC of Bensonhurst
National Runner-up team 1961
Ronnie Axelrod, Eddie
Diamondstein, Marty Urand,
Larry Wasserman, Coach Artie
Press, & Stan Mackover

After graduation, for which I never walked across the stage because I did not pass the exit exam, we moved once again. We moved to a nicer location in Brooklyn on Avenue J and East 7ᵗʰ Street, just off Ocean Parkway. It was in the Midwood High area.

My ankle healed with Doc Sherman's help, and he convinced me to play basketball for the "J" because their teams travel and maybe someone would see me playing and pick me up on a scholarship. Soon after, I joined the "J". It was looking like we would have a great team, and it was my last resort! If this did not work, I decided I was heading to the Far East and the armed forces.

One of the older men who was a basketball fan when I played at the "J" got me a job working on Wall Street with Newburger and Lobe, cleaning ticker tape machines and sweeping the cigarette butts off the floor. When they saw that I could handle myself, they sent me to night school three nights a week to learn how to be a stockbroker. I began working on the "Floor" pushing and shoving for the broker that was buying and selling. It was fun, fulfilling, and educational; I enjoyed learning as well as the rough housing that went on in the "brass circle" on the stock market floor.

At the "J", we had great coaching from Artie Press and he gave me the basketball basics that I had been lacking. During the season, I went on several dates with his daughter, Adrian. I knew her from the year before when she was a cheerleader at Lafayette. The neat thing about meeting her was that Stu, my best friend, was introduced to her best friend, Anita. Several years later, Stuie and Anita were married!

Stu did not go to high school with me. He had known what he wanted, and he traveled almost three hours a day to and from Stuyvesant High School, which was well respected for its academics, and was located in downtown Brooklyn. He then went to Brooklyn College and received two Masters from CCNY, School of Business. Stu was an excellent basketball player but was not lured into organized basketball. He limited his free time to just pickup games at Marlboro Project. There were always tournaments that he could play in if he were interested, but Stu stayed focused on academics and chose to play football in high school. He kept his eyes on the academic prize and was never sidetracked, finishing school at an early age while we were still just trying to "play in another city tournament".

Needless to say, after he graduated college, Stu was hired by a great company that saw the upside of him. Stu always had a heart of gold and he donated funds to build high-rise apartments that were to be attached to the "J!" The housing was to help Jewish immigrants coming from other countries. The moral of this story is; where you live has nothing to do with what you become or where you go....It is your desire, motivation, and willingness to work for a good life that gives you opportunities to move forward. I learned this a little late, but I did benefit by not giving up.

Many of my friends (Philly Myra, Johnny Cinanjulli, Joey Hurstreet, Carl De Franco, Myrna and Phyliss Schloss, Marty Appell, and others) from the projects attended college and are very successful today.

Nevertheless, the fact remained, I still needed to get away from my parents, and I had no plan in place yet. It was obvious that the only thing I had in place was to work harder with my ball playing and get some sort of scholarship, because my parents did not have enough money at that time to assist with college. My dad started a new business/hobby that was brewing for several years. He became a handicapper for a well known Brooklyn bookie!

When the bookie accepts a large bet, he asks the handicapper if that horse has a substantially high percentage of winning. If it is determined that it does, the bookie will "dump" the bet, giving it to a "runner" who brings the bet to the track and places the bet.

If the horse wins, then the track pays off the bet rather than the bookie. It is a fine art that requires great insight and the ability to take many variables into consideration, such as track location, trainer, weight of the jockey, post position, previous races, weather conditions, dropping down in classification, and the ability of the jockey, etc.

This opened a new door for me to make some cash. I became one of about ten runners who waited at Dubrow's Cafeteria on Stillwell Avenue for a bet to be "dumped". The size of the bet would determine who was the most qualified to make the run. The largest bets were given to me because no one was bonded, and the bookie knew where to find my dad.

A young woman delivered the envelope to me, and then I took it to my dad's car and opened the envelope to begin my plan for how I was going to make the bets. Meaning which windows did I need to place the bets: at the $2, or $100 windows. In the envelope was the cash to place their bets, and a smaller envelope with my $10 for making the trip, plus $2 for getting into the track and for parking.

If it was really a large amount of cash, a couple of thousand or higher, then I knew the horse had a real good chance of winning and I would place the big bet and head over to the $2 dollar window to place my $10 bet on that horse. I always tried to stay for the race and collect my bet if it won. The rules were to bring the pari-mutuel tickets back, win or lose. I guess it was their way to make sure a runner did not decide to keep the bet in the hopes that it would lose and then he would just keep the money!

I took advantage of being at the track whenever I found time away from basketball practice, games, and work. It gave my dad and me a lot to talk about; it really brought us closer together.

I was 17 at the time, and in N.Y., a person needed to be 18 to drive legally. I had made enough money at the track to buy a 1952 Buick convertible. It was blue with a white ragtop, a big chrome grill, radio, and blue leather seats. I loved the car and kept it in a ten dollar a month rented garage space across the street from where we were living. Since my mother did not drive, she spent a lot of her time shopping nearby or sitting out in front of the apartment visiting with friends. Therefore, I could seldom chance taking the car out for fear she would see me driving it. I would go into the garage to wax and polish my car, and to start the car to keep the battery charged. I listened to the radio while waxing the car each week, and remember that the most popular song at the time was "A Hundred Pounds of Clay".

During the day however, I was busy with the stock market, which was a bit archaic by today's standards. Communication at the time was certainly not even close to where we are today. Technology-wise, when the market would close with a volume of a million transactions, the scotch would be brought out to celebrate the feat. Today's transactions are in the hundreds of millions each day!

But ironically, there was a stock my boss was trying desperately to encourage me to borrow money, so I could buy this stock. He said it was a revolutionary type company that could change the way the world would operate, literally! It was classified as a "Paradigm" shift in culture. For one, it put the Swiss out of the work of making the majority of watches. This company, Texas Instruments, claimed to make a watch with absolutely no moving parts. When I approached my dad with this man's "tip", it offended him. Throughout my life, all the "tips" had been supplied by my dad, not by a stranger from Wall Street.

Dad tried to use his handicapping skills on the "Texas Instruments" stock, but he assured me that TI did not have "a chance in hell" of making it. So obviously, I did nothing toward purchasing any stock because I thought my dad had better insight than the people who I worked for on "Wall Street!" But not this time.

No sense in talking about it; I missed a great chance of making some big cash. I only asked my dad one time if he followed that company and he said, "Forget about it!"

Back at the "J", our basketball team did very well, good enough to get to the playoffs in Allentown, PA! Unfortunately, we lost in the finals when a player on the other team shot a half-court shot that cost us the National Championship. Jerry Starr was the player who hit that winning basket and I will never forget his name!

I made the All-Tournament team, but was never contacted by any scouts while I was there. I was beginning to have doubts that I would ever be recruited. However, it was about three weeks later when I received a call from a man named Marvin Blumenthal. He explained that he saw me play in Allentown, and asked if I was willing to go to Houston to discuss the possibilities of playing in Texas. I replied, "Let's cut through the shit, do you know what my grades look like?" He said, "Yes! But they could work through that." I hated to keep questioning him about my education, but I did not want to make a trip around the world only to get discouraged! He assured me that he knew my situation.

He sent a plane ticket from Kennedy Airport to Hobby Airport in Houston, Texas, and I was told to look for the ugliest person in the airport! When I arrived, (my first plane trip ever!) he was waiting for me. Marvin Blumenthal was not the best-looking person, but he certainly was not a "Woody!"

We never left the airport. I had my workout stuff with me and was ready for anything. Being desperate for a chance, I guess my level of suspicion lessened, and my willingness to travel seventeen hundred miles for the chance to fulfill a dream come true was worth the risk!

In the four hours that we visited, he presented three college options - all within Texas. They were The University of Houston, Texas Western in El Paso, and Pan American College in Edinburg at the bottom of the state. He talked about his plans to supply each college with players who would bring National Championships to each of those schools. His plans were to work with the coaches of each of the schools and get the players who would make this happen. His plan was simple: he would get the brawn from the south, (Louisiana,

Mississippi, Alabama and Houston) and the brains from the east (Indiana and New York). Sounded like a great plan to me as long as I fit in there somehow.

We carefully discussed each college, who was there already, and how I would fit into each of their situations. We also discussed the value and need for an education. Marvin's insight and honesty were reassuring. He was a genuinely good person. He told me never to lose sight of the prize, which was to graduate from college. Marvin brought up each college, and we discussed who I would have to beat out if I attended that school.

The school we settled on was "Pan American College" in Edinburg, Texas. Marvin felt that because of my limited use of the English language, (I speak "Brooklynese") I would fit best in the Rio Grande Valley, seven miles north of Mexico! I would have agreed to attend South Texas State College of Bible Studies if that was a place that would pay for my school and get me out of New York! Location was not my priority as long as it was away from New York!!

Within days, I received the letter from Coach Sam Williams offering books, tuition, housing, meals, and a laundry stipend of twelve dollars per month.

What a feeling I had opening that letter on Pan American College stationary! I still have that letter framed in my home.

As for my sisters and their quest to get a new start, that was also accomplished! A little unorthodox, but just the same it worked! Enid left home to tour Europe and the Far East where she met her future husband. Ilene met and dated Bob Frasso, and they ran Brooklyn! Both were very happy in their own ways and I truly thanked God for these very fortunate opportunities for the girls!

On May 5, 1961, I received the letter that changed my life!

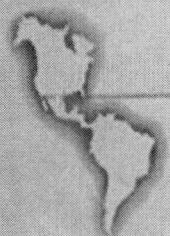

PAN AMERICAN COLLEGE   WHERE TWO CULTURES BLEND

EDINBURG, TEXAS

May 5, 1961

Mr. Marty Urand
1216 East 7 St.
Brooklyn 30, New York

Dear Marty:

Enclosed are the scholarship forms for you to fill out along
with this letter. You will receive tuition, room, board, books,
and fees. As you know, we are looking forward to having a good
season in 1961. We have the height and balance to do real well.
You will get a real opportunity to break into the starting lineup
as a freshman because we are weakest at the guard position, and
under NAIA rules, freshmen can play in varsity competition.

Would you send me a copy of you high school transcript as soon
as possible? I don't believe that we will have any trouble in
getting you into our school. Also, in a later letter, I will
give you the addresses of Vince Marino and Jim McClurk who live in
the Bronx and play for me. You can get more information from them
than I can write. They seem to be real happy down here.

Please rush the transcript so that we can get an o.k. on the entrance. I will send you a catalog under separate cover.

Yours truly,

Sam Williams
Basketball Coach

QUARTER TWO

College & Basketball

1962-1966

Texas Bound!

So in 1961, I began the second quarter of my game of life and was finally getting the chance I had been dreaming of. With two suitcases packed with everything that I owned, I said good-bye to my sisters, mom, dad, and Brooklyn! My dad drove me to meet two Pan American College basketball players from the Bronx, Vinnie Marino and Jim McGurk, who were driving me to Pan American College, in Edinburg, Texas for my first year of college. They had played on the basketball team at Pan American the previous year, and were on their way back to Pan Am for another year of college and ball playing. I should have guessed that these guys would have lived in the Bronx! So on my first trip to Texas; we drove through "Yankee" land towards a completely new and different lifestyle! Little did I know how different it would be?

Vinnie and Jim had gone to the same high school together, St. Helena's in the Bronx. I knew one thing for sure, not to tell them the Italian and Irish "crap" joke! These guys were really nice to me and were excited that there would be another New Yorker on the team. Both had started for the Pan Am Broncos, and Vinnie 5'11" and I eyed each other all the way to Texas. It would be he and I battling for a guard starting position for the years to come.

Jim, a 6'4", blue eyed, blond, was an all-American type guy who played forward. Jim and Vinnie were both stereotypical "Bronx players", who were referred to as "BIC'S", Bronx Irish Catholics. Vinnie was a miniature hulk, with a fighter's nose, cannons for arms, and huge wrists and fists.

On our trip to South Texas, referred to as "The Valley", it took me only to the end of Concourse Avenue to realize that people do not want to mess with Vinnie Marino.

Our trip was very educational since I had been out of N.Y. only a few times; once to play basketball in Allentown, Pennsylvania, and the other times were the summers that I spent at camp in Honesdale, PA.

Vinnie and Jim were making the trip for the first time by car. They had flown to and from Texas the previous year, but this year Vinnie's dad had given him a new '62 white Impala with red leather interior. What a way to go. Both shared the driving, and more than halfway there, when they thought they knew me better, they asked if I wanted to drive. I said "sure", although I had had no experience driving on anything other than on side streets in Brooklyn! After ten minutes of me driving and passing a car on the wrong side, using the emergency lane Vinnie quickly asked that I pull over to switch drivers. My feelings were not hurt! I was very nervous driving, and even more so in a brand new car. I was not asked to drive again all the way to Texas. Thank goodness!

It was a great trip and one that I will never forget, as I learned many specifics about geography and other facts that I should have already learned throughout my schooling. All the way to McAllen, Texas, I questioned both of them on what the college was like, how were the "women" and of course I had a million questions about the team. Never once did I think of asking any questions that referred to academics or school itself. I was naively assuming that what I had heard on the streets in Brooklyn was true. The basketball "jocks" in the parks had claimed "athletes" with college scholarships only had to play ball and did not have to attend classes. The word on the street was if athletes win games in college, the athletes would automatically be given passing grades. I was assuming that Jim and Vinnie were in the same boat I was in, "No grades, but plenty of ability!" I should have realized that coming from parochial schools; they would probably have at least some decent academic smarts.

1961-1962
"The Freshman Year"

Front Row: Mgr. Gordon Forester, Jim McGurk, Ellis Appling, Joe Karam, Walter Yates, Coach Williams **Middle Row:** Ramiro Vegas, Marty Urand, Vinnie Marino, Adon Perez, Paul Friddle, **Back Row:** Athletic Director James Brooks, Howard Montgomery, Jim Harter, Luke Jackson, Mitchell Edwards and Bill Crenshaw

RECORD 25 - 5

My entrance to college and dorm life certainly did not start out the way that I had imagined...that was for sure. We pulled up to the so-called dormitory and it was a pink, wooden, lopsided building with a sign dangling in front that said, *Belrose Hotel.* "No shit!" I said to the guys. I thought they were pulling some of the upper class bullshit that I had been warned would happen to incoming freshman. It certainly was a far cry from this great hotel I had been told was housing the basketball and baseball teams. This structure, I was assured, was a holdover until the new dorm that was being built was completed. I have to admit, there was plenty of construction going on at the campus.

After traveling 1,900 miles, it was quite a surprise pulling up to the "dormitory!"

We were surprised when Coach Williams, the basketball coach, came out to the car and greeted us. That was very nice, except we had to hide our cigarettes quickly under the front seat. Vinnie and I were the smokers. The coach acted like he never saw the cigarettes, but Vinnie was shooting me the finger behind the coach's back, since I was the one who had left the pack of cigarettes on the seat.

Coach Williams had a very strong East Texas drawl, making small chitchat while he thoroughly looked me over. We had never met. I had been sent to him sight unseen: a Blumenthal deal. The coach asked if I would stick around after seeing the "dorm". He had a great sense of humor and was always laughing and joking, but I could tell the others were being very polite and had dropped their cussing back to zero! Even their New York slang and accents were cleaned up a bit as well. We carried our bags in while Coach measured me up from my bowed legs to the 150 pounds that I weighed. It was obvious he wanted to ask me a lot of questions to try to evaluate my abilities. He said that some of the other basketball players were coming in from Houston later that evening and if we wanted to shoot around, we should drop by the gym the next day after breakfast.

"Well this ought to be good", I was thinking. "If this is the dorm, I can't wait to see the cafeteria!" But guess what!? There was not a cafeteria! The cafeteria was also under construction, and arrangements had been made at a few restaurants in Edinburg for us to give them one of our meal tickets and they would give us our meals. The *Highway Grill* was one of the places we could eat with our special Pan Am Athlete dining cards. We got the cards punched each time we came to eat, and the college took care of the finances.

L to R: Ellis Appling, Me, Jim McGurk, & Luke Jackson
Just one of the shocks that we faced was that there was not a school cafeteria!
It was three meals a day at the "Greasy Spoon".

There were three restaurants where we could eat using our food cards, but all specialized in "Tex-Mex" cuisine. So instead of cereal on my first morning, I was introduced to "Huevos Rancheros" and these little green things the guys told me were hot "pickles". At lunch we jumped all over some tacos and enchiladas with "the hot pickles". For dinner, we ate cabrito (goat), a meat often eaten in the Rio Grande Valley. By the time I went to the bathroom, I had to roll my socks down just to take a crap! I learned a lesson and chose my food more carefully thereafter.

When the Houston guys rolled in that evening, I found out why there were only three restaurants that would serve our entire team. Integration was on the move, but the Rio Grande Valley was not fully there yet. This was only the third year that Pan Am had added color to their teams. When I came to Pan American College, we had more black players than any other college in Texas. That included "The Glory Days" Texas Western who had been incorrectly portrayed as the first "breakthrough" integrated school in the state. Bull crap, WE WERE! And we were proud of being a part of that. Color was not an issue with any one of us.... We did not see color, we were united, a team... that's all that counted to us!

When a black 1954 Ford from Houston pulled up to the Belrose at 12:30 a.m., everyone, including the tennis players who had not qualified to play at the US Open Championships in Forest Hills with our championship Tennis Team, went downstairs to greet the Houston arrivals: Walter Yates, Mitch Edwards, Ellis Appling and Howard Montgomery. It was a great feeling seeing how well liked they were and how everyone seemed to get along so well.

Then a voice from hell came from the room closest to the front door. I heard the God awful curdle of a voice yelling from behind the door, "Boooooyz, don't let me have to come out there and get upset with y'all, hear?!!!" Everyone at the same time chimed in as if we were in a chorus, "yessssss, Ms. Alston!" From the sound of her voice, she had to be 90 going on 120. It really was frightful to know that and THIS was our "dorm mother"!!!

I roomed with Vinnie, and Jim roomed with Ned. Ned was not on the team and I never knew what his position was there, but he was an upper classman who was well respected by the athletes and students at Pan American. I was beat and I zonked out on a bed that had no sheets or pillows! However, in the middle of night, some scratching on the wall near my head awakened me. In fact, I saw several holes of different diameters scattered around the walls. There was no telling what in the hell was behind or in these walls. I woke Vinnie, yelling, "What the hell was that noise?" He muttered, "You will get used to it; they are dumb-ass possums that can't find the holes to get out". He told me to get back to sleep; that the opossums were probably making their rounds greeting everyone who came back after the summer!

The morning came and my butt was still on fire from all those "pickles", which I'd learned from this experience were actually jalapeño's, very, very hot peppers. I had foolishly been eating them to impress the other ballplayers with my "toughness". Nevertheless, I had to get over this and focus on getting ready to show my game to Coach Williams and to the other players. We went to what they called the "Field House" which was on the same plane as the other venues that I had already encountered. Although the gym floor was in good shape with good lighting, there were no seats at all. The gym had huge garage doors on both sides that were raised up so all of the 98+ degrees could pass through the court at ten o'clock in the freaking morning. It was my first "basketball" look at Vinnie, Jim, sophomore Walter Yates, 6'5", his freshman cousin Mitchell Edwards also 6'5", and Howard Montgomery, 6'6", "an animal" with a wing span of a 7'2." The story on him was that he could bring the ball up court and play as a strong forward. Banty Rooster, (Paul Friddle), showed up not too long afterwards, and I could tell he was very popular and respected by the other team members as well. He was a 5'8", skinny guy from Indiana who sounded like he did not have a care in the world. He would say something that always began with, "You know", and finish it by laughing. He was older than the rest of us, and he looked and acted more mature as well. I had received a "scouting report" from Jim McGurk and Vinnie on everyone except Mitchell while we drove down to the Valley. I heard great things about Friddle, mainly from Vinnie. When Friddle took his first jumper, I thought he must have been screwing around. That could not be his shot! It was a two handed, over the head shot, and before the ball even left his hands, he was yelling, "boards"! He had a funny way of talking, especially when he was hollering out the word, "booooooaaaaaards"! Another player, Jim Harder, a big kid from Little Falls, New York, had not arrived yet. He was a 6'11", blond kid who was coming to Edinburg with his wife. A local player, Joe Karam, a 6'2" shooter, was a player from McAllen High School.

Coach selected one player from the Valley each season for a one-year scholarship. Joe was the second player who was local on the team. The other local player was Ramiro Villegas from Rio Grande City, another guard who could shoot well and had played at Pan Am the year before. And along with me, that rounded out our basketball class for 1961-62.

When our first pickup game was about over, another player walked over to one of the "basketball gym's garage doors" and sat half in and half out under the door. The court cleared as everyone went over to greet "Appleseed". Ellis Appling was his real name, and he was by far the oldest player on the team. He looked like an NBA player right off the bat! I was thinking that we were in good shape already without him; however, with him... Howard Montgomery was the best player that I had ever seen. From the stories, "Seed" was the top dog!

Then we had my car mates from New York. McGurk was very strong with a great touch and Vinnie was a handful! I couldn't imagine what this team was going to look like with "Seed" included.

Everyone was as good as I had imagined; Mitchell was lights out, hitting on 65% from the outside. He had two gold caps on his front teeth and I could not understand one word that he said. He spoke so fast that his words ran together. I just made believe that I understood everything and kept playing. Yates was sleek and well developed with defined and powerful legs, like a thoroughbred racehorse! He was a bright kid with a great personality and most importantly to me was his easy friendliness.

Coach Williams brought Mitchell, who we were now calling "Topper" because he always seemed to have a hat on, to meet Coach Brooks, our Athletic Director. Coach Brooks was a large man who had a great background in football. He had been an assistant to Bear Bryant at Alabama, and had coached a football team at Pan Am College when it was a junior college. The football program had been dropped and replaced with basketball by the time I met Coach Brooks. I was nervous. He had a tendency to wrinkle his nose just before his thumb and forefinger pinched his nose. He did not mind beginning each sentence by saying, "Shit" almost as a prefix! On the occasion that he did not begin with "Shit", it was, "God Damn! God Damn you all are going to be tough," he growled when he met Topper, but then he looked at me and he immediately opened the side drawer in his desk and pulled out a bottle of syrup. He pushed it toward me and exclaimed, "They don't sell this 'shit' in Brooklyn! This syrup is called sorghum, made from black strap molasses; it will fatten you up kid!" He gave me the bottle and I smelt it. It was like taking a whiff of pure iron that had been melted down. He said that within a month on this stuff, I could be a starting back in football for Alabama. Coach Williams laughed and rolled his eyes and let loose with a rare vulgarity. Coach's worst words in all the time that I knew him was "gosh damn"!

However, his favorite was "Shiii..! I'll tell ya now", and Coach said that all the time. It was as if he was going to say shit, but cut the "it" from the end. When he was standing and saying, "shiii..!", he shuffled his feet on the floor and looked down as if he were trying to erase a word or kill a bug on the ground. Every time he said and did his shuffle, it would catch our attention and we found ourselves all staring down at his foot.

Clair Bee

Coach Williams was an exemplary student of the game of basketball. He had a multitude of theories and unique ways of doing things. He had a high school coaching background at Donna and McAllen High Schools when Brooks asked him to be the first basketball coach at the four-year school. Coach Williams always went to great lengths to learn, increase his teaching style, and spread that to others. It was certainly evident when he invited Clair Bee down for basketball clinics to improve our basketball skills. He also had Coach Bee put on clinics for the coaches in the Valley, but Williams lost his ass financially on the venture. The Valley and for the most part, Texas, is a football state. The high school coaches focused on football, not basketball. For many years, at the high school level, if a student did not play football in high school, he could forget about playing basketball. The HS football athletes were not even allowed to try out for another sport.

Coach Williams always wanted to get away from that kind of thinking and wanted to improve instruction for the basketball coaches in the Valley. What Coach Williams added to our team by bringing Clair Bee in was a big case of the "smarts".

Coach Bee was one of the best basketball minds in the country. He was the basketball coach at Long Island University and Rider University from 1932 to 1951. He won over 82% of his games, the best percentage ever for a college coach. He was the originator of the 1-3-1 zone defense and of the three-second call. Claire Bee was considered a moralist in the days of point shaving. Although no blame ever fell on him for any cheating, blame did fall on some of the players on his team. It was reported that by being such a moralist acted like blindfolds for him against the intrusion of such bad decision-making by some of his players! The larger share of wrong doings at the time was the entire 1950-51 Cinderella team of CCNY, Alex Groza, and Ralph Beard of Kentucky. Adolph Rupp was quoted at the time of the scandals that, "no one could touch our boys with a ten foot pole!" He was shocked when the "point shaving" hit his team as well!

In articles written by Sports Illustrated (*Jack McCallum, January 1980*), McCallum points to the fact that "Nobody was more devastated by the scandal than Bee."

Coach Williams surrounded himself with smart, honest, productive people. He was a no-nonsense kind of person. He was also young enough that he himself played three on three with us and set picks on us that would rattle our teeth. He was a lefty who could not shoot well unless it was near the foul line. Coach, before long, had created plays and defenses that were way ahead of his time.

Known nationally for his basketball wisdom, Clair Bee came to Pan American to conduct practices with "Skull Sessions". Pictured are Paul Friddle, me, and Joe Karam

In the middle of August, Coach Williams brought Coach Bee to conduct a clinic, and we could tell that Coach Bee was a "mastermind". He would conduct what he called skull sessions utilizing a blackboard and chalk to make his points. He was old, wrinkly, shaky, eye twitching, bent over, and had to use a microphone to talk while at the chalkboard. Nevertheless, he was a basketball genius!

I kept staring at Coach Bee during skull sessions, watching him piece together defenses in such a simplistic way. However, I could not help but feel that I had heard of some of these plays before. However, it seemed impossible. I had never met Coach Bee, nor watched his teams play. I was too young to have seen him coaching his teams that played in the early 50's. The old time coaches such as Red Aurbach and Hank Iba always fascinated me. I cried like hell when the Russians beat the USA with Iba coaching. I wished that he had taken his players off the court when the game ended. Then USA might have won and not had to return when the officials said there was still time on the clock.

After Coach Bee's first practice of the two weeks ended, he asked Coach Williams if he could go fishing. Coach asked us about it, and Jim McGurk said that his girlfriend, Linda, had a rowboat sitting out at Edinburg Lake. Somehow, it was decided that a freshman player would take him. There were four freshmen; Joe Karam was not there, so it was up to Topper, Jim Harter (Swede) and me. Topper yelled out something that indicated he did not know how to swim, and Swede had a family, so off I went, pretending I was disappointed. But to me, it was a great opportunity for me to get into a rowboat with Clair Bee. I was totally impressed with his knowledge, and I still had the feeling that I somehow knew him, but I just couldn't figure out how or where. His request was to go fishing. Being the only freshman standing there, I received the duty!

Vinnie drove us to the lake and dropped us off, looking at me with a pitying look, saying he would be back later. Claire Bee had not said a word in the car heading to the lake. It was as if he could not talk about anything other than basketball. Once in the boat, I pulled out no stops and said, "Coach, I feel that I know you so well." Before I could finish the sentence he said, "Kid, I am trying to relax, give me a break". Our conversation was very limited once he realized that I knew nothing about fishing! Therefore, we fished in silence for two hours!

Vinnie and me watching Clair Bee loading the rowboat on Edinburg Lake

After those two weeks, it was the last time I saw Coach Bee, and years later, in 1980, I read of his death in *Sports Illustrated*. As I read the article, I was touched with memories of the past. When I turned to the last page of the article about Coach Bee, I was shocked. I could not believe what I was reading! Across two pages of the article, was a display of the very familiar jackets of the books that I grew up reading, "The Chip Hilton Sports Series" with Coach Bee's name on the bottom of each of the books (see jacket cover that illustrates his books). What a shock to see that he was the author of The Chip Hilton Series, and had created the fictitious characters of "Chip Hilton", the all-around great player and his coach Hank Rockwell!

My stomach was turning as fast as my mind was focusing on each book cover and thinking that I had been in the middle of a lake with this man, this author. Unbelievable! I wish I had known so I could have told him what those books meant to me and so I could have gained more insight into the characters, etc.

Sports Illustrated, January, 1980,
"A Hero for All Times,
by Jack McCallum

So, in 1980, I made it a lifetime goal to find the 23 volumes in the series. My wife was also on the search through the internet and various other sources, buying any of his books she could find and saving some of these volumes to give me on my birthdays, for Christmas or other special occasions. Cami Jones, my children's kindergarten teacher, was moved by my story and also located many of the editions for me. It seemed that anyone who heard the story joined in the search. Artie Kamaya, a friend from North Carolina discovered a copy of one of Coach Bee's books, purchased the copy, and sent it to me. His note said, "You may already have this edition, but I couldn't pass it up just in case."

It was the last one I needed to complete the series. "Thanks Artie!"

The Franchise

By the time "Bronco Days" came around in November, just before Thanksgiving, it was still hot as Hell! The annual event, Bronco Days, began and both Vinnie and Jim warned me that I was in for an eye opener. It was great! It was like nothing that I had ever seen before. In some ways, it reminded me of the Macy's Thanksgiving Parade on 5th Avenue in New York. The only difference was that these were real cowboys riding on their horses. We had a Rodeo Team at our school, and I probably spent too much time watching them practice instead of studying. I could not believe I was attending school with these maniac cowboys! They would get on real bulls and rope and tie calves faster that I could tie my sneakers.

The girls sitting on the floats were out of this world. These Texas college girls, representing campus clubs, fraternities, or sororities, etc, were beautiful, wholesome, and spoke with sexy southern accents. Everyone on campus, the girls and the guys, dressed in western gear during this event, all the way to their holsters and guns! I am talking guns with blanks, and they were shooting everywhere we turned. The boys chased the girls all over campus, and if caught, the girls had to kiss the boy or be put into the campus "jail" until someone bailed them out. That is all it took for

Vinnie and me to dress up and get in on the chasing! Jim McGurk did not want any part of this, nor did any of my other teammates, but Vinnie and I had a blast!!

Later, after the festivities and back to basketball practice, Coach announced that we had another player who was coming down from Houston, via Louisiana, to join our team.

Big Jack had a unique way of introducing himself to opposing teams!

We all waited for this new ball player by the Field House on a Saturday morning, just before officially starting practice. Coach was sitting with us and we could tell it was going to be a big Christmas for the Williams' family. Coach Williams was more fidgety than ever, holding his "Shhhhhiii" longer. Coach really did not know a lot about this player, Jack; but just enough I guess. He was 6'9", fast, strong and could jump. When he arrived, he was so tall that it looked like every inch of him came out of the car in sections. He walked over to us and began shaking hands while saying, "Jackson's the name, Luke Jackson." He had such a low voice that by the time he finished his sentence, we were looking for toilet paper! This was a big, big man.

I will never forget that day, meeting Luke, who soon became known as "Big Jack". He became eligible at mid-season and with him, I honestly felt like we could have beaten the New York Knicks on any given night!

Our practices were just short of a war with fights breaking out at each practice! Everyone was intense, fighting for a spot on this potentially great team. The fights came to an abrupt halt at the end of practice when we hit the locker room. Then the joking began! We really got along well with each other socially.

Making fun of each other, laughing at each comment made, and then the jokes carried into the showers! It did not take long to learn that if we were going to wash our hair with soap, we had better keep our eyes opened. Otherwise, who knew what practical jokes would be played on us. We were a very closely-knit group to say the least. And unless you have played on an organized team before, you would never believe the events that took place on and off the court! This is probably the first time that I have shared this story with anyone other than my teammates, but some of the laughter and humor was often accompanied by the more gross events, which, good and bad, are remembered for life!

No one wanted to shampoo his hair in the gym showers with this group of guys. As soon as one of us closed our eyes to prevent the soap from entering them, that person might get "pissed" on by anyone who was showering! Gross.... I know, but that was the "sense of humor" of those of us participating in athletics! Nothing was too gross, for a bunch of athletes who were bonded like brothers by sports!

The "Magic" Begins for me: "The Sting"

The season began just about the time that our grades were becoming our focal points! I was all into school and attending my "favorite" classes, but mainly it was to check out the girls. The professors were nice, but kept getting on me about attendance. "You know, you are going to miss plenty once the season starts. If you want to pass you need to come to class when you can," warned several of my professors.

However, the basketball workouts were tough and they were kicking my ass, so I needed more sleep.

Something had to give... and you can imagine which I decided to give up....classes!

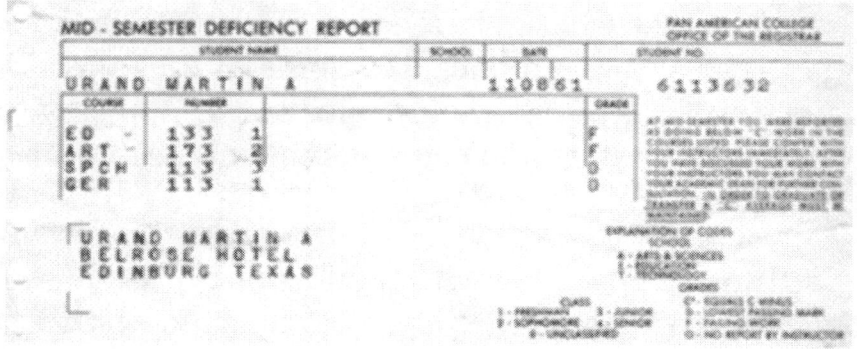

You really have to know when to hold them and when to fold them...

By mid-semester, I was ahead of everyone, holding two pair: 2F's and 2D's. There were several players with two pair, but I was proud of my hand and held pat. I was sure someone, somewhere, was going to come and assist me with passing grades. I obviously did not know or understand how that was going to work since no one had really discussed what happened if we were not passing.

Well to my surprise, Coach Williams came to the Belrose, and he was solemn. He informed me that I had flunked out and that he would get me a plane ticket to return to New York on the coming Saturday. I was shocked. "Surely this is a joke, Coach?" However, he did not laugh as I was accustomed to see him do when kidding around. I asked why nobody had warned me about this. "Why in the Hell is somebody not giving me "help" with the grades?" I asked. That was my belief about college athletes, and I just did not know the real game rules when I came to Pan Am, just seven miles north of the border of Mexico to play college basketball! Coach just said, "Pack your bags"! Coach Williams also growled that my ticket would be delivered to me at the airport. I was angry and could not believe that he was doing this to me! I blamed all of them, and it did not even enter my mind that I could be to blame.

So reluctantly, but angrily, I packed, said good-bye to everyone on the team, and headed to the McAllen Airport on Saturday morning. One of the tennis players gave me a ride to the airport since the basketball team had their Saturday practice. It was a very lonely feeling.

I had been sitting in the airport for thirty minutes or so, consumed with anger and sadness, when I glanced up at the entrance to the airport and recognized Dr. Ralph Morgan, my white-haired, education professor wearing an off-white suit with a black rope tie, boots, and an LBJ Stetson as he stepped through the door. He also wore granny glasses and had a long Sherlock smoking pipe. He stopped, just staring at me, before he asked me, "What are you doing here? Where are you going?" My reply was anything but nice. "Give me a break, you gotta be shitting me!" I growled. Then I told him that his grades had caused me to flunk out! Then, to salvage my pride, I said, "No big deal, I will simply enroll at St. John's and play for them". He was very thoughtful as he listened to my mad bullshit. After he had listened to me ranting about how pissed I was, he just turned and said, "Good luck to you, Marty," and walked away! I sat there another 30 minutes expecting my airline ticket to arrive, when Dr. Morgan came back in for a second time. I pretended that I did not see him and acted as if I was reading the sports page. He kicked my sneakers and I put the paper down. Once again I was rude to him and cursed at him using my best-pronounced Italian words and arm movements. He stood there while I had my tantrum, and when I finished he said, "You seem like a gambler, and I've got a proposition for you. If you give up your scholarship and come live with me and my family while I guide you academically, that is if you study with me, do your school work, and bring up your grades, I will change your 2 F's to C's".. You won't believe what a stupid thing I said to him after this unbelievable offer: "What are you, a queer?" Is that what this is all about? How could I not see this coming?"

He said, "No, I have a wife and a son! You would be living with my family.

"We live on a farm and we could use some help with the chores, and I will tutor you and help you with your study skills as well." I never replied, I just picked up my two bags, walked with him to his white truck, and threw my bags into the back. I was overcome with relief.

It was a blessing for me. His wife taught elementary school, and after reading and studying with her, I felt like a curtain was lifting in my mind. I was reading and even understanding! I had never before studied so hard or put in so much effort. Actually, I had never studied period! Dr. and Mrs. Morgan taught me how to study, plan, prepare, and think on a different level. I had always worked hard and never given up in sports, and I now realized I needed to do the same with my schoolwork.

The Morgan's big thing was to write in their diaries every day. They called it their "self-reflection"! They asked me to do this for myself also, it was all about thinking, writing, and then reading, and thinking about what I had written, that really assisted me with my reading issues.

Therefore Coach let me back on the basketball team, and I resumed practice, diligently preparing for my first game back while also preparing for my midterm finals, And we all celebrated when I passed my classes at the end of the "real" mid-term and I moved back to the Belrose to live with the team again. I cannot believe that I had actually thought I could flunk out at mid-semester. With all the pranks and crap that I pulled in New York, I fell for this lame "sting" that Coach and Doc laid on me! And I am so grateful that I did.

Doc Morgan died several years later, and I asked his wife if this had been a sudden thing. He had been so full of life; I wanted to understand what happened? Why? She just shook her head and told me that he had throat cancer from the "damn pipe" he had smoked all the time. "Then why would he take me on with all that adversity in your lives?" She replied, *"Because you were his greatest educational challenge!"* He said he saw more in you than you saw in yourself. This is something I will never forget and will forever appreciate.

The Valley truly is "Magical!"

My first college Season

Vinnie and I battled for the spot as starting number two guard with "Banty Rooster" (Paul Friddle) starting at the point. At forward were Jim McGurk and Howard Montgomery (Monty), and Ellis Appling (Seed) played a high post center. None of us really knew how old Seed was. He wore a steel knee brace that could be heard coming from a block away. He was 6'5, and did it all. "Seed" was from Detroit and supposedly had played for the Globetrotters at one time or another. He was a trip: A smooth operator who probably averaged more three's than anyone in Pan American College's history. I am not talking about three pointers from the outside, (they did not have them in the 60's), they came from the inside. Seed would drive and hang up around the rim, waiting to be fouled before he would release the shot. I loved watching and certainly playing with "Seed". Coming off the bench were Topper and Trim at forward, Swede at center, and Vegas ("V") would come in for Banty when things got rough.

We were a great basketball team and we prepared diligently for our games. We focused on winning the National Championship in Kansas City, and that was our goal, our motivation. Before the games, our pre-game meals often consisted of enchiladas with plenty of tortillas and cold Dr. Peppers, and that would do it. I kept a bottle of sorghum at each of the places where we ate and always had three or four tortillas to dip into the sorghum, like a dessert. After eating, we would rush over to the Belrose and conduct our team's ritual before every home game. We would circle around on the carpeted floor and sing with the music, "Going to Kansas City", blaring. Mrs. Alston always screamed from her room about the noise, but she never came out. We all knew she was afraid of us as a group and would not come out if we were all gathered together. We were pumped! We headed to our cars and hauled out past the Courthouse, heading for the Junior High Gymnasium where we played our "home" games.

I'm talking old, when I describe the gym...it was all wood - everything: Ceiling, bleachers (all of five rows high), and a scoreboard that must have been there during Clair Bee's days! Lafayette HS in Brooklyn had a much better gym, even with all the bars showing on their windows.

Halftimes of each game were much different from what I had experienced in high school. Coach read up on the latest fads for replenishing our energy and tried them on us during half-times to see if one thing helped any better than another. Throughout the season, we tried a variety of energy building supplements. We tried energy tablets, mixed protein drinks, and energy and protein bars of all kinds, and then Coach Sam would decide if any one of them helped us any more than the other did. But the refreshments we favored were simply oranges which a couple of young boys, JJ. Avila and David Garza brought to us during our practices. JJ and David "picked" oranges from the orchards across the street from the gym, peeled them for us, sectioned them, placed them on ice with napkins over them to keep the slices cold, and then walked around the locker room standing in front of each player, waiting for each of us to take a handful.

We all appreciated and loved these kids and we could definitely see how much they loved basketball, competition, and most of all, us!

Our team manager, Gordon Forester, was an extremely bright person, and well-liked by all of us. If any of the guys messed with Gordon, I always stood up for him, although he was capable of holding his own. He was from the Valley... I think Edcouch-Elsa. His parents and sister attended most of the home games and they always made themselves available at the end of each game to say hello and speak to the players. Gordon was a long distance runner, and I only saw him shoot a basketball a few times in all the years that I knew him. I eventually roomed with him because I was such a head case, and he had a knack of working with me and getting me focused in the right direction. The other reason Gordon was a good roommate was that I needed my sleep and when I had Vinnie as a roommate he was coming in late after dates almost every night, and the noise woke me up!

I guess the story for which Gordon is best remembered happened during my sophomore year when he had a scuffle with one of our players, Andy Carney. "G" was not one to fight, he was pretty laid back, and he could usually reason himself out of anything. Andy on the other hand came from New York, which meant he was a wise-ass like so many of us were. In fact, everyone assumed that being a wise-ass was a prerequisite for having lived in N.Y.

"G" was always looking for unique ways of doing things that took balance, coordination, or brainpower. With that in mind, he was coming back from washing his clothes at the field house, had the clothes folded nice and neatly in a basket that he was balancing on his head... no hands, just the basket sitting on his head as he walked in full stride as he entered the Belrose. We were all watching the one television in the main lobby when Andy jumped up and knocked the basket off Gordon's head. Everyone laughed for maybe fifteen seconds before "G" jumped up and punched Andy in the mouth! "Holy Shit!" we yelled. It shocked everyone because Gordon was anything but violent! Andy hit the deck hard and laid there for a minute before standing up and apologizing to Gordon. "G" did not say a word, just collected his clothes off the carpeted floor, dumped them into the basket, and went to his room to refold the clothes. From that day forward, we all respected him even more and any kidding or teasing from the entire team lessened.

On early basketball trips, 99% of the time we traveled in a Weenie Wagon, which Gordon drove. The wagon was quite long and received plenty of comments from people on the street. It carried ten players and a coach. "The Weenie Wagon" was cramped and probably a health hazard with all the farting that went on after meals. We put a lot of miles on the wagon for two years before we got our "Silver Bullet" coach bus. Now we were going in style in the "Silver Bullet", which gave us room to open a book or do homework.... If we wanted.

The Silver Bullet was more like an RV and very useful since getting lodging for us was often difficult in the South. When traveling, the two main locations that we frequented for lodging were Houston and Grand Prairie, Texas. During that time, due to segregation, when traveling through east Texas we were just crap out of luck, and that's when we really appreciated being able to sleep in the RV!

I remember traveling to Houston with the team, after playing East Texas State in Commerce, Texas. It was about 6:00 AM, and we were getting ready for breakfast after having driven for several hours. Coach asked Trim, who was sitting across from him, "Hey Walt, get out and ask those two guys where we can eat?" I could see "Trim" through the window talking to these two farmers in their overalls. As they answered him, they were pointing toward a location down the street. I sat up and was getting my crap together to get off the bus when Trim jumped into the bus and said, "Coach, let's get the hell out of here!" Coach asked him what was the matter and I could see how upset Trim was because his eyes were bigger then I had ever seen them. He was "usually" so cool. He exclaimed, "I asked those guys where the black folks hung out, and they pointed to that big oak tree!" The bus driver, trying to find first gear, broke out with laughter as Trim crouched down in his big cushioned seat.

It was common to run into these situations in the early 60's. When the cheerleaders followed us to games we were playing in Texas, they would follow the same rules as all of us! We had several instances when we were either questioned or just thrown out after entering a restaurant because of our interracial team. Sometimes after we sat down at a table, a waiter nervously would come over and ask or tell us to leave! The exact words were usually, "You boys are not welcome here!" Our team wanted no problems; we tried to focus on basketball games and staying together as a team. Therefore, we looked for places where we were all welcome. Moreover, the food was often better at the places that welcomed us anyway! We were all good with that.

There was never a doubt in my mind that this kind of treatment strengthened our relationships with each other. It was "all for one and one for all". As far as I know, never once did any one of us ever feel resentment toward our own players. We were a team, and what hurt one of us, hurt all the others. This was how it was about any difficulties we faced. It made us that much closer and stronger as individuals and as a team. I cannot think of one "all black team", including when we played Tennessee State on their home court that we ever lost to. We were one of the "first" integrated teams of that era, and it was not a front. We truly loved each other like brothers!

Back in Edinburg, we kicked ass during our basketball games and usually had our big after game meal at Don Diego's Steak House in Edinburg. Then we frequently went to *Otis and Bernice's*, a black honky tonk for dancing. Our cheerleaders would come over for a while, and later, after they left, we would drink some beer and shoot pool. Around two a.m. we'd head back to the good Ole' Belrose Hotel.

Each and every holiday and school break was an experience. During the mid-semester break, we never went home for our "break", but rather we played in some sort of a Christmas/Holiday Basketball Tournament. This was a tradition for each of the four years that I attended school at Pan American College.

The Winning Pass

During my first year in Edinburg, we hosted our own college tournament that we played in the McAllen High School gym. This gym was one of those airplane hangar looking structures with rafters everywhere. We made it to the finals of the four-team event. During the final game, the score was tied and Banty fouled out, so I was put in with about a minute to go. Then with only six seconds left, we were down by one after Southeast Oklahoma had just scored. We had the ball under their basket after the time out, and Coach called us over and made up a last second play. He told everyone where to go except me! The referee blew his whistle to end the time out, and I still had no clue as to where Coach wanted me. I yelled over to McGurk, and I will always remember his response, "I guess you are taking the ball out". The ref handed me the ball, and his hand went up as he began counting the five seconds to get the ball in bounds, while I was still trying to figure out how or to whom I was going to pass. I had been so nervous during the time out that I never really listened to the play that coach had drawn up.

Now, with only five seconds left, I looked for Vinnie, but he was not playing. With four seconds, I looked for Seed, but he was covered! With three seconds, I began to panic, afraid that I was going to turn the ball over to the other team. With two seconds left, I finally saw Monty by our foul line. With one second left, I heaved the ball as hard as I could to be sure that it got to the other end of the court without hitting any of the overhead rafters. Thankfully it went sailing through three rafters without touching any of the cross bars in the rafters, and came one foot from the basket, as Monty, who could jump high, practically out of the gym, leaped up high, grabbed the ball in the air, and laid it in to win the game for us.

I watched our bench clear and jump all over Monty as I sat on the floor wondering if I had just crapped in my shorts. The story of the "rafter pass" traveled all the way to the "Alamo" city of San Antonio and with each day, the story grew like a folktale and traveled further north to more colleges by the day.

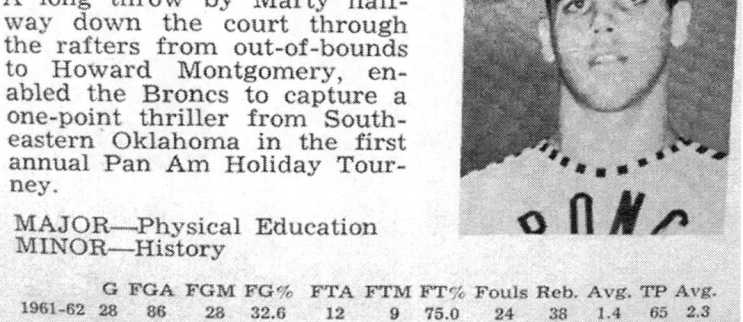

Sophomore Guard, 6-0, 19
Brooklyn, N. Y.

The only frosh to letter last year, Urand is ticketed for a possible starting berth at guard. A long throw by Marty halfway down the court through the rafters from out-of-bounds to Howard Montgomery, enabled the Broncs to capture a one-point thriller from Southeastern Oklahoma in the first annual Pan Am Holiday Tourney.

MAJOR—Physical Education
MINOR—History

	G	FGA	FGM	FG%	FTA	FTM	FT%	Fouls	Reb.	Avg.	TP	Avg.
1961-62	28	86	28	32.6	12	9	75.0	24	38	1.4	65	2.3

The second amazing event happened at the Echo Hotel, the one and only hotel located in Edinburg, Texas. It was where all of the visiting teams stayed when they came to play Pan American. Marvin Blumenthal (the recruiter who brought me to Texas) came down to watch the tournament and he invited me over for lunch. The hotel was nice for those days. It had very large glass windows wrapped in a semi-circle that looked out onto the pool, which was surrounded by palm trees. The Valley had palm trees up and down each main street that were huge and you would always see men trimming and pruning the dead branches. I still have a passion for palm although I have come to appreciate how difficult pruning them can be.

There was always a full house eating at the hotel, many of them workers from town, usually wearing the Dickey khaki pants and shirts that matched, as they talked about their crops or other adventures. Therefore, when Marvin Blumenthal was in the hotel, it was always easy to spot him with his baldhead and wearing his sport jacket.

Marvin and I had finished our lunch, and we went up to his room because he was expecting a long distance call. After about ten minutes of me giving him a scouting report on our team and season, the phone rang, and from what I could tell, it was from someone in the New York Knicks office. I would have loved to hear the entire conversation, but with hearing only my half, I still about "crapped out!"

Marvin's conversation went something like this: "Sorry to hear about the problems", and then he listened for a while and said, "I am sure you all can find someone with more experience."

He continued listening and rolled his eyes at me. Marvin continued his phone conversation, "I am pretty sure, and who in the hell would want to live in New York?" Realizing at that point that I was from N.Y., he made a grimacing face, holding up his palm as if to say, "Relax kid". He ended his conversation saying, "I really appreciate you all thinking of me, but you better count me out!"

He got off the phone and said, "I guess you heard that I just turned down the Knicks' coaching job? All I could muster out of my mouth was "Shhhhhhhhhhhhi..." Six weeks after the Knicks talked to Marvin, the Knicks hired Red Holzman as the Knicks coach. Marvin never once looked back!

Marvin was on a mission in Houston to help raise money to build a new JCC building and move out of the small JCC building located a half a block from the Houston Zoo on Hermann Drive. Just about every great ball player had worked out there under his guidance and counseling at one time or another. Marvin was an above board kind of person who had a heart as big as Texas! I loved talking with him and listening to his stories. He would tell me about his two daughters and family and I always (with my NY insensitive stupidity) razzed him about not having boys. After having my own treasured daughters, I realized that he could not have cared less. I totally understand and appreciate the pride he felt for his daughters. Deanna and I thank God every day for our fantastic children. Only after we had children did I realize that the marvel of having our children in our lives rose above any other need or achievement I had ever had.

Marvin celebrated with Pan American's basketball players during the years to come. He always came down to check on "his" kids! Many of the players on our team were in some way connected with him. Marvin was well known all over the nation for recognizing and recruiting exceptional basketball talent.

After all of Marvin Blumenthal's hard work in supporting, leading, and securing many donations and financial support for the new JCC, the majestic JCC opened without him! Marvin had a heart attack playing racquetball at the old JCC, and he died the day before the opening of the new JCC! I attended his funeral with many other college and NBA players to honor and remember the man who had been such an important part of our lives. I often think back and remember watching the historical game between UCLA and University of Houston on television, and seeing glimpses of Marvin in his sport jacket, sitting on the bench next to Guy V and his polka-dotted towel. I will never forget all the help and guidance he gave to me.

"There is a fine line between a leader and someone that is being chased"

At Pan American College, every freshman had to wear a "beanie" at all times. This little green, round hat was like a "skull cap". This was a form of hazing, but at the same time, it created friendships and loyalty with the other freshmen at the college.

I decided to run for freshman class president, and was proud to have made it into a runoff against one of my teammates, Joe Karam from McAllen, Texas, a town next to Edinburg. Joe was well liked, respected and had a great name in the Valley. After the runoff, Joe became President and did a great job. And if I had to lose, I'm glad it was to Joe. In my running for this position, I underwent a feeling of satisfaction in the challenge and in the comradeship, I had experienced with the other students running for offices. I felt positive about the entire experience.

Back in my high school days, I had never run for anything. I always took a back seat to everyone unless it had involved sports. I felt I had some good ideas, I had organized games and sometimes even fights within the "projects" in Brooklyn. However, I had also been worried that the kids would see my weaknesses, afraid that taking the lead would allow my peers to find flaws. Consequently, I seldom stood up, so just taking the "chance" in something other than athletics felt like an accomplishment!

I give a lot of credit to Pan American College, to Bronc's basketball, and to the people in the Valley for "upping" my feelings of self-worth.

The Magic Begins for Our Team and School

The goals were clear: win the "Big State Conference" and head to Kansas City for the N.A.I.A. National Championship for the first time in the history of Pan American College. By the end of the season, we did reach our goals and this planted the seeds for the outstanding records that continued in the ensuing years to come!

We took one game at a time and the "W's" added up quickly! Lucious Jackson's name spread to all parts of the country as well. Things were happening very fast. We had beaten a team in the mid-west, and after that game proudly got on our bus to come home. At breakfast, we read that we were ranked 7th nationally! From there it was all smooth sailing as we had now qualified to compete in Kansas City for the Championship!

We caught a train out of Harlingen, 30 miles east of the college, and headed to Kansas City, MO. Our first stop was Houston. The buzz on the train reached us in the back, but it was not about us; it was about the team from Prairie View A&M.

Taking a train to Kansas City from Harlingen, Texas, was a first for us.

From Left to Right: Front row —Marty Urand, Vinnie Marino, Gordon Forester, Back Row: Jim Harter, Luke Jackson, Mitchell Edwards, Joe Karam, Walter Yates, Paul Friddle, and Ramero Villegas.

Kansas City had the number one ranked team in the nation, with Tennessee State ranked second. We all looked out the windows without showing that we were a bit interested. The muscles in our eyes were straining as we kept our heads focused in front, but we were using our best peripheral vision to peek at Zelmo Beaty, the 6'9" All-American who would become the number one draft choice of the St. Louis Hawks! We were all trying to act like we were pretty cool from the back of the train. We could hear, very clearly from up front, the sound of "Shhhhhhhhii" from Coach.

By the time we hit Kansas City, there was no question in our minds that we would be able to stay there for an entire week: kicking ass. The tournament was set up to play five games in six days at the Municipal Auditorium. The first day there was one festivity after another with workouts squeezed in. One event was the "Dinner of Champions", which was kind of neat. Each team was introduced as they sat at one of the thirty-two tables. When a school's name was called, that team stood up together and the players nodded their heads and waved a hand, trying to sit down as fast as they could. When we stood, we heard soft murmurs as our team's name was called. Jack was always the last of our team to stand. He started out standing up with us, but he had a knack of doing it so slowly, unfolding his towering body, that by the time Jack was fully erect, everyone was gasping, and ooh's and ah's were coming from everyone's mouths!

We played Belmont Abbey in the first round. They were best known for their coach, an ex-pro NBA player, Al McGuire (Knicks). Coach McGuire, as a basketball player, was a reckless player who I had watched play at the Garden, and he had this team of his, thinking and playing the same way! When their team was called, in response to us, they stood up on their chairs. This brought laughter to the audience of teams.

Alex Groza, a player from Kentucky, delivered the dinner speech. He was one of the players who had been on the take on Rupp's team in the early 50's. I heard only his first line, since it was his best anyway. He started off by saying, "I would like to welcome you all . . . . My name is Alex Groza. My parents remind me that I am the "heel" of the family, while my brother is the "toe". We all knew that his brother (Lou Groza) was a place kicker in the NFL.

Bottom line of the tournament was that we lost in the second round to Ferris Institute from Big Rapids, MI. and Prairie View from Houston went on to win the whole thing, but we were pumped up for the upcoming year.

Little did I know at the time that our 1962-63 team would be the best team that I would play on during my four years at Pan Am! Our other teams were extremely good, but this particular year's team was fantastic! We had no right losing in the second round in this tournament with the talent that we had. On the train ride home we had three different camps of thought as we traveled through the open fields of the Mid-West and South.

Our first thoughts were that we were happy to have made it to K.C. and to get our foot in the door. The next thought was that we were still pissed for dropping the game that sent us home. Appleseed was especially frustrated since he was from Detroit and he did not let up on us all the way back to Texas! Luckily for us, he slept for much of the trip home, but occasionally, when he woke up, probably craving a smoke, we would hear, "You bunch of asses, shit!"

My first college baseball season

*Jim McGurk tallest in the back row and
me kneeling in front in the middle*

Everyone on the basketball team headed in different directions when the basketball season ended, but I decided to play baseball with the Pan American College baseball team. McGurk had played the year before and said he had enjoyed it, so I gave it shot. What McGurk failed to tell me was that his first year he had been coached by Coach Williams. This year, however, we had a new baseball coach who came in from Alabama. He was a hard-nosed son-of-a-bitch who never seemed to smile. He just spit his tobacco out when he was going to laugh to himself. One of the terms that I never really understood in the transition to the South, was the term "Redneck". I am sure this term was around before Jeff Foxworthy was even born. When I met our baseball coach, Coach Earl Gartman, I found out in a hurry what the term meant! Nevertheless the more we were around him, the more we began to admire him. I don't know of anyone who did not respect his work ethic. He worked the devil out of us and knew his stuff! So I thought, "What the hell"! Therefore, I decided to give baseball a year and get some sun, which I really did not need since I was darker than half of the African Americans who were on scholarship!

I tried out for third base and I was excited to win that spot on the starting team. McGurk had already nailed down the catching spot, and we were off for fun, hard work, and an interesting season. And, Jim and I were not the only two basketball players to join the team! Big Jack decided to play baseball as well. However, I didn't take him seriously when he said he wanted to play. The first problem of course was finding baseball pants to fit his 6'9" frame with a 32-inch waist. Other than the three of us, the team was primarily made up of players from the Valley.

Big Jack made practice interesting! He was a right-handed hitter and he pulled the shit out of the ball. Jack jerked line drives off the left field fence, and on several occasions knocked the wooden fence slats down! He was an animal to say the least. While everyone stood in amazement at his hitting feats, I took about ten giant steps back onto the grass from my position at third base every time he came up to bat. The thought of standing in front of one of his line drives scared the crap out of me.

Batting practice consisted of about fifteen cuts, and then we would take off running the bases. I could not wait for Big Jack's batting turn to end! I only had one of his baseballs that came at me, and naturally, it was a short hopper that hit no more than a foot in front of me. I gasped so loud and hard that my gonads got stuck in my stomach! By the time I could even make an attempt at getting out of the way, the baseball had zoomed past me on the way to the outfield.

However, there was one time that I did not mind playing third during Jack's batting practice, and that was when I heard Gartman say, "Jack, work on your bunting, you will never be able to dig in playing in the South." I took that to mean that the pitchers were going to throw at his head much of the time. The jerk-offs on the other team were always calling out shit to him to make him lose focus on his hitting. I am sure Jackie Robinson had some of these same jerk-off comments when he was first playing for the Dodgers. The only difference was that Jack was 6'9, and meaner than shit if you pissed him off! He took his fair amount of crap before he turned, stood straight up, and glared. And with nothing else said, the incident was quickly resolved!

There was plenty of talent on our baseball team, and I probably got the spot at third base because I had a very strong-arm. I remember Gartman coming over to me after I made a rushing error at third, saying, "I'll tell ya, from now on I want you to read the label on the ball before you fire it out." It really helped me to slow down, and I committed fewer errors. He always had a unique way of explaining things that made sense to us.

It was probably my third game since the basketball season had ended, and we were playing St. Edward's in Austin. I got up with bases loaded and two outs when Coach Gartman called time and approached the batter's box. When Coach Gartman was nervous, he never remembered our names, and when he came up to me, he called me Dodger. I hoped it was because I was from Brooklyn and not because I dodged a few hot ones to third. I had heard him refer to Jim as Yankee when he got upset with Jim for not throwing someone out. Anyway, as he approached, I was thinking that since I was so new to the team, and didn't know the signals well, that he was going to verbally tell me to lay down a bunt and try to squeeze "Knot" Garcia in from third.

However, to my surprise, his plan for me was fairly simple. He said, "Dodger, you can't hit worth a shit; the first close pitch... get hit". Then he looked at me and said, "You got the idée?" ... not idea, but idée. Then he spit a load of brown juice out from his mouth and began walking back to the coaching box. So sure enough, on the second pitch that came close, I stuck my shoulder in and got the walk, which brought in Garcia.

Since my birthday was in April, baseball season was in full swing. Pan American was always being invited to Mexico to play some sport and we usually accepted so we could try to encourage and recruit students from further north of Edinburg to attend our school. Hearing that we played in another country was an incentive to any possible recruits. Therefore, each year, we played baseball at Monterrey Tech in Mexico City, and it was always a trip our team enjoyed taking. This particular year's trip was fabulous! We played hard and partied just as hard! With my birthday coming up toward the end of the week's games, focus shifted from baseball to partying. The celebration of my 20th birthday was great. Dancing, drinking, ... too much drinking in fact, and before I knew it, I was running on the Monterrey Tech campus in my undies!

We are not talking about campus police here; we are talking "Federales" in Mexico coming after me! The Hispanic players knew this better than anyone and were trying to save my life by not letting them catch me. Although I did not get caught by the the Federales, Gartman found out and was all over me. At that moment, I wished the Federalist HAD caught me.

Gartman turned me into Jim Brooks, the athletic director at Pan Am. Both of them were extremely unhappy with me, and even our college President, Ralph Schilling, who had played football for the

Redskins, became involved. He had also received calls from officials in Mexico about my sprints through their campus. However, looking back at these trips, overall, we had a great time, and it was even better the next year when I celebrated my 21st birthday.

The First Year Round-Up

What a sensational year it had been. I was fulfilling my wish of getting out of New York and having a new start in life. I actually became closer with my family through our letters and phone calls, without all the drama of living in New York. God had sent me two remarkable mentors in Coach Sam Williams and Dr. Ralph Morgan. I actually enjoyed reading now for the first time in my life, found sorghum from the farming communities in the South, and left 30 pounds heavier at 180 lbs!

Freshman year in the old Edinburg Junior High gym. "Appleseed" (32) boxing out as I shoot a jumper.

Probably the most positive thing that happened to me was my maturing due to the wonderful teammates and coaches who became a part of my life!

I felt like it was the first time in my life that I had people, other than my family, who showed they cared for me by exhibiting such high expectations for me. They believed in me! Many of us were in the same boat: Poor, struggling through school the best we could, and giving everything we had to baseball and/or basketball!

I truly looked forward to the next season and ...of all things...school.

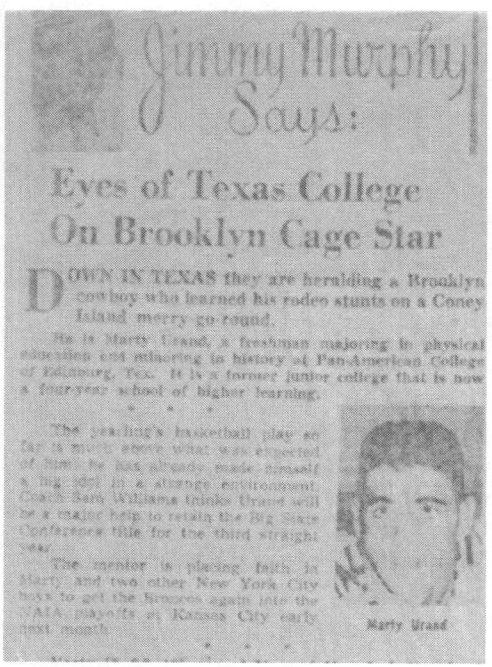

Jimmy Murphy Says:

Eyes of Texas College On Brooklyn Cage Star

DOWN IN TEXAS they are heralding a Brooklyn cowboy who learned his rodeo stunts on a Coney Island merry-go-round.

He is Marty Urand, a freshman majoring in physical education and minoring in history at Pan-American College of Edinburg, Tex. It is a former junior college that is now a four-year school of higher learning.

The yearling's basketball play so far is much above what was expected of him, he has already made himself a big shot in a strange environment. Coach Sam Williams thinks Urand will be a major help to retain the Big State Conference title for the third straight year.

The mentor is placing faith in Marty and two other New York City boys to get the Broncos again into the NAIA playoffs in Kansas City early next month.

Marty Urand

One Last defining moment!

One last thing happened in that first monumental year away from home. I never turned my radio off, even when I left the room so my radio played music 24 hours a day. I loved listening to the radio, and my favorite group was *Tom and Jerry*. Gordon and I had the same taste in music so the radio was never really touched except to turn the sound down when we went to bed. Most of the time I was around a radio and not the TV.

We had one TV in the main lobby, but I did not have the time to watch it unless it was a special sporting event. My dorm mates and I enjoyed each other's company, comments, and most of all the athletic humor that is associated with watching or playing sports.

Probably one of our most serious TV sessions was when we were watching two tennis players from Pan American who also lived at the Belrose with us, playing tennis in Forest Hills. They were amazing! We, Pan American College, had the number one ranked tennis team in the nation in 1961-62. Our players were from Argentina, England, Switzerland, South Africa, Australia, and California.

For some reason, the only other TV show we watched was *The Ed Sullivan Show*. We usually did not take the performers seriously and we joked and made fun of any acts that did not meet with our approval. But unexpectedly, one of the acts on the Ed Sullivan show caught my attention!

"And now, straight from the streets of New York, please welcome the singing sensation of Tom and Jerry." I jumped up and excitingly yelled out, "These guys are great." When they came out on stage, I went into shock! My next words that came out of my mouth were, "Well, I'll be dipped in shit. I grew up with these guys!" It was Paul Simon and Art Garfunkel, from my neighborhood baseball team! I listened, but I don't think I heard one word they were singing. I could not keep my eyes off of Paul without remembering all the encouragement he had given me when I was younger. I had been concerned about my lack of height because I had wanted to play basketball! I thought to myself, as they were singing his song, "I am a Rock", how we both truly "made it", each in our own ways!

Summer in New York

As soon as my last freshman final exams were finished, I flew to New York and was surprised at how excited I was to see my parents and sisters. My two sisters had really grown; they were now sixteen and fourteen. My parents had moved to another place in Brooklyn, this time closer to Coney Island, overlooking Sheepshead Bay and Emmons Avenue. My parents' apartment was very nice with an outside terrace. We had fun together each evening sitting on their terrace. The nights were pleasant, with a great breeze, and our terrace was up high enough that we did not hear the honking of cars or taxis: it was the best location of all their moves so far.

Little Enid, my younger sister, was growing up and she was thinking about taking a trip abroad. She had a fascination with living in and visiting other countries. I could see that things had not really changed with my sisters. Enid wanted out to go traveling abroad, and Ilene wanted out to be on her own in New York.

Ilene, my oldest sister, had met a guy who was a bit older, and was what we called a "Gavone". Bob was from a very large Italian family, and he had one sister, three brothers, and a multitude of other relatives, each one a bit crazier than the other. But Bob was funny, friendly, and really a lot of fun! He had just opened his new plumbing business and gave me a business card that read: "Bob's Plumbing: You Shit, I Eat!" Now you know what a "gavone" is!

His dad was a first class man who spent most of his time cleaning up the trouble his sons frequently got themselves into. His mom was at the other end of the spectrum from his stereotypical family members. She was a piano teacher, played at church services, and sang opera!

About this time, my dad was in the middle of major car problems. It was all he talked about. He had to have a reliable car and he was making life miserable for all of us. His Ford had seen its last days, and my dad had to either trade the car in, or stop grumbling and get it fixed. Because it was not working at all, we had to call cabs or take our lives into our own hands with Ilene's husband, Bob, driving us around. Bob had won many titles for auto racing, and drag racing in particular, and he drove as if he was drag racing even when in the streets of New York. My mother drove with Bob only one time and then declared that would be the first and last time she would ever get into a car if he were driving.

One evening we had planned to celebrate my homecoming with a trip to Roosevelt Raceway out on the Island. We were going out to have dinner and the whole works! On that afternoon, my parents, my sisters, Bob, and I were all standing on the terrace when in the distance we heard sirens getting louder and closer and closer to the area of our apartments on Emmons Ave. My father said it sounded like a four-alarm fire. We always had restaurants having fires across the street, so we were not overly concerned.

When the fire engines reached our street and were preparing to fight this fire, smoke was rising up to the fifth floor where we were, and my mother began to get nervous that it might be in our apartment building. And when my mother gets nervous, it is time to do something because she carries on like a mad woman. On her third scream of "Jack!" we were all ready to evacuate the building, but Bob yelled out, "It's not the building, "Ma," (he had become like one of my family while I was gone). Bob waited a few seconds to say, "Don't get shook, it's only your piece of crap car, Dad!" My father responded, "What in the hell did you do?" However, I knew my dad was really proud of Bob for this "first class "east side" job, and my dad just began laughing and repeating, "You gotta be kidding me!" while calculating what kind of new reliable car he would have by the next night!

Bob was the kind of son my dad always wanted! My dad wanted a "gavone"; instead, he had a son who was more interested in sports and education. He loved me and was proud of me, but he could not fathom me wanting to play sports and not wanting to continue being part of the "streets", like he and Bob. He was proud of my goals, but it just wasn't part of my dad's background or interests. I also was fond of Bob, along with the rest of my family. When we would go to the track with him, no one dared get in his way, and we just followed my dad and Bob as they lead the way. My dad "owned" the track whether it was the trotters or the flats (no harness).

Bob Frasso (and his brothers) ran
Sheepshead Bay in Brooklyn!

When driving with Bob, I could see why my mom nominated him for "Worst" driver of the year! He thought he owned the streets! Brooklyn cops knew him and his brothers, so they usually looked the other way and just left him alone. No one was too high in the society chain to receive a piece of Bob's "system" of repayment!

Driving down Nostrand Avenue, he looked for a drag race at each light. He had a quick car, both powerful and sleek. It was so powerful that he bet me that while he was driving, I would be unable to reach the dashboard and grab the twenty-dollar bill he had put on it before he took off! Whenever I would begin to reach forward, Bob would throw the car into a higher gear, jerking me back into my seat. I tried to grab the twenty so many times that I was becoming nauseous, but I did not want to give up and show him what a wimp I was. Later he laughed as he put the bill in his shirt pocket, and we cruised over to *Big Bow-Wow Drive-In* to get into some serious drag races.

The cops ignored the drag racing on Rockaway Boulevard, where the drive-in was located. It was away from everyday traffic so the police patrolled other areas where innocent traffic might become involved. That left Rockaway Boulevard with wide-open streets, and it was crazy as hell!

At the light, on the corner of Rockaway Blvd, a car next to us jumped the light and beat Bob to the next light. When Bob reached that light, he calmly reached under his seat, pulled out a rubber mallet from under the seat, and smashed the other car's passenger side of the windshield. He stood there in the street after a blow or two and waited for this guy to get out of his car, which he never did. He must not have wanted an altercation with "Crazy Bob". The street was crowded and I am sure this event did not go unnoticed, but everyone looked the other way, not wanting to get involved. Then the light turned green, and the driver of the car with shattered glass still falling from the window turned left down a side street. Bob took his time getting back into his car. No one behind him honked their horns as he nonchalantly got into his car, causing everyone behind him to miss the light!

Although personalized plates were not available at that time, I would have liked to have seen what personalized license plates Bob might have chosen if they had been available. I would expect Bob's plates might be the same as the name of Tony Soprano's boat, "Stugots!"

I had been in New York for ten weeks before it was time for me to go back to Pan American College to get in shape for basketball again. I practiced mainly on bringing the ball up the floor and shooting. Banty always brought the ball up against presses, and I felt I also had the ability to occasionally bring the ball down also. I was dribbling fast down court, but my issue was that I often got out of control. I had played many games in the projects during the summer, and could not wait to get back to Pan American and show Coach Williams my improvement in ball control.

While in New York for the summers, I worked the night shift at the store until about 12:30 AM. I would then ride the train home and at 11:00 the next morning, I headed over to Dubrow's restaurant off of Bay Parkway. Not to eat or play basketball, but to pick up some cash "running" bets for my dad. I tried to get in three trips to Aqueduct Raceway before going to work each day.

I did this "running" seven days a week and was making some good cash to use for placing my own bets. I dumped my "running money" on the same horse that I was "tipped" to dump other bets on. I was also beginning to increase my income by betting on the horses my dad bet on. I respected my dad's judgment on horses! On some good days, I could rat-hole three or four hundred dollars. So by the end of the summer, I had around thirty five-hundred dollars with my goal to do well again the following summer and use my winnings to buy a new car for my junior year.

1962-1963
The Sophomore Year

*After losing in Kansas City with what I
considered our best team we ever had,
going 26-6 was a real highlight!*
Record 26-6

I returned to the Valley in mid-August with hopes of
getting some good basketball work done on my own,
and then to progress more with Coach Williams' help.
I knew I needed work on bringing the ball up since

Banty was going to graduate after this year, and then it would be up to me to break pressing defenses. Actually, Vinnie had better ball handling skills and I figured he would probably take the point on those occasions.

People cannot possibly understand what hot is until they come to the Valley in mid-August. There is a reason the "Siesta" is a way of life in Mexico! Since the Belrose was not air conditioned, staying indoors was not a smart option. The South Padre Island Resort area, located on the Gulf of Mexico was also a great idea of a place to "retreat" and only a little over an hour away. However, unless there was a plan to go to the ocean by someone who had wheels, we were messing around in the field house, lifting, practicing, or talking with Selso, our gym custodian and basketball bus driver. I had so many positive experiences with the custodians who had often helped me out and had tried to guide me in the right direction when I was in school, that I had a great thankfulness and to all custodians. Selso fit into the mold of always helping and reminding us of what was important, and what we would lose if we lost our focus. I often assisted Selso with his chores when I had any short breaks from practicing. He was such a good, caring man I liked reciprocating for all he did by helping him out when I could.

Louis Devries (Director of Maintenance) came by the field house, and after watching me helping Selso with some of his chores, on the spot offered me a part-time job to assist Selso! He was impressed that a scholarship athlete would be getting his hands dirty and voluntarily helping Selso. So I became an assistant to Selso in maintaining the gym, which Selso usually kept spotless in the first place. I did errands and was there for him when he did need me. It was the perfect, flexible part-time job for me. While I was helping him, Selso would give me ten minutes every hour to shoot baskets or dribble through the various garbage cans that he had already setup for my dribbling practice.

Within a few weeks, as my other teammates arrived, three on three games began each day around 4:00 PM, when it began to get cooler.... like 97 degrees! It was great seeing everyone and talks began about the upcoming season. We all knew that we were getting better with age, but I could not help thinking how difficult it was going to be without Seed and Monty! Monty had planned to come back for his fourth year of eligibility, but fortunately for him, the San Francisco Warriors drafted him. Other than those two, we had virtually the same team.

MONTGOMERY—ALL-AMERICAN AND ALL-BIG STATE CONFERENCE SELECTION

Montgomery

Houston's Howard Montgomery, now a member of the San Francisco Warriors, was named to two all-teams at the close of the 1961-62 campaign.

Monty became the first Bronc to be selected on the UPI small college All-American team as an honorable mention choice.

Although the Broncs captured the Big State Conference crown, only Montgomery placed on the all-conference team. Howard and Bill White of Texas Wesleyan were unanimous selections for the first team.

Monty was a great catch for San Francisco, but Monty was cut and no one picked up his options. Monty had been hanging around with Wilt Chamberlain, and in hanging around with "Wilty", Monty must have thought he had the same privileges as Wilt. However, he had not earned them yet. It got out to the league that Monty was a cut-up, although many others believed he was really just the scapegoat for Wilt.

Appleseed had joined the Globetrotters again and stayed with them until they realized how old he was!

Trying to believe that this would be a better basketball year, even after losing two players like "Seed" and Monty, and also after having lost in the second round last year, was not too encouraging. However, everyone had a good mindset for the upcoming year. "Trim" always put things in perspective and kept our minds on obtaining the "prize": and the goal for this year was to win it all! The UPI Poll had us ranked 9th in the Nation (after they saw Big Jack in Kansas City) and we were ready to work harder than ever before.

Banty and Big Jack with Coach
were chosen as our captains

A great surprise was that we had a transfer student from St. Edwards joining our team who would utilize the current year to become eligible. This player, Jim Board, was good! He was about 5'8", stopped on a dime, and could shoot the lights out. Jim was All-Conference first team selection in the Lone star Conference and was pure hell to guard in practice or in a game. During practices, Coach would get so pissed at the first team if Vinnie and Board, who were on the second team, tore up the press that the first team was throwing against them. I felt that playing against Board on a daily basis certainly helped me improve defensively. I guarded Jim while Banty guarded Vinnie. On defense, Vinnie guarded me which meant that I would be fouled before, during, and after I shot the ball! Vinnie was tough, and as a result, during games, he got into foul trouble quite often. When I talk about people being tough, I always think of Vinnie.

Outside of the gym, we, along with all Pan Am students, were participating in "Bronco Days", a yearly traditional celebration in September. During this year's activities, two amazing things happened. The first was an example of Vinnie's toughness, which occurred when we were sitting in the cafeteria looking out of a huge glass window facing the spacious lawn and manicured grounds lined with palm trees.

Bronco Days was something totally new to us but it was not a game to the locals at Pan Am, they were the real deal! Those of us who were not from the area decided to try to fit in and dress the part, trying to dress like a cowboy. But somehow we just made the other students laugh when they saw us trying to dress and act like "cowboys". One of the sites built for the event was a makeshift jail in the middle of the campus. If any students were not dressed "western" or did some dumb thing wrong, they were escorted to jail. The "arrested" guys had to chew tobacco to be released, but the girls in jail had to kiss the Sherriff who was on duty in order to be released.

Banty, Me, and Vinnie in our
western gear for Bronco Days!

Campus jail for the women who had
to kiss the sheriff to be released!

It was fun to watch unless it happened to be your girlfriend who was kissing these bearded cowboys! Girls were being chased and caught, and some even carried over a shoulder to the jail. Sure enough, we saw Vinnie's girlfriend Sarah running for her life! The guy chasing her had won the State Golden Glove Championship in Dallas a week prior to this event. While this was happening, Vinnie had jumped up from the table yelling he would be back in a minute. We all watched through the window as Vince (not Vinnie when it is serious business) went out and talked with this guy. Vince waited for him to take off his gun holster and leather vest, and put his hands up in a fighting position. It took one punch to destroy, the Texas State Boxing Champion! From that point, all anyone saw was the bottom of the other guy's boots as he landed on his back! After the Rodeo cowboy found his breath, he got up unsteadily and wobbled off.

Another event happened during the Bronco Day Parade, which began in the middle of town and finished at the "Bronco Day" jail. The "TKE" fraternity had the winning float and I remember it very well because there was a gorgeous blond sitting in the front of this float. She was wearing a white outfit with one bright star on her short western skirt. I asked around campus, but no one knew her other than she lived off-campus and drove an old green car. She was a new girl on campus, having just moved to the Valley from San Antonio, Texas, and the "Frat Rats" picked her as their queen!

My first glimpse of the "Girl on the float."

As the season rolled around, our team was doing really well. Travel was still long and presented a few problems here and there with schoolwork, but probably not as much trouble as our new team uniforms. Coach was always the good guy, wearing the so-called "White Hat". He believed in being polite to officials, and maintaining outstanding sportsmanship while playing with tremendous intensity. His motto was to help an opponent off the ground after you had knocked him down during a game! During the previous year, Coach Williams stayed on us about tucking our shirts in at every timeout. It got old after a while, having to mess with our shirts. Therefore, he designed a new shirt with snaps at the bottom of the jersey to keep the shirts taut and in place, within our shorts! The problem was that these silver, steel snaps were fastened in the crotch. If we were not in shape, it would show due to the tightness of the shirts on our bodies. Everyone hated these shirts except for Coach; he was proud of how we looked even though our nuts were somewhere up in our chests!

While traveling during basketball season, we played at Tennessee and we had our hands full with some of the higher-rated teams, but for the most part, we were steadily climbing in rankings. Our team was up to 5th and heading into Kansas for three games. We started out in Kansas City with a loss against Rockhurst College, 60-59. We had a hard time matching up with them - they were a super defensive team. They had a player named Ralph Telkin, who ate my lunch. He was a 6'2" defensive specialist. He was not much on offense, but he was a good solid kid! And in our next games of the tournament, we beat Kansas State 83-67, and ended Fort Hays State's home record of 26 straight wins by beating them 85-73!

By the time we arrived back in Edinburg, and had dropped off one of the drivers in Red Gate (8 miles North of Edinburg) at 2:30 AM, and then arrived at the Belrose, we were ranked 4th. We were excited about the new ranking, but even more excited about the plans to move into the new "Southwick" Dormitory in two weeks. We always had to be very quiet entering the Belrose. We didn't want to wake Mrs. Alston, and above all, we certainly didn't want to wake the scary little possums. Yes, a new dorm sounded great.

We hit classes for three weeks before our next road trip came along. This time we were off to Kansas City, once again trying to improve on last year's second round exit from the N.A.I.A. National Championship. We all felt we could make it through the week and hopefully play Grambling with Willis Reed, in the finals. The match makers had it all figured out, Big Jack against Willis! I really couldn't wait either! Both of our teams did what we were supposed to do and we did meet in the Semi-Finals! I had watched so much footage on Reed that I began imitating the exact way Willis walked down the floor. He would place his hands on his hips, turn his back to the ball, turn his feet out, and then he would slowly walk toward our basket after his team scored.

Well sure enough, we got to play Grambling again, and Jack and Reed had a battle, with each scoring 33 points, with both getting short jumpers and a dunk here and there. I probably gave my best defensive effort of the year and held Frazier to 42 points!

We were up by four when they scored, cutting our score to two, and there it was, just like I had seen it in my mind during that week. After their basket, Grambling's team was walking back toward our basket, with their backs to me while I had the ball moving up quickly, thinking about two things while closing in on them. Debating with myself whether I should pull it out and start a play, or sneak by them while they were not looking. I chose the second, even though my life was flashing in front of my eyes. I heard Coach Williams yelling in the background, "Shhhhhhhhhhiii!"

I was two steps past the foul line when Frazier yelled to Grambling's player, "Albert, turn around!" By that time I was airborne going in for a layup as Albert finally turned. He looked at me for maybe a tenth of a second, and he then reacted in a way that I never expected. He suddenly bent over so as not to take the charge! When he realized that he would look like a candy ass by ducking, he stood up quickly while I was off the ground taking the lay-up. As he stood straight up, he undercut me so my legs went straight up toward the backboard and my arms were straight out from my sides as I was heading downward headfirst. The caption under the UPI photo of me performing this play read, "Pan Am flies low!"

The foul was called on Johnson, and I went to the line, hitting one of two. We went on to win the game 90-83 with Coach Williams walking behind me to the dressing room, repeating loudly, "What the hell were you thinking, Urand?"

The next night we were in the finals against Western Carolina and the NAIA Championship was ours! The Final Game was a tight game until the last three minutes when Big Jack lit them up! We won 73-62!

Proud Champions!

Coming back into the Valley by bus was a hoot! We had the Confederate Air Force flying over us as we hit Edinburg. The bus headed directly to the town square, and we were greeted by most of the student body and crowds of people from the town. We were all so proud of what we had accomplished. Even Lupe and Tito, the bus drivers were feeling the energy that was building. There were speeches from the Mayor, University President, Coaches, etc. It was like a page

MARTY URAND

from the movie "Grease". Cheerleaders were jumping and getting the crowd screaming and chanting encouragement, appreciation, and support. That is the beauty of attending a college that does not have football and treats basketball as the number one sport.

Walter Yates and Jim Mc Gurk didn't let the Trophy out of their sight while sitting on the stage in the downtown square.

But probably the single best present we received, easily outdoing the small basketball charm with "NAIA Champs" engraved on it, (the charm was only a shade better than the roller skates!) was the Board of Regents Safari Hunt! The Safari Hunt was fantastic!

A few weeks after the basketball season ended, we had breakfast served to us at our new dormitory on campus, "Southwick Hall". And in honor of our basketball team's success, we were invited to The King Ranch for some Texas Fun!

Upon reaching the ranch, about forty minutes north of Edinburg, we were met by the Board of Regents from Pan American University. Many handshakes and short speeches were made highlighting the success that our basketball championship our basketball team had brought to South Texas and our college, Pan American. In honor of this achievement, the Board felt that this particular event was truly "fit for a champion", and they began the activities by issuing us four items:

1. *One four-wheel drive Jeep for each two players*
2. *Shotguns with several boxes of shells per player*
3. *A map of the Ranch*
4. *The "Menu" for the hunt!*
    A. *A Rattlesnake earned you ($50.00)*
    B. *A Boar or wild turkey ($75.00)*
    C. *Any kind of bird ($25.00)*
    D. *Fox or Wild Pig ($100)*
    E. *Coyote brought ($150)*

We took off in all directions, mainly to get away from each other for our own safety! Vinnie and I went together and we shot at everything... including cactus bushes. We managed to get a couple of snakes, but they were not rattlers. Trim and Jack had a big day, bagging a turkey and several road kill type animals, so they won the most cash for the event. Topper did not want to hunt, and traveled in the back seat with the coaches. It was interesting that none of us had had any idea what was in store for us. We were told to wear jeans or long pants with long sleeve shirts. and almost all of us wore baseball caps except for Topper. He wore a green safari hat with flaps tied up on the sides. Everyone laughed when Topper showed up with that "lid"! But he had the last laugh when he was given a hundred dollar bill for the most appropriate hat for the hunt!

This did not happen by chance! Topper, (Mitchell Edwards) frequently had premonitions about almost everything. Of all the guys on our team, he methodically took in everything. At social events he said very little, but observed everything that was happening. He was especially observant of opposing teams as he carefully sized up their basketball players as they were warming up. Many times during basketball practice, when the rest of us were too proud or nervous to ask coach about a technique or play, Topper would be the one to say, "Hey,"Cortch" (this is how he pronounced coach), can you repeat that?" And when it came to plays, he was the first to learn them. Mitchell was a unique person and was possibly the best shooter in the history of the school. This must have been because of his high level of concentration.

Another thing about Topper was that he was always watching his money so he could buy a new "lid" when we traveled to a new city. The story we all seem to remember about him and his frugal ways was during the year when we had the basketball food cards to use when eating around the Edinburg Square. We had just played a home game and were heading straight to *Don Diego's* to eat, when a man approached him wanting to buy him dinner for the great game that Topper had just played. Topper thought for a second and said, "Say man, can I have the money for the meal, because I have a food card?" We all fell out when we heard him say that to the guy. He never broke a smile, thanked the man for the "dinner", and went in while we were still outside cracking up!

Dinner that night was what you would expect on a ranch: All the steak and baked potatoes we could possibly stick down our throats. I mean huge steaks, with some at least 60 ounces! They had five very large barbeque pits smoking away, with corn and potatoes on one pit with a vat of beans and sausage, and you know there had to be corn bread! We stayed there eating most of the night, telling good stories about Kansas City. At 10:30 PM, we were still bragging and sometimes exaggerating to each other with our stories, and the only light we had came from a massive bonfire. We didn't see anything while we sat there, but we heard strange noises all around us, and I have to admit that I was nervous sitting in the middle of nowhere, USA! The King Ranch is the largest in Texas and there was nothing else around us for fifty miles in either direction.

We finally left the ranch around 2:00 AM, and headed straight to the all-night Highway Grill in Edinburg. Since the dormitory and cafeteria had been built, we hadn't been around the square getting our meals anymore, and we kind of missed the Grill and the great smell of Mexican food. This day would have to go down as one of the most memorable days we had in the "Magical Rio Grande Valley".

> *a curious mixture of oil, citrus, cattle, and cotton; of hillbilly music and touring opera companies; of rodeos and of bullfights; of these and miles of desert-like sand; of institution of higher learning and of illiteracy; of all of these elements which combine to create "The Magic Valley." (El Bronco, 1963. Gwin Evans)*

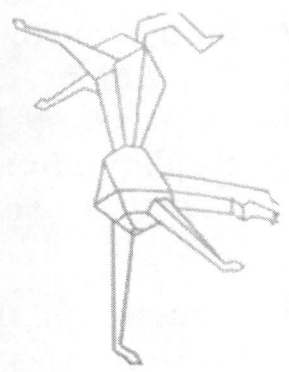

Baseball Career Comes to an End!

My second season of baseball at Pan Am was off to a slow start because we had so many celebrations and ceremonies that our championship basketball team needed to attend, which included a trip to Austin. Governor Connelly greeted us and declared the day, "Pan American College Day!" The original plans were to be introduced on the floor of Congress, but for some reason or another, it was moved up to the Governor's closed door office!

1963 was a difficult year for our political leaders. The Kennedy assassination in Dallas created a personal hardship for every Texan! Our championship brought a positive climate to the Governor's Office.

With the baseball season starting, Jack, McGurk, and I caught up with Pan Am's baseball team after the team had already played their fifth baseball game of the season. We were not in any kind of baseball shape to say the least. Coach Gartman sat us out of the next three games and told us that if we got ourselves into baseball shape he would play us in San Antonio when we played St. Mary's University.

We worked hard and Gartman finally gave us "thumbs up, letting us know he believed we were in shape and ready to play baseball. The team bus, "The Silver Bullet", was to leave from the Pan Am Field House at 6:30 AM. However, when the three of us arrived, the baseball team had already left! We got to the field house at 6:50, 20 minutes late and there was no sign of them. All we knew was that we needed to get to San Antonio! We went back to Southwick Hall to see if we could borrow a car to make the trip. However, everyone had plans and we had no recourse other than to call Coach Williams to see if he would help us with our problem. He agreed to let us use his car, and we were off to the Alamo! Before we even left, I knew there were two more major problems facing us: first, we had no money whatsoever, and secondly, coach's car was a small, beetle Volkswagen and our group had to somehow squeeze into it. But we eventually jammed ourselves in and were off! Jim drove, I sat in the passenger seat, and Jack somehow crunched himself into the back seat.

We had a half a tank of gas, which got us as far as Alice, TX. We needed more gas, and a cold drink would have been nice as well. But the fact remained, we had no cash. So I did what I did best; what I had done for so many years, "Sell baseballs!" Between McGurk and me, we had four pretty good baseballs and two bats. I sold them walking from store to store. Filled the ugly little car with gas, and off we went. What a sight! I know I would be speaking for many of the players when I tell you that no one liked the sight of that little piece of crap car.

The reason that the car brought bad memories was that after our basketball workouts with Coach Williams, he had required us to run three miles after the practice. Coach was shrewd; he knew the cafeteria closed at 7:00 PM so he started us out at 6:15, if we ran a 7 minute mile, then it took 21 minutes to run the three miles, 10 minutes to shower (Now 6:46), jump in a car and get to the cafeteria in five minutes (Now 6:51). We now had a minute to relax and walk into the cafeteria in a seemingly leisurely manner.

We provided the entertainment for the students watching this ritual each evening! Tony De la Pena was the fastest runner at an average of a 6 minute mile, and he was part of the students who had already reached the cafeteria and were eating as they watched the "rest of the team" come into the cafeteria. Swede always had a tough time with the run, but he didn't have to get to the cafeteria before it quit serving because he was married and lived in a duplex across from the Field House. When he finished his run, he would go home to eat with his family. The guys who ran a 9 minute mile had a rough time each evening, trying to get into the cafeteria before they stopped serving. But, on a positive note, it did motivate us to improve our time running the mile.

So we had the "Bug" flying up to Rattler Field (St. Mary's), but when we finally arrived, Pan Am was just taking the field for batting practice. As Gartman looked up and saw us, he never said a word, then or ever! We had great respect for him and it was not in our hearts to let him down. We made the trip realizing that we were not going to play, just so he'd know we'd cared enough to be there. During the four hour trip, we discussed what we thought he'd do or say when we finally showed up.

The cool thing was that the starting lineup card was up in the dugout from the time the team came out of the locker room, and when we came from the parking lot we were shocked that the card had our names on it! He had had faith in us. "He expected us to break our asses getting to the field!" It felt good to know that in spite of our "tardiness," he had that much faith in us and it felt even better winning 3-1.

Pan American's baseball team had a good year going into Spring Break, and we headed to Monterrey, Mexico for another baseball tournament. The Silver Bullet was feeling the effects of the long trips during basketball season and it really had a hard time with the Pemex gas and the mountains that it had to climb in Mexico! Coming around Saddle Back Mountain, the Bullet died a few times, and we coasted down the mountain to the first garage we came to.

Our baseball team did well winning the three games that we played. The downfall was that it was my 21st birthday which meant celebrating with Carta Blanca beer, and a few margaritas were also thrown in here and there! Before the night came to an end, I was once again feeling the *spirits* like I had when I was a kid running from the cops at the hospital grounds in East Brooklyn. This was very similar. Until this day, McGurk says that if it were not for him, I might be in a Mexican jail. I don't remember anything other than him buying the rounds at a local cantina!

Coach Williams was pissed and there was "talk" about me not playing in the Goodwill Basketball Games in Mexico City at the beginning of May (Two weeks away).

Goodwill Games—"Mexico City"

When we returned from Mexico, I was with the team, but I stayed away from the A.D. as much as I could so he wouldn't weigh his decision of letting me go or not go to Mexico to play with the basketball team at the Goodwill Games. A day before the team hit McAllen Airport for the flight, Coach Brooks called me and said that he was willing to let me go since Coach Williams was not going to make the trip. His wife became extremely ill and, he stayed with her rather than making the trip. He said he expected more appropriate behavior from me, and I was relieved and exceedingly thankful that Brooks included me.

Trans Texas Airways, with our team seated within, was rocking all the way to Mexico City. Everyone was having a great time. Coach Brooks was so nervous that he might have had too much of those little bottles of

Scotch, and he slept the entire flight. He was not a fan of flying! Our team was met by the Mexican Officials and we were treated like royalty. We all climbed into long limos with flags of Mexico on each side of the cars. Registration for our rooms had already been taken care of when we arrived at this wonderful hotel. First class all the way!

I had heard that after practice at the local Armory, we would be guests at a swanky restaurant. We had frog legs, cabrito or steak, and as much as we wanted. Once again, speeches and pats on our backs, and we were good to go... to a party that is! We heard that after dinner, other teams were hosting a party so we went there also. Joe Karam and Villegas had made some "headway" on the TTA flight and had invited the flight stewardess, who then in turn invited some friends, and those friends brought more friends, and it was an all-nighter!

Our first game was against the Mexican Olympic team with the winner playing Guatemala. With the Olympics coming up the next year (1964) in Mexico City, it was a good opportunity for us to play their number one team. We held our own for most of the game but eventually lost by 12. The crowds in Mexico are very different from those in the states. The crowds in Mexico are a bit more vocal, but we did not know what they were saying. Olympic rules allow for more aggressive play, and it was very new to us. Coach Brooks kept saying, "You guys stay away from fouling and let them do the fouling." "Yea right, that's what we will do..."

We soon learned the hard way, and we also began slamming heads as the crowd got even more out of control. It was obvious that we were not the favorites here, and all sportsmanship floated out to the Gulf of Mexico! The game ended with us running off the floor covering our heads for safety.

The next night was not any easier. The crowd got on us from the minute we began taking layups. All we could hear were loud whistles as plastic seat cushions were thrown out onto the court. These were cushions that people had paid extra money for so that they had a cushion between them and the cement bleachers. I am still fuzzy as to what Trim did to one of their players who had gone in for an easy basket, but it brought the house down! Trim's last name is Yates and all we heard over the loud speaker was "Valter Yahtez", over and over. And then every seat cushion in the house came flying down onto the court.

These flying "saucers" (cushions) were hitting us with pretty good accuracy. They surely must have had plenty of practice throwing those "damn things"! When Brooks got hit in the head, he ran onto the court yelling at us to, "Let's get the shit out of here". About 15 Federalists were on the court with clubs, guns, and shields fighting to take control. They knew the drill inside and out! From that day forward, I have called Trim, Yahtez! It was a very scary evening and the game was never finished. We were all so thankful to Brooks for standing up for us and getting us safely out of there.

The tournament officials were all over Coach Brooks for not bringing our team back for the next game, but he stood his ground. Hank Iba should have taken a lesson from James A. Brooks during the USA and Russian game!

We returned home the next day and both Jim McGurk and Luke Jackson left for Dallas where they played on a special basketball team that was going to play a practice game with the Russians. We were all very proud that we had two players from our team representing the United States.

Luke and Jim had a send off by coach
Williams at the McAllen Airport.
The following day, they played the Russian
Olympic Basketball team in Dallas, Texas.

My Second Year Round-Up

It was a great year for me academically. I declared my major, which was Education with physical education as my minor, and my grades were getting better. I pulled a full house, but this time it was Aces and Bulls and with "no flags".

My baseball career came to an end, although I tried out with the Houston Colt 45's at an open tryout. I jerked several balls out of the park and was catching some nods here and there, until Grady Hatton, the Manager motioned to the pitcher to throw curves.

That was the end of the tryout. "Can't hit the curve" was what they told me!"

My social life was even better than my freshman year, although I still had not seen the girl from the float on campus yet! But the year was a blast, and I was selected "Playboy" from the Ladies of Camelot Sorority. What else can you ask for?

As far as basketball was concerned, my heel had finally mended after I had smashed it against the backboard during the Grambling game, and I was so excited when at our annual basketball banquet, I was selected as the "Most Improved Player."

Most Improved player at the
Awards Banquet (1963)

But most of all, it is the thrill of my life to have been a part of such a great team, made up of so many talented athletes coming together from various parts of the country. One quote that meant a lot to all of was when Coach Sam Williams stated, "We are all so proud of these young men, who work so hard to sharpen their skills, minds, and to keep their focus to try to make basketball history for this small Texas college." Coach Sam Williams emotionally expressed his belief in the future of Pan American College basketball! He continued by saying, "I am especially excited with our current players as talented individuals and for their outstanding potential as a team." Coach Williams' belief in the college, the basketball program, and the dedication and quality of the basketball athletes

MARTY URAND

was magic to us. His excitement and conviction came through when he vowed that the program had something special going on down here. With those auspicious words, guys left their homes and their families from both small and large cities to follow this dream that was inspired by Coach Williams!

During this special year (1963), our hard work and perseverance paid off! This culturally diverse group of men set precedence for the Valley and Pan American College!

What an accomplishment! After losing Appleseed to the Globetrotters and Montgomery to the San Francisco Warriors, we go 26-6 and win the National N.A.I.A. Basketball Championship!!!

The summer was devoted to Wheels

The summer was a great getaway from classes and practices. I caught a flight home to Kennedy Airport and it was a flight from hell. We hit a huge lightning storm, and after circling Long Island for an hour, we finally had to land in Baltimore. We stayed on the plane until the "all clear" was given from Kennedy Airport, and we were finally able to take off from Baltimore. Everyone on the plane cheered as we landed safely at Kennedy Airport.

By the time I saw my parents, they were both acting crazy, like the weather delay was my fault or something. All the people who had to wait on their families and friends were in frenzy as well. Naturally, my dad was the most vocal. "What a damn swindle this is!" he was yelling at the top of his lungs. It was as if we were all just returning from Vietnam or something! Everyone was hugging and kissing, visibly shaken but relieved! However, it did remind me how dramatic my parents could be and just for a second it gave me confirmation that going so far from home had been a good idea!

Once we got home from the airport, things got back to normal, and I was back on 42nd Street one day later. Everyone at the Malt Shop and old friends on 42nd said the same exact thing when I would see them, "Jesus, has it been a year already?" The most affection came from the "perv's" who ran the street. They knew everyone's business. I was supplying them with basketball pictures of the players on our team without the players knowing! And of course I wouldn't send the pictures without autographing each picture as if it were the players' signatures, which was netting me 50 bucks for each Kodak. Those who had purchased the "autographed" pictures felt like they knew the players and actually stayed up with the results from each of the players' basketball games. Communication was bad at that time, no ESPN or internet, and any news came slowly through the newspaper articles. I sent articles from time to time to run up the "autographed" picture sales. I was driven to make more sales, motivated by my desire to earn money to buy a car to drive back to Texas when I returned to Pan American College at the end of the summer! I had my savings to put toward a car, and also would be able to bring back some of the proceeds from my "PP" business (photos for Perves).

The crap hit the fan when my dad asked me to bring some of the basketball players to work in the store during the evenings. My dad knew that business was always better when college guys were serving, showing their newly acquired Texas mannerisms and slight southern drawls when talking to each customer. My dad paid the college guys good money and it worked out well for all of us until one perv saw one of the guys and realized he had a signed autographed picture of this person. A picture he had bought from me, of a boy I'd said had the same interests as the buyer. He thought of the boy in the picture as his dream "sweetheart" and just about went into ventricular fibulation when he saw the real person!

When the guys saw their pictures being held up in the street, they thought it was really funny, asking me how these people got the photos? The perves were not allowed in the store by my dad, so I always thought I was in good shape with just the long distance fascination. However some of my Pan Am College friends, trying to figure out what was going on, asked a guy holding his picture to come in. And when my friend saw the writing on the picture, I was off and running. I had signed, "Thanks for your support, love... and then I had signed my teammates name."

Fortunately my friends took it all in fun, and in the end it had netted me about $800 toward the Ford Fairlane that I had my eye on. This car was solid black with red leather upholstery and had a red stripe on each side of the car. The car was "hot", and I finally made the money I needed for the $5,600 purchase of MY brand new car!

MARTY URAND

It took lots of "running" to the track, at least two to three trips per day and one to two pick-up basketball games at Reese Beach to help "earn" my car purchase money. There was not any time for dating, just horses and pickup games seven days a week. The only set back I had was that I had to replace my front teeth again after being pushed into the basketball pole at Rockaway Beach. And it was $250 to fix my front teeth for the third time. I had such good spaghetti cutters when they were first chipped out. It was a perfect upside down V that made a great slicer, but I felt like the girls were not going to go for that look!

August 15th, 1963, I was driving back down to Texas with Coach William's new basketball recruit from New York, Elliot Werber. I had vouched for his talent and work ethic to Coach Williams. Excited from what he had read and been told, Coach had followed my recommendation and Elliot was to be a Pan American College Bronc. I then contacted Elliot to see if he wanted to ride with me down to the Rio Grande Valley, to Pan American College. Elliott Werber was a 6'4" kid from the "J." He was a lefty and was a talented player, but he needed some work. I was excited that coach had taken my word for his talent and had given Elliott a scholarship with the hopes that he would become a banger off the glass. I kept telling Werber that I had nothing but positive thoughts of repeating as National Champs and he was fortunate to be on this team as a freshman.

My "Black Beauty!" 1963 Ford Fairlane 500.
I was on a roll and looking
for my beauty queen!

1963-64
The Junior Year

Front Row: Student Assistant Ramiro Vegas, Jim Board, Andy Carney, Vinnie Marino, Marty Urand, Raul Salinas, Mgr. Fidel Del Barrio, Middle Row: Mitch Edwards, Tony Dela Pena, Walter Yates, Elliot Werber, Gary Loff. A.D. Jim Brooks. Top Row: Coach Sam Williams, Anthony Eatmon, Jim McGurk, Luke Jackson, and Stan Bonewitz
RECORD: 28-6

New basketball player, Jim Board, was the talk of the town and the papers had high standards set for the upcoming year. JB was a transfer from St. Edwards in Austin, and had a wife and two little girls, Dawn and Tina, who everyone fell in love with. His wife Donna was very sharp and had us laughing whenever we were around her. The Boards were from Indiana, New Albany, where his dad had a local barbershop. Jim had picked up some of his dad's barber skills, and on Saturdays we were all over at his duplex waiting to get our flat tops for three dollars a cut. Jim "Swede" Harter, (6'11" from Little Falls, New York) who was also married, lived right next door to Jim and Donna. Since both Donna and Swede's wife were young, cute, and full of personality, we didn't mind waiting for our turns to get our haircuts!

As for our team, we were recognized by the AP and UPI wire services as "The Team to beat!" Coach Williams was selected as the N.A.I.A. Coach of the Year and Big Jack was a unanimous All-American Selection. All of the pieces were in place for a repeat!

Christmas Tourney

Our Christmas Tournament was in Quincy, Illinois. We took care of Central State of Ohio, 93-80. Jack fouled out early in the second half and I went for 27 points in that game. In the second game, we finally beat Western Illinois 82-77. In the finals, we beat

Rockhurst, from Missouri, 79-70, and Big Jack and I both made the All-Tournament team.

Luke Jackson and I made the Pan American Holiday All-Tournament Team (1963)

Trip to the East

This trip was really going to be fun, especially for the New Yorkers! Our team was heading to Upstate New York and the families of those of us who came from the area were driving up to watch us play. This was a first for our families as well as for us. My parents had last seen me play when I was in Little League. They never came to any of my basketball games when I was in New York because my dad was always working, and my mom was taking care of the kids.

Our trip east was a great recruiting tool as well as a "Perk" for the New Yorkers who were on the team.

New Yorkers; Vinnie Marino, Elliott Werber, Jim McGurk, Marty Urand, & Andy Carney

We flew into Buffalo, N.Y. to play St. Bonaventure, and it was a shock coming from our tropical weather to 15 below zero! We played in a coliseum rather than the Armory where the "Bonnies" normally play, but it did not help us as they beat us 84-77. The next night we beat St. Francis in Erie, PA. 104-90, and after a day off, drove to Gannon College and beat them 80-74. When we came back from the tournament with a record of 15-3, our ranking went up to third, behind Grambling and Tennessee State.

We had a great opportunity to improve our ranking again, if we could beat Texas Western University (UTEP) at their field house, which was in El Paso on the border of Mexico. El Paso's team had a big banger by the name of Jim "Bad News" Barnes, a 6'9" power center who really knocked heads with Jack. This game was for bragging rights in Texas. Both Jack, from Pan American College and Barnes, from Texas Western, had great games, scoring 36 each. However, we lost the war, 78-67. Every scout in the NBA was there to watch the two go at it. It was exciting just being on the court, although I almost did not make it to the game.

I had taken my meal money, along with some money I had brought myself, and I took the Sun Transit bus across the Mexican border from El Paso to bet on the horses at *Sun Down Raceway* in Mexico. I wanted to leave after the 7th race to get back for our game, but I could find no buses heading into El Paso at that time. When I finally caught a bus to the field house, I had already missed the pre-game meal and I told the coach that I had overslept. He looked somewhat skeptical, but he let it go. If I had mentioned the racetrack, I would have been picking wood out of my ass from sitting on the bench.

The Big One Got Away

We lost two times to Phillip's 66ers, the eleven time AAU champions, 98-79 and 82-57. We got our asses kicked twice by these NBA dropouts! Coach liked playing them because they were so good and it gave us exciting, high caliber games, which provided us with a great chance to learn and improve from them.

However, the real competition came during our basketball practices, which included practicing with our second team and our ineligible players. We had a more difficult time at these practices than we did playing the Texas teams or even from playing the Phillip 66'ers for that matter!

We had more pro scouts watching our practices each day than people attending our games. The NBA scouts followed Barnes (Texas Western), Willis Reed (Grambling), Luke Jackson (Pan American), and Tom Hoover (Pan American). They especially watched each battle that occurred in our practice gym on a daily basis. We were better during practice than at games mainly due to the playing of both Lucious Jackson and one of our ineligible players, Tom Hoover, a 6'11" transfer student from Villanova who weighed 280 pounds and was a beast! He could jump "out of the building". Since he was not currently eligible to play, few people knew about him. He was on the same size and skill level as Lucious and the best of the "Bigs" in the country.

If Tom Hoover had stayed eligible, we would have been unstoppable. Jack and Tom beat each other to death in practice daily! It was a war. As much as I relied on driving the ball, I began shooting from the outside rather than being caught in that line of fire under the basket. Jack was quicker and drove around Hoover, but Hoover went through Jack! That was something we had not seen happen during the two previous years.

Both Jack and Hoover became first round draft picks in the pro basketball draft.

Back at Pam American College, many of the players once again went to Mexico and ran into problems there. Almost every weekend we headed south seven miles to a border town called Reynosa, Mexico. It was a small town of about 125,000 people with a booming red light district, but it also had wonderful restaurants where families from nearby Rio Grande Valley towns came to eat and also to purchase tax free booze at these very fancy restaurants.

Some other types of businesses in the area were fancy dance clubs and shop areas people could walk through and purchase liquor, sterling silver jewelry, and souvenirs from Mexico. The back of these shops often opened into nicely decorated bars with waterfalls, and great facilities for dancing with tables for snacking and drinking. However, it was always an adventure to go over the border with our multi-racial team. If the United States in the mid-sixties was considered to be backward with their racial prejudice, then Mexico was even light years behind us!

One night we were at a bar in Mexico, and Tom Hoover, was dancing with a white girl, when an old redneck decided to separate the two. Hoover, being from South Philly, was used to fighting, and he laid this guy out with one punch, which cost that gringo thirty some odd stitches in his face. Unfortunately for ole Tom, that gringo was an Edinburg Judge!

And it was off to a Reynosa jail for Hoover! Going to jail is not like in the states, where a person pays bail and he is sprung! In Mexico, one never knows what the "Policia" will do. A person could be in a Mexican jail indefinitely, unless someone pulls a string or two using money to get him out. We called Coach Williams and Coach Brooks for help. They both came to Reynosa early the next morning to "plead their case for Hoover...to win Hoover's release".

The judge, after personally receiving a partial payment of "bail" money, finally approved Hoover's release based on the judge receiving the rest of the money for his release. Therefore, Coaches Brooks and Coach Williams had to return to Edinburg to "collect" more money to help pay the rest of the fine needed for Hoover's release. Both coaches collected what they could from numerous sources in Edinburg, including from alumni, a few Rio Grande Valley politicians, and various other backers.

A couple of days later Coach Williams and Coach Brooks finally had collected enough money and returned to Reynosa. The judge pocketed some of the money and told them to give the rest of the money to the jailer. He left the coaches sitting while he went to get someone to take them to the jail.

After a long wait, a Mexican soldier drove them to Reynosa's heavily guarded jail. Coach Williams and Coach Brooks got Tom out of the worst nightmare of his life!

Hoover's release had taken longer than anticipated, but Coach Williams and Brooks finally got him. Hoover owed both coaches for his life! And after he got back to the states, he left the valley and I never saw Hoover again until I watched him on television when he was playing for the Knicks.

At the completion of that season, the four big men for the NBA were Luke Jackson, Reed, Barnes, and Hoover. Philly had the first draft choice and they picked Luke. The Knicks took Jim "Bad News" Barnes and in the second round, the Knicks picked Reed. Hoover was taken in the third round, also by the Knicks. That season, Jack was selected as the Rookie of the Year after he had joined Wilt Chamberlain with the 76ers, and they had won the NBA Championship with my Erasmus High buddy, Billy Cunningham, at the other forward spot. Big Jack was the prototype for the new classification of "Power Forward."

Back to Kansas City: Will it be back-To-back?

As we prepared for the five day basketball marathon, we could not help feel that this was in the bag! We felt pretty confident in our bracket and were looking for Grambling to meet up with us again. But, unfortunately they got slammed in the third round and that ended another chance of another match up.

Pan American College began by blowing out La Crosse State, from Wisconsin, by 14 (94-82). The next evening we were having a tough time with St. Cloud (Minn), but won 81-76. We then blew by Mansfield State 82-69 and we had Carson-Newman College next. Nobody expected them to be very tough although they were a strong, hard-nosed group, with a motion offense that had no quit in them. However, they came on stronger than we expected. With the game tied at 82, we had the ball with seven seconds left and Topper hit a shot from the sideline by our bench. Nothing but net, and we were in the finals against Rockhurst, who we had beaten once during the Christmas break at the Quincy Tournament in Illinois.

The game against Rockhurst was a tougher game than we had expected! During the final four minutes, I felt we were playing the game in slow motion. We were trying, but we seemed to have lost our focus. We seemed to be just messing around. We were not even making a game of this when we should have taken care of business and danced to the tune of "Repeat!"

When we were down by six points with three minutes to go, I recall telling my teammates during a time out, that we would remember this game for the rest of our lives. I was trying to motivate everyone for a last ditch effort. I remember saying that we owed this to Jim Board. He was the only one of us who would not have the opportunity to play on a National Championship team unless we woke up right now! But as hard as we tried to get it together, we lost 66-56, and it was a heartbreaker for all of us! But we were proud of all we had accomplished. We were proud to have finished the year with the best record in the history of the school, 28-6!

My Wife to Be?

With no baseball season to look forward to, Padre Island was the place we wanted to be during our Spring Break. Many of us from the team drove to the beach just for the day, or if I got 'lucky', I would stay the night. Of all the women on the beach, I linked up with a high school girl. Being that she was still in high school, I needed to get her home early, so we caught a ride with some of the cheerleaders from Pan American and dropped her off in Pharr.

During the ride, I kept looking at this cute blond cheerleader in the front seat, who looked like the most wholesome girl I had ever seen. She was so shy, never once spoke to me or even looked at me. She hardly wore any make-up, had great legs and not an inch of fat to speak of. Then it hit me, she was the girl on the float who I had been crazy about earlier in the year! This was nuts! What a coincidence this was. Her name was Deanna Powell and she drove an old 56' green Oldsmobile to and from school. When they dropped me off, I spoke to everyone but her!

Deanna Powell, from Alamo, Texas

I asked around, and to my surprise no one I talked to knew anything about her. Eventually, I found out that she was going to try out for cheerleader with help from Betty Jo Sansing, a current cheerleader. So I went to her practice and waited for her to finish so I could "officially" meet her.... and forty-nine years later, I am still married to her!

MARTY URAND

Third Year Round-Up

1963 Pan American Univ.

Other than losing a heart-breaker to a team that we had already beaten during the year, the season had been very good. I had made two All-Tournament teams; my dribbling had improved as well as my outside shot. I was selected to the Who's Who in American Colleges with Trim, and we were pretty proud of that. McGurk and Linda, his girlfriend, had been in Who's Who the year before. I was maintaining my grades, and began enjoying teaching Physical Education at a local elementary school as part of a course that I was taking.

Coach Williams, Amelia Thomas, Diane Sturdevant, and Janette Hawkins, teachers from the Kinesiology Department attended the Texas Association for

Health, Physical Education, Recreation and Dance State Convention each year. They took the majors to this high energy event which was held in San Antonio that year. The conference was three days and it was then that I fell in love with teaching and wanting to become a member of TAHPERD.

It was like being in the next chapters in the "Chip Hilton Series", drawing me closer to my life's work of teaching and coaching children.

The very first presentation I attended at the TAHPERD convention was as a student, and it really hooked me! The large area was filled with teachers and I was standing on a chair in the back watching a guy with curly hair bouncing around with children, tumbling all over the place. His name was Dr. Garland O'Quinn, the Master! I attended every workshop he put on over the years that followed and read his books on how to teach children. I discovered that he had been on the Olympics' Gymnastics Team during the 1960 games.

School was really becoming a lot of fun and I was loving it. Maybe Deanna had something to do with that. After she made the cheer squad, playing basketball became even more fun for me. The cheerleaders did not travel to all of our out of town games, but the few that they did attend were enjoyable.

*New cheerleaders were: Cleo Garza, Linda
Rogers, Deanna Powell, and Georgian Sheriff
Their limited travel included experiencing
segregation that we faced at each meal!*

My social life had some real meaning now. Deanna
had a great family with a younger brother, Charlie,
who was 8 years old, and he was really into sports.
Deanna also had a married sister, Jackie, who was
nervous much of the time since her husband Tim was
a helicopter pilot in Vietnam.

Deanna's mom and dad were military and everything
was done on a schedule. I obeyed the schedule each
Saturday evening! That was the night that "The
Colonel" would cook up steaks, great steaks. He was
a stern, but loving family man, and if he felt anyone
was doing his family wrong, he became a stern SOB!
I should have guessed from his personality that he
had been a warden at a military prison for a few
years while in the Army. He ran a tight ship and that

included his beautiful daughter. I brought her home on time, "Yes sir, no Sir," and we were buds! After dinner one Saturday, he looked me in the eye and said, "You know Marty, a woman may fool me, but a man can't!" I have believed that mantra during all the years that I had known him. I felt that he was born to "Bust Balls!" But if he trusted and liked someone, the person had it made, and he liked me!

He was one of the best golfers in the Valley and loved sports in general. He was pretty easy to talk to unless he was watching the news or the Dallas Cowboys. He would also cut you off in the middle of a sentence and bang his shot glass on the coffee table and yell out, "Mate," and his wife, Nell would come running. Nell was a genuine, genuine sweetheart. Not a bad bone or thought in her body! They always say to look at the mama to project your wife's looks. I thought she was a beautiful woman, but I may have been partially influenced by her "good heart."

The Colonel was opinionated, but a very bright old codger who loved to write "Letters to the Editor" in McAllen's local newspaper, and when really agitated, he thought nothing of writing his opinions to the United States President.

Deanna's father would take Deanna's mother Nell and her little brother Charles to each of the basketball games to watch her cheer and to see me play. Since he knew we were dating steadily, he felt that our games warranted his presence. He was probably my biggest backer.

As the season and our friendship grew, so did his dislike for my coach. All of which was only based on my playing time. If Coach Williams benched me for something I did, or did not do, the "Colonel" would state his feelings ... loudly! He called him "Sam", not coach, to show his displeasure. Everyone could hear his voice: (scratch that, his "command"), anywhere in the gymnasium. He would scream out, "Hey Sam, sit down and put Marty back in the game!" I was embarrassed many times, but before the season was out, he had a new name for coach. It was Liberace!! Coach Williams wore a sports coat and always flipped up the back of his jacket when he went to sit on the bench. It got bad! I would always say something to coach to show that I did not approve of Deanna's dad yelling at him.. Although Coach always said that it didn't bother him, it sure the hell bothered me! My father-in-law to be wasn't nearly that old then, but the best way that I could describe what he looked like and even more so, acted like, was Clint Eastwood. In the movie, "Grand Torino," they could have used the Colonel for a double, no shit. He never went anywhere without his pistol! He stayed up with his "toys." Every Wednesday after dinner, at about "1800 hours", he was off to the target range with an arsenal of hardware. I am positive that this ritual was in my mind when it came to any thoughts of sex with Dee! There was a reason that my wife had our first child three years after we got married!

The summer was a piece of Crap!

I drove home to New York for the first time with Elliott Werber, and that was one of the highlights for the summer to come! My parents were still living on Emmons Avenue, and their apartment was nicely furnished. But it seems that my dad and his brothers, after twenty five years, had closed down *Famous Malted milk Inc.* The City had decided to clean up Times Square and that meant the stores, the all-night peep shows, and the theaters that had welcomed every "perv" in the city were eliminated from the area.

My mother went back to work after all her years of being a stay at home mother and homemaker. She began working for *Morgan Trust and Securities* in the city and was very happy. For the first time in her married life, she did not have an "allowance" from my dad to abide by each week. Her allowance had covered food for the house and whatever was left had become her allowance for her needs. Now she was earning a paycheck and it all went to her for clothes, entertainment, and furniture.

Enid was in the process of trying to leave the USA to find herself. She was dating a very talented musician who was in a band called "Sweet Smoke" and he and the other band members were talking about going overseas to perform. By October of the upcoming year, Enid was hitching around the world having the time of her life. She fell in love with Andy, the base guitarist in the musical group. A high official within the "Sweet Smoke" family ("Sri Ananda Murti") married them.

My sister, Ilene, and her boyfriend, Bob tied the knot as well and by the end of the summer, my parents were looking to move into a smaller apartment on the Brooklyn side of the Brooklyn Bridge. The bridge connected Brooklyn and Manhattan's lower East side! My dad was in heaven.

Due to the heat placed on him by the police, and the gaming laws, my dad decided to buy his own yellow cab and to purchase the silver medallion that must be on the taxicab in order for the cab to be legal in New York. My father, the man with possibly the worst temper in New York City, was now going to drive people in city traffic! I would hate to have been any of his passengers. His driving was "interesting". He has always made the shortest right hand turns known to man! I cannot tell you how many garbage cans and cars he scratched when driving. There were probably hundreds of people that he "almost" hit on a daily basis. His passion was scaring the crap out of would-be "jay walkers "as they stepped off curbs. His car windows were always open. First, because the cars were un-air-conditioned and the other was so he could yell at the pedestrians that he almost hit! He loved sticking his head out his cab window to call people "Schmucks!"

He lasted a total of one year as a New York cabby! He was robbed three times, beaten up once, and eventually lost his license for driving "stick-up". The term "stick-up" refers to the meter in each cab not being turned on when a new customer is picked up. When a passenger is seated in a cab, the first thing that is required is for the cab driver to turn on the meter by lowering the flag (Stick). That turns off the light on the top of the cab, showing a customer is in the taxi, and car fare is being recorded. If the light on top of the cab is not lit, but a customer is in the cab, it means the driver is scamming the company and keeping the fare himself, and probably reporting lower income for taxes.

After being caught doing these irregularities three times, the cab driver is automatically fired, and taxi-driving privileges are canceled! My dad came close to being caught several times, but made it through. Despite all the bad adventures my dad experienced, he enjoyed driving the cab and being somewhat on his own. He loved waiting for passengers while reading the Telegraph. He felt like this was the best job in the world!

He looked into purchasing his own cab but found out that the medallion on the hood, indicating a private cab, costs fifty-two thousand dollars! With that goal in mind, my dad kept going back to the bookies and to Aqueduct to keep raising cash so he could gain independence. Having his own cab was now his goal. That is where I started and ended my summer as a "Runner" once again.

I tried to talk Deanna's dad, the Colonel, into letting his daughter come with me to N.Y. for a visit, but he wouldn't hear of it! He always tried to protect Deanna from what he considered the "wild side of life". It made for a very long summer for me. Basketball, for the first time, was not a priority in my life. Getting back to Texas and Deanna was all that was on my mind, 24/7. I hit on a couple of good races, taking on some more advanced financial risks and found out that I could win more often with small bets, but usually lost on the big ones. I realized then that luck is not always good luck, and I lost my share of bets! I felt that if the "horse Gods" were on my side, that it didn't mean I'd hit a big one more often than a little one. It just didn't work that way, and I stayed with under fifty buck bets and stayed clear of one hundred dollar window regardless of how many times I'd hear, "This damn horse can't possibly lose." Or they'd say, "If this horse loses, I will eat this Telegraph!" So making small bets, winning, and getting back to Texas was my objective.

1964-1965
The Senior Year

Front Row: Assistant coach Walter Yates, Mgr. Fidel Del Bario, Marty Urand, Jim Board, Coach Sam Williams. Middle Row: Raul Salinas, Alex Gillum, Bill Garrison, Tony Dela Pena, Gary Loff, Mitchell Edwards, Top Row: Anthony Eatmon, Richard Horowitz, John Harbison, Jim Harter, Otto Moore, and Elliot Werber.
RECORD: 19 – 7

My final year of basketball! My last year of eligibility, my basketball career as a player was nine months from ending! Other than my thoughts of Deanna, the year was missing the optimism of the past years. Our team had lost Jack, Trim, Villegas, McGurk and my best friend Vinnie to graduation.

Captains: Jim Board, Mitchell Edwards,
Marty Urand with Coach Williams

Jack went on to have a great year, winning the NBA Championship with the 76ers and earning "Rookie of the Year." Ramero Villegas, Walter Yates (Trim), and McGurk began their coaching careers. Yates was in Houston and McGurk and Vinnie in the Valley. Later Vinnie went back to N.Y.C. and became a Police Officer.

Three new players were added to help Jim Board, Mitchell Edwards, and me get back to Kansas City. Of the three freshmen, Otto Moore, 6'11" from Houston had the most potential. Anthony Eatmon, a 6'6" power forward, and 6'4", Alex Gillium, (Mud) rounded out the players. Tony DelaPena, Elliot Werber, Jim Harter, and Joe Karam also returned. To say we missed Jack was an understatement!

We went 19-7 that year and for the first time in my career, we did not make it to Kansas City for the playoffs!

We opened against UTEP in El Paso, and our hopes went down with our loss of 66-58. We did manage to take Tennessee State at home (69-65) but dropped one to them in Nashville as well as losing to Tennessee Tech in Cookeville, 76-68. That did it for our travel that year. It was the least amount of travel in my four years at Pan American College.

As the year progressed, so did my plans for getting married. It became official in October. Once I had made my decision that Deanna was for me, I had to get up the nerve to talk with the Colonel! God, he hated Yankees . . . I was in for one Hell of a stressful time.

After spending 20 minutes with "the Colonel" in his backyard, it must have been nearing the news on TV, because he just blurted out to me, "Spit it out Marty!" I did, and all went well... and he didn't miss any of the news. Dee and I set the wedding a day after finals were over, May 25, 1965. The wedding was going to be in a small church in Alamo, Texas and the reception was planned for the Texan Hotel in Pharr, Texas on US Hwy 281, less than three miles from Mexico.

Deanne Lynn Powell Pledges Vows With Martin A. Urand

I Finally found that "Cowgirl" from the float and married her on May 21, 1965

The plan was to get married and then head to New York City for the honeymoon. Unfortunately, one small problem arose. My mother was ill and my parents couldn't make the trip! I decided I wanted the two people who were like my "Texas parents" to stand in for mine. This is where I earned a **TECHNICAL FOUL** with my poor judgment! Instead of asking

Coach Williams and his wife, I asked Coach Gartman, the baseball coach, and his wife Pat. I would have been happy with either coach standing up for me, but what a slap in the face it was to Coach Williams! He had been my main coach and done so much for me. But it's something I did without thinking things through. Both coaches meant so much to me.

With the plans under way, and my parents feeling guilty for being unable to come, they began planning a second wedding reception for us in NY. The party was a dandy! My entire family and our close friends attended the reception which included dinner, drinks band and dancing. It was great seeing all of my family celebrating our happy occasion.

The reception was a hit with the family, and my dad's brothers were in rare form! There was lots of laughter and many hugs. Deanna was very nervous coming to meet the family. She was usually a very quiet, "Southern Bell". She was not a drinker, but was given "scotch and ginger-ale "throughout the night and surprised us both by dancing, hugging and laughing it up. She was without a doubt, the belle of the ball! The reception was a success for all of us.

Although she was very nervous, Dee impressed the eighty family members at the New York reception.

My Fourth Year Round-Up

Back on campus, Dee and I were selected as the Bell and Beau for the senior dance and everything was fitting into our storybook romance! Of course the pressure at the time was on me and graduating. Dee had another half semester in the fall, but with any luck, I could graduate in May!

Dee and I received the "Bell
and Beau" recognition
Just before getting married in May.

I was taking nine hours during the second semester of my senior year. One of those courses, Freshman English, had been my curse, and I was taking it for the third time. And from the looks of things at the time, I was going to need to take it again in September!

With pro basketball not being an option, coaching and teaching children became my reality. Coach Williams kept me on scholarship as a freshman assistant coach so that I could graduate with Deanna at mid-term of 1966. Texas was now my home and I owe a great deal of the success to Pan American University, Coach Williams, Coach Brooks, Doc Morgan, Marvin Blumenthal and the Lone Star State of Texas!

My life of Basketball gets Sunsetted

This quarter of my life would go down as certainly the most important part of my life. It was my season of maturing and coming to a realization of how important an education and the right woman is toward succeeding in life!

Coach of the year, Sam Williams
with Coach James Brooks
Put Pan American College on the
National basketball map.

NOT RECOMMENDED FOR COLLEGE

Only in Texas

This is a must read for all Texans, used-to-be Texans, adopted Texans or wanna-be Texans:

Just Texas

Pep, Texas 79353
Smiley, Texas 78159
Paradise, Texas 76073
Rainbow, Texas 76077
Sweet Home, Texas 77987
Comfort, Texas 78013
Friendship, Texas 76530

Love the sun

Sun City, Texas 78628
Sunrise, Texas 76661
Sunset, Texas 76270
Sundown, Texas 79372
Sunray, Texas 79086
Sunny Side, Texas 77423

Want something to eat?

Bacon, Texas 76301
Noodle, Texas 79536
Oatmeal, Texas 78605
Turkey, Texas 79261
Trout, Texas 75789
Sugar Land, Texas 77479
Salty, Texas 76567

Rice, Texas 75155
Pearland, Texas 77581
Orange, Texas 77630
And top it off with:
Sweetwater, Texas 79556

Why travel to other cities? Texas has them all!

Detroit, Texas 75436
Cleveland, Texas 75436
Colorado City, Texas 79512
Denver City, Texas 79323
Klondike, Texas 75448
Pittsburg, Texas 75686
Newark, Texas 76071
Nevada, Texas 75173
Memphis, Texas 79245
Miami, Texas 79059
Boston, Texas 75570
Santa Fe, Texas 77517
Tennessee Colony, Texas 75861
Reno, Texas 75462
Pasadena, Texas 77506
Columbus, Texas 78934

Feel like traveling outside the country?

Athens, Texas 75751
Canadian, Texas 79014
China, Texas 77613
Dublin, Texas 76446
Egypt, Texas 77436
Ireland, Texas 76538

Italy, Texas 76538
Turkey, Texas 79261
London, Texas 76854
New London, Texas 75682
Paris, Texas 75460
Palestine, Texas 75801

No need to travel to Washington D.C.

Whitehouse, Texas 75791

We even have a city named after our planet!

Earth, Texas 79031

We have a city named after our state:

Texas City, Texas 77590

Exhausted?

Energy, Texas 76452

Cold?

Blanket, Texas 76432
Winters, Texas 79567

Like to read about History?

Santa Anna, Texas 76878
Goliad, Texas 77963

MARTY URAND

Alamo, Texas 78516
Gun Barrel City, Texas 75156
Robert Lee, Texas 76945

Need Office Supplies?

Staples, Texas 78670

Want to go into outer space?

Venus, Texas 76084
Mars, Texas 79062

You guessed it. It's on the state line.

Texline, Texas 79087

For the kids . . .

Kermit, Texas 79745
Elmo, Texas 75118
Nemo, Texas 76070
Tarzan, Texas 79783
Winnie, Texas 77665
Sylvester, Texas 79560

*Other city names in Texas, to
make you smile . . . .*

Frognot, Texas 75424
Bigfoot, Texas 78005
Hogeye, Texas 75423

Cactus, Texas 79013
Notrees, Texas 79759
Best, Texas 76932
Veribest, Texas 76886
Kickapoo, Texas 75763
Dime Box, Texas 77853
Old Dime Box, Texas 77853
Telephone, Texas 75488
Telegraph, Texas 76883
Whiteface, Texas 79379
Twitty, Texas 79079

And last but not least, the Anti-Al Gore City

Kilgore, Texas 75662

And our favorites. . .

Cut and Shoot, Texas 77303
Gun Barrel City, Texas 75147
Ding Dong, Texas
West, Texas (it's in Central Texas)
and, of course,
Muleshoe, Texas 79347

THIRD QUARTER

My Career

1965-2004

My first Job Interview

As soon as Deanna and I returned from our honeymoon, I again spent the majority of my time studying, but it was a different kind of studying that was occupying my time now. A coaching vacancy at Edinburg High School was going to be available in September, and Edinburg's Superintendent, Mr. Cowens, asked me to apply for the J.V. basketball job. It was a perfect start-up job for me because I would be working with "Frito" Flores who was the Varsity basketball coach and he had been a friend to our college teams for years. However, the problem was that they were not actually hiring a basketball coach. They were hiring a *football* coach to coach their lower-level football team, and the second part of the assignment was to coach the Junior Varsity basketball team.

The studying came about because the coaching assignment I had to apply for was to coach the school's lowest level football team, and I had to study and add football terms and football plays to my vocabulary so I could be convincing. Since I had never played football or even worn a football helmet, I knew it was going to be difficult. I had to be prepared to convince the athletic director that I was the "perfect" applicant to coach the beginning football team, and just coincidentally, that I could also coach basketball. I was going to "mention" that I would not mind coaching JV basketball along with the football, since I knew there was a vacancy for that position. However, football was the "required" sport. For those not familiar with the Texas football hype on Friday nights, you are really missing out on a real "sports culture".

In many districts, the underlying policy back then was that beginning in junior high school, if a boy did not play, or at least try out for football, then he was not allowed to play another sport. Therefore, the role I had to play was that of a college graduate applying for the football position based on my football knowledge, and that is where the studying became a factor. Nickel defense, slants, inside and outside blocking schemes, zone coverage versus man-to-man, and passing defenses became a part of my nightly studying. Even "Frito" was bringing over material from his football coaching duties for me to study to prepare for the interview.

As the interview approached, I had doubts that I would be able to pull off being an imposter as a football coach. With some last words of wisdom and a pat on the back from Sam Evans (Assistant Superintendent), I entered the A.D.'s office. Fred Akers was not what people sometimes think of as the typical football coach/athletic director. He was in shape, no big belly, an immaculate dresser, academically bright, and he had a great personality. There was no doubt about it; Coach Akers was all business and all about winning.

I thought that if there was anyone who could see through me, it would be him!

At the interview, naturally, all questions were about football. I answered every question whether I knew the answer or not, hoping my "sports" intuition would help me bluff my way through it. I guess my interview went well because Coach Akers offered me the job as the assistant freshman football coach at the end of the interview. Even though I had just been hired for the lowest football coaching position at the high school, I was thrilled. However, Coach Akers never mentioned the basketball position that I was really seeking, which had me worried. As I started for the door to leave his office, Coach Akers asked, "Do you know anything about basketball?" I answered by shaking my head in a yes motion, having a hard time even saying the word, "yes". At that time, my hand was around the doorknob when I heard him say, "Good, you will have to take that JV basketball coaching job as well!"

My First Basketball Team
Edinburg High School

EDINBURG H.S.
DISTRICT CHAMPS
1965   19-1

I spent the entire summer preparing for coaching
football of course, but I was also excitedly preparing
for my first basketball team as well. I had never before
experienced this kind of excitement. My head was filled
with the knowledge from all my previous basketball
coaches I had played for through college, high school,
the "J", and of course, I had the Chip Hilton Series to
fall back on.

In Texas, any employee who wants to coach must also teach. I had no idea what I was going to teach, and I was shocked when I eventually received my teaching assignment at Edinburg High School! It was somewhat ironic that I would be teaching "Programmed Learning" English to the children of migrant workers. I stayed a step ahead of my four classes and I learned a great deal in the process.

There was not a basketball around as we began preparing for football season. I had some neat, hardworking kids to work with and became attached to these players, especially to the boys who accepted my offer to play basketball.

Lyles Guess, the head coach of the freshman football team, realized within five minutes, that I knew absolutely nothing about football. I was lost on the field! He started me out by giving me coaching assignments such as organizing water breaks and handing out salt tablets. I pretty much worked with the team manager, Amancio Garza. I took a liking to Amancio, who was a quiet, shy boy. I asked him if he would manage my basketball team also, and through this, our friendship became stronger through the years to come.

When basketball season began, my Junior Varsity team was short-handed. Since the Varsity football team had made the playoffs, all players I currently had for basketball were the freshmen who did not have much experience. Because they were so behind in their skills, I taught only defense and lay-ups, and did not even allow the boys to take outside shots. They worked hard on those skills and began taking and having more control of their games. Soon our typical scores were below thirty points, but that was more than most of our opponents made. With the boys' hard work and enthusiasm, we ended up having a great season and finished the season at 19-1, only losing in the playoffs in double overtime.

Overall, it was a fun year. There was no pressure on me in being an "imposter" in football since Coach Akers left in July, before school even began. I had known that he was a good coach, but I had never realized how good he was until he became the head coach at the University of Wyoming.

As the school year ran down, I was having second thoughts of coaching football at the high school again for the next year. After talking to some other coaches, I realized that to coach basketball only, I would need to coach at the college level. It was a great thought, but coaching at that level required a master's degree. The big question was...did I want to go back to school again? I gave it a considerable amount of thought, and said goodbye to my $5,200 a year salary, which included my coaching stipend!

At the end of school in May, Dee and I drove to New York to visit my family, and on the way, I visited several universities and inquired about me getting a Master's Degree. We first traveled to San Antonio, where I turned down an offer for a high school varsity basketball job at Churchill High, a new school that was to open at the end of that summer. However, the A.D. said I would have to coach football at a low level as well as coach basketball. It was a good start, but I wanted to keep looking to see if I could find a job without football as part of my assignment. I told them I would let them know when I came back from New York.

Then at my second stop, I met with Coach Archie Porter at Sam Houston State University in Huntsville, Texas. After my visit to the campus with Coach Porter, our future was set. What finalized the deal was when I told him that Deanna and I were going to New York to visit my family. Coach Porter pulled me over and said, "I have two scholarships available for two talented basketball players, so if you see two truly good players get them! They can be black or white because we have room for two blacks on our newly integrated team. At that time, many of the people in Huntsville were very bigoted, and the segregation issue was firmly in play. We had not realized how bad it actually was when we had gone to recruit a couple of New York ball players for Sam Houston State University.

Once in New York, I searched at community centers, beaches, and schoolyards, looking for some first-rate talented players to recruit for the SHSU basketball team. At one of the community centers run by Ray Felix, a retired New York Knicks player, I watched Calvin Oliver, a 6'7", All-City basketball talent from Boy's High School shooting and dunking. I was impressed! I was able to identify with him because of my New York background and especially with his similar predicament with his low grades in school. His high school grades were no better than my high school grades had been. Calvin and I hit it off well, and Deanna and I went to talk with his mother about Calvin coming to Sam Houston State in Texas on a basketball scholarship. Deanna helped close the deal as she and Calvin's mom talked with each other and got along well. Calvin's mother was a very bright, single woman, who, after much discussion with us, probably had more confidence in Deanna than in me. Then Calvin told me that he had a friend who was an outstanding guard, and that this friend was interested in coming to Texas to play basketball as well. After meeting with Calvin's friend and watching his friend play, I called Coach Porter and told him I had his two basketball players and that I believed these two players could bring his team up to the next level.

Back to School Again!

Dee and I drove back to Huntsville and I registered at Sam Houston State University to begin classes toward my Master's degree. We moved into the athletic dormitory where I earned tuition and books as the Graduate Assistant for the Sam Houston State basketball team, and the manager of the athletic dorm and the Gymnasium.

Huntsville is a unique, small college town. On one side of Huntsville is the Sam Houston State National Park and a block from the campus in the northern direction is the Huntsville State Prison. Both places played an instrumental role during my year of studies.

While at SHSU, Dee and I purchased our first dog, a border collie and we named her Alfie. Dee and I also bought a second car, an MG midget convertible that I used to get around in Huntsville. Deanna was teaching in Klein ISD in Houston so she needed our main car to travel to work. She drove the 60 miles into Houston to teach at her school, and then she drove the 60 miles back to Huntsville. Deanna, Alfie, and I used the MG when we headed out to Huntsville State Park to relax and enjoy nature, which we did as often as possible.

On the weekends and holidays, Huntsville State Park was our escape for our "family of three".

I played on a recreation basketball team and some of my friends and I drove over to the prison and played basketball against a prison "team" during the week if possible. One of our players was a guard at the prison and he set up the games against some the low security prisoners. The inmates were great fans and appreciated watching these hard fought games. The prison brought in two experienced referees to keep the games "honest"! After the games, the prison provided our team with a great lunch, which usually consisted of corn on the cob and all the steak we could eat. That was how they thanked us, and it kept us coming back for the challenge of the game, but especially for the great meals! At the time, this was one of the few places in town where people did not discriminate. Athletics seems to break down barriers in most venues. Huntsville, located in East Texas, was a few steps behind most of the rest of Texas in race relations, although it has changed dramatically in that area since then.

I realized when I traveled through Texas, while playing for Pan American that things were not quite like New York. It was certainly different from the North. Discrimination is still a revelation for me, no matter how often I encounter it: no matter what race a person is!

I will always appreciate that Archie Porter and Sam Houston State University gave me the opportunity to earn a Master's Degree and the chance to begin my college coaching profession. I was taking a few classes, teaching a few physical education classes, coaching, and I was on the road scouting and recruiting for the basketball team. The person in charge was an assistant football coach by the name of Dr. Billy Tidwell. He had five graduate assistants under his direction and he made teachers and leaders out of each of us. He introduced us and immersed us into the science of teaching, "Pedagogy". His leadership led the three of us into outstanding careers in education:

Mike Bobo had a tremendous career at Texas Tech and became President of the Texas Association of Health, Physical education, Recreation, and Dance (TAHPERD).

Bobby Deidoss, from New Jersey, became a state leader in Jersey.

Gerald Gusti became a principal and was an innovative leader.

Dick Cuey was late to report to school since he was playing pro baseball. He spent his entire career at Baylor University in Kinesiology.

As for myself, I have always given Dr. Billy Tidwell the credit as the one educator who most motivated me to give my heart and soul to education: to teaching!

There were *four* incidents during that year that should not go untold. The *first* came after I picked up our two recruits from New York, Calvin Oliver, and Anthony Jones at Hobby Airport when they arrived from their flight into Houston. We drove straight to Coach Porter's house so the coach could meet them. Archie was having dinner, but came out to our car and put his head slightly through the open car window to meet his two new recruits. He immediately pulled his head out and quietly said, "I'll take the big one, Calvin, but I'm not wasting my other black scholarship on the "little one". I looked at Archie, exclaimed that the "little one" as he called him, was great, and could probably be the best college guard in Texas. Shaking his head with a perturbed expression on his face, he once again said, "Send him to some other college."

Nothing I said or did would change Coach Porter's mind, so I made a few calls: first to Coach Williams at Pan American University, and then to some other small Texas colleges. Coach Williams did not have an opening on his team, so the next morning, Anthony was on a bus heading to Alpine, Texas, to play for Sul Ross University. Sul Ross needed a guard and they were willing to give Anthony a chance. At the end of the season, the Sul Ross coaches were ecstatic about Anthony, who while playing at Sul Ross, led the Lone Star Conference in scoring.

Archie later recruited Frank Lawthridge, a 6'8" young man from East Texas, to play for Sam Houston State and to replace Anthony on the basketball team. Frank was a "banger", and Archie was happy to have two talented, big kids to fill his "quota"!

During the season, Archie occasionally talked to the Sul Ross coach about Anthony, and on one occasion, after he hung up, he got up from his desk and came over to me, turned around, and as he lifted his sports jacket up in the back, he said, "Go ahead, kick me! I can't believe I let Anthony go!"

The *second* event came shortly after Calvin complained to us about the harsh treatment he was encountering in town because of his race. Some restaurants would not serve him and some churches did not allow him to come in to worship. This was a difficult situation and hard for him and Frank. They were both also having difficulties with their studies. I knew I had to do something to get their academic problems under control at least.

Deanna and I had the only two-room apartment in the athletic dorm. The second room was actually a washroom where we kept our dog, Alfie, and Deanna had created a little office for herself where she did her schoolwork. Sometimes Deanna, being an English teacher, would tutor Calvin and Frank in this back room.

An incident happened during one of their study sessions with Deanna. While Deanna was tutoring them, someone began pounding loudly on our apartment door. I saw Archie and his assistant Lance

Stevens, but before I could get the door fully open, Archie was screaming, "Do you know where the black guys are? A girl was raped in the park and the police are searching for two black men!" As I was trying to calm him down and ask him to lower his voice, Calvin and Frank came out, "pissed off", to say the least, that they were suspected just because they were black. Trying to calm everyone down I pulled the coaches out of the hall and into our room as other athletes were beginning to gather in the hallway. When the coaches, Calvin, and Frank left, no one was happy!

The next day, after Calvin told me he wanted out of Huntsville and SHSU, I told Archie that we needed a plan to piece everything back together, beginning with an apology to them. Archie agreed and provided his car to Calvin and Frank on weekends, so they could drive into Houston and socialize. I called Yates (Trim), my old teammate who was now coaching in Houston. I explained the problem, and I asked him to help Calvin and Frank find some kind of a social life in Houston. Walter introduced Calvin and Frank to some basketball players with whom Walter played pick-up games in Houston, and they continued to make more friends and acquaintances in Houston through their involvement in these recreational sports. This not only helped them socially, but it also improved their basketball skills. I hoped that as Calvin and Frank became more content, they would be happier and stay at SHSU. I knew a social life was important for them as they studied and worked to complete their freshman years. In addition, helping them remain on

MARTY URAND

scholarship would also be helping me retain my good standing with Archie. However, most importantly, I felt like I owed the boys another chance. We wanted to do everything we could to support Calvin and Frank in this difficult time in race relations in the area. Realizing the importance of a social life and the importance of passing grades in their classes, we felt the Houston situation would help us all.

The *third* episode involved my dorm duties and coaching duties. There were times when Archie, Lance, and I would spend our weekends traveling to scout basketball games. One day Lance and I met to "flip" to see who was going to scout Stephen F. Austin University's game or which of us would watch a high school prospect in Houston. As it turned out, I "won the toss" and chose to attend the SFASU game, which was 75 miles east, while Lance went to the south side of Houston, which was about the same distance.

In the morning, around 3 am, Lance's wife called Archie because Lance had not come home from his scouting trip yet, so Archie called me and asked if I had heard from Lance or knew where Lance might be. Archie said he had already called the police, but he was following through to find out what he could on his own. Lance should have arrived at his house hours ago, but he had not shown up or called. Knowing Lance was a devoted family man, that his wife was expecting a child, and that Lance was a non-drinker, I was confident that alcohol could not be involved. It was frightening as we tried to think of other possibilities.

Lance was a responsible person who always called his wife if he was running late. We were extremely worried that he might be in some terrible situation, but we tried to remain positive as we made phone calls and waited for updates from the police. Finally, at 4:30 a.m. we received the information we had not wanted to hear. The Highway Patrol had found Lance still in his car, which had gone over a bridge just past Conroe on Highway 45. He had evidently fallen asleep on the way home from the game.

Lance had severe brain damage from the accident, and it was several years before he was even able to stand up and walk on his own. His brain damage was irreversible. Lance had played center for the Canadian Olympic team in 1960 and had a great future in coaching ahead of him. Other than his coaching duties, Lance had also managed the swimming pool in the student union building, which I took over for the remainder of the school year. I will never forget the awful feeling of that experience. The disbelief, my helplessness in being unable to change the circumstances kept me down for a long while. His family is in my thoughts and prayers.

The *fourth* event came at the end of the year when I graduated from Sam Houston State University with my Master's degree, and Coach Williams asked me to become the freshman basketball coach and his assistant at Pan American College. This was bitter sweet. I had accepted a position at a school I loved, and having an opportunity to coach with a man I respected. Although this was a fantastic opportunity, my thoughts of Lance living in a hospital never left my mind. It was difficult to leave as Dee and I packed to leave Huntsville!

The colossal statue 70-ft. tall of Sam Houston is located on I-45, outside of Huntsville, Texas.

My First College Coaching Job Coaching @ Pan American College, 1966

MARTIN
URAND
ASSISTANT BASKETBALL
COACH

Before going back to Pan American, Dee, our dog Alfie, and I took off to California to visit my sister, Ilene and "Wild Bob", her husband. Bob was finishing his stint in the armed forces, and we took the opportunity to visit them in Oxnard, California, and then we all went to Vegas until our money ran out, which wasn't long.

As we started back to Texas to begin the next chapter of our lives, which included "College Coaching", little did we realize that we were heading into a predicament that would haunt me.

Coach Williams and I shared a very small office, which was attached to the outside of the Field house. I reported to Coach Williams on my first day on the job at Pan Am, but when I opened the door to our office, I froze in shock. I stared at both Calvin and Frank, the basketball players from NY who had just finished their freshman years at Sam Houston State, who were both sitting and talking with Coach Williams.

It did not take me long to realize that they both were here, in Edinburg, to transfer to Pan American to go to school and play basketball at Pan American College. I am sure that when Trim entertained them in Houston, he told Calvin and Frank great stories about his time playing at Pan American, and both of them had decided to try out for the Pan American team without telling Archie or me. Calvin gave me a hug and said, "Well Coach, we're all back together, and thanks for introducing us to Trim!"

Although I was happy for them, I tried hard not to show my confusion or the disappointment I felt for Archie. At that time, it did not occur to me that I would no longer be able to show my face around SHSU. However, I understood how it looked, and why Archie never believed that I had not been involved. He and his staff, naturally, thought I had lured Calvin and

Frank away and they could not see it any other way. Archie and I never spoke to each other again. It was several years later when I learned that Archie had died in his sleep. I will always regret that we parted with bad feelings.

1968 – 1969
My first year as an assistant coach at the university level.

Bottom: *L-R Lonnie Reynolds, Drew Chernow, Kenny Jones, Frank Lawthridge, Walt Schoenberg, Steve McCormack, Lloyd Mitchell, Howard Fuller*
Back Row: *Coach Williams, Mike Tackett, Ed Mathis, Calvin Oliver, Gilbert Walker, Billy Rivas, Fred Taylor, Coach Urand*

Not pictured was our basketball manager, Jack Shanks, who was an outstanding figure among the players. He was intelligent and had a quick wit about him that amused coaches and the players. When on the road there were times when he was mistaken for the coach. Jack was usually the first to come out of the locker room and I followed him. Since Coach Williams was always the last coach out, it was easy for the officials to assume that Jack was the head coach. Jack always wore a suit and tie, was very proper, and pretty much had all the answers and basic situations in hand! It amused Coach Williams when the officials realized their error.

After graduation, Jack Shanks went into the field of education and quickly worked his way up to become a superintendent and has worked in several school districts in Texas.

The dean at Pan American College decided which courses I would be teaching. The dean understood my deep desire to teach, and "God only knows" why, but he chose the three classes that I had come close to failing during the mid-semester of my freshman year at Pan American, when Dr. Morgan and his wife had worked with me to help me bring up my grades which had allow me to stay eligible!

I worked at Pan American College for five years and loved every minute of it. Deanna and I had our first daughter, Marti, in April and 18 months later in October we had our second daughter, Jacqui ... both major, wonderful milestones in our lives.

It was tough spending so little time with my family since I was on the road continually recruiting and traveling with both Pan American's varsity and freshman basketball teams. Marvin Blumenthal, from Houston, helped me pick up extra money scouting for college players for the Boston Celtics, Kansas City Royals, and San Diego Rockets, who had moved to Houston and become known as the Houston Rockets. Marvin was still watching out for me after all these years; he was such a wheeler-dealer! Marvin brought in Pro teams to play exhibition games at Pan Am and always took time to introduce me to their coaching staffs. He was involved with several young men who were trying to break into coaching, including me, and helped us by planting seeds on our behalves.

Marvin B. knew my favorite coach was Hank Iba, who was coaching at Oklahoma State in Stillwater at the time. Marvin often got me scouting jobs that involved OSU. I always sat right behind Coach Iba and watched his every move. He usually did the same thing at every game. He would take off his suit jacket or his fleece, white with orange lettering, about five minutes into the second half and placed it over his chair. His voice sounded old as he yelled instructions to his team in a harsh, demanding voice. It sounded like death when he yelled, with a six-point lead and five minutes left, "Let the Air Out!" In basketball terms, it simply meant not to dribble but to pass the ball with absolutely no shooting! He would yell it twice and then sit back down. There were not any shot clocks in those days, so the OSU Cowboys would pass and pass and seldom dribble as they ran the clock out!

Although I never observed Clair Bee coaching, I could visualize that Iba and Clair Bee would have similar coaching styles that were evident from the disciplined players they had both produced.

I was scouting in Stillwater, Oklahoma shortly before Christmas. Snow was falling and I was talking to Dee on the phone about Marti and our newly born daughter, Jacqui, when it came into my thoughts that, although scouting was exciting and rewarding, I would rather be home than on this lonely road. I had a hollow feeling, and knew I was tired of being away from Deanna and my little girls. I called Dee almost every hour apologizing for having to leave her alone at this time, and made the four-hour trip home in two and a half hours.

There had been other signs of my discontent as well. I was so busy with my scouting and my family that I had not called any of my current basketball prospects during that time. Well, sure enough, I received a call from a mother of one of my prospects in San Antonio. The call was about Mike McVey an exceptional, 6'4" guard. I had spent many hours with both him and his mother, and I believed that this boy was a "lock" to sign with Pan American College. She told me Mike had been talking to a coach from another college and was considering changing his commitment

When I arrived in San Antonio at 7 pm to meet with Mike, he was not there and I spoke with his mother. She said he had been talking to another coach, and she thought he was going to sign with that coach. She did not know the coach's name, but described the coach to whom I lost Mike as a recruit to Pan American College. The coach Mike Levy had gone to play for was Carol Dawson from UT Arlington. Although coaches told me I needed to get used to this type of thing happening in recruiting wars, I still took it personally. Years later Carol became the General Manager for the Houston Rockets. Thirty years after this happened with Mike Levy; I attended an event for Guy V. Lewis, the basketball coach at the University of Houston. I saw Coach Dawson, who was also at this event and I went over and told him he was the one who had driven me out of coaching and why! We both laughed, but I think he laughed the loudest.

The recruiting of players, obtaining their commitments, and then losing the commitments to another coach is part of the game. However, it had bothered me so much that my feelings and thoughts began shifting away from my devotion to recruiting, and consequently also from coaching. I had several prospective players who had not given me the time of day, and I took it in stride. However, it had never bothered me as much as losing Mike, to whom I had felt close. I still loved Pan American and the actual coaching, but the emotional "ups and downs" of recruiting and the amount of time away from my family had gotten to me.

Not all recruiting was negative. We had several recruits who were extremely dedicated and working with them was enjoyable. For example, Dick Backfish, 6'9" from Tenafly, New Jersey and 6'7" Richard Tate from North Carolina were among the exceptional young men who came to Pan American through basketball, did well, and went on to graduate and benefit from the college education. I also continued to be optimistic and strove to recruit basketball players I knew I did not have much of a chance of recruiting, but I felt they were worth the effort of trying. While in North Carolina with Tate. I attended a basketball game at Gardner Webb where I tried to recruit Artis Gilmore was as far as I got. While in California, I called Sam Williams, so excited that I had just watched the best big man that I have ever seen and I had approached him. His name was Bill Walton. Coach Williams never let me live that one down.... That I would even attempt to compete against the large well-known basketball programs in major colleges around the states!

During my fourth year of college coaching and recruiting, I received a couple of feelers from other colleges to switch to their schools, but they never caught my interest enough to follow through on any of their offers. As my attitude was changing about coaching, and my interest level fading, I received a call from Corpus Christi University, asking if I would be willing to coach for them. It sounded like something that I would like to do, a place I'd like to live, and a time to get out on my own. The campus is on the Gulf of Mexico, with strong Baptist backing, and just 150 miles north of Edinburg, Texas. Deanna and her family had lived in Corpus only a few miles from the college while she was in junior high through her freshman year at WB Ray High School. She was excited about the possibility of returning to Corpus.

Dee and I met with the Maroni brothers from UCC and they went house hunting with us, showing us how great things would be if I accepted the job. They were that positive that their recommendation to hire me would be approved. The School Board met that night to approve me for the position, but even that went wrong! H.E. Butt (H.E.B food chain) was the president of the school board at the time and he was very strong with the Baptist church. He asked me if I had a letter from the Baptist church I attended that I could give to him. I explained that I did not belong to the Baptist church, but I attended a non-denominational church in Houston. When the man who had recruited me for the job at UCC called me, he said the strong Baptist hold on the school board would not approve me because they wanted someone with a strong, active Baptist background! It did not turn me off from religion, but it did turn me off on the members of that school board! Fortunately, things have changed at UCC since then.

All signs were pointing toward me to search for another career! With all of these setbacks, I began to question this direction of me giving so much of my time to just fifteen guys on a basketball court! That is when I began looking into returning to school and working toward a Doctorate Degree. Once again, I turned to

Marvin and he set up a meeting at the University of Houston with Harry Fouke, the Athletic Director, to see about giving me some advice, and to see if he had any openings for a position as a graduate assistant to help me begin the process of gaining admittance.

Back at Pan American, The School Board announced that the college would be offering a Master's program beginning in September. Around the same time, Coach Williams broke the news to me that with all we had going on, we needed help with recruiting, and he was bringing "Mud" to assist us with recruiting. I never said a word one way or the other to Coach, but knowing about Mud's past behaviors, I went home and told Dee the circumstances at Pan Am and that I wanted to move to Houston so I could begin working on a Doctorate degree that summer.

I told Coach that I did not think it was wise bringing "Mud" in, and I told him about Mud's bad reputation. However, Coach disregarded my thoughts and probably felt like I was jealous, selfish, and not taking it the right way. I told him that this would be my last semester at Pan American College; that I was going back to school in Houston to work on my Doctorate degree at UH.

During my last five years (1967-1972) in Edinburg, Texas, I had many wonderful and memorable moments attributed to coaching and working with the players. One of my fondest memories was when some of my previous players from Edinburg High (Ralph West,

Amancio Garza, Adon Rendon, Lupe Salinas, and others) came to me and asked if I would be the faculty sponsor for their newly developed fraternity (Phi Kappa Theta) at Pan American College. At that time, Hispanics had been blackballed from joining most of the frats on campus, so these young men decided to start their own chapter! I was so proud of them for "manning up" and going through the red tape that was necessary to initiate their own fraternity chapter! During those years, one of the honors their fraternity attained was to have never lost an intramural game in any sport!

Another especially memorable moment was when I was still coaching at Edinburg HS and I appointed Amancio, a senior at Edinburg High School, to be the manager of my high school freshman football and basketball teams. When he graduated from EHS, Amancio received a full scholarship to Pan American for his hard work and good grades at Edinburg High School. I was very proud of Amancio for having worked so diligently, attending college for four years, and proudly graduating.

When the summer came for my family and me to move to Houston, several members from Phi Kappa Theta, a fraternity at Pan American, helped move me to Houston. They helped pack the rental truck and then drove it to Houston so I could drive Dee and the girls. Once in Houston, they also helped unload our belongings and then returned the U-Haul for us when they drove it back to Edinburg! These young men were great people and we had a mutual admiration for each other. I feel so privileged to have been surrounded by so many great people.

Post Graduate Studies
University of Houston

The year in Houston was a very difficult year with the girls in day care and Dee teaching again to help put me through graduate school. We lived in a small apartment on the Gulf Freeway close to UH. I was teaching as a Graduate Assistant once again, making just three hundred dollars a month. Dee was working in HISD at Lyons Elementary off of U.S. 59.

Deanna and I were both very busy, but found the time to join the crowds "cheering on" our UH basketball team as they wrecked the other teams they played against. This group of players became more than a team, but also a fraternity in its own right, with its own name. Crowds filled the U of H gym to see U of H's own *"Phi Slamma Jama"*, overcome all competitors.

The only other basketball related activity after we had moved to Houston at the end of March, with a phone call from the NCAA. It seemed that Pan American University was being investigated for recruiting violations! The NCAA was calling to find out if I had any information leading to the infamous "sexually explicit interracial photo album that had been used in recruitment by some at Pan American College!

They asked me questions such as, "What relationship did I have with Mud when I was at Pan American College?" They also asked why I had left Pan American College. Despite my true feelings about "Mud", and his negative parts in the recruitment program, my only honest answer was, "I am sorry, but I don't know anything!" And, this was true. I really did not have any information other than the rumors that had floated around. I had separated myself from him as much as possible while at Pan American, so I figured if anyone was interested and needed more detailed information, they would have come to Houston and set up a meeting with me. I could not have helped anyway, and they had plenty of information already.

The "recruiting book" was nowhere to be found during the five-month court investigation. However, when it came down to Mud going to prison, the "book" mysteriously showed up! This "book" had been Mud's way of recruiting minorities to attend Pan American. Each of the photos illustrated different college men, or players, in sexual situations having sexual encounters with women of different races.

As a result, Jim Brooks, and Sam Williams, two of the most righteous, SOB's in the world, were burned by "Mud Loose!" The years our dedicated coaches spent bringing Pan American College basketball from a small, little known NAIA college to a respected Division I college slowly circled the drain.

Despite bringing in big name coaches to turn the basketball program back in the right direction, Pan American College basketball suffered. Among Pan American's well-known coaches, have been Abe Lemons from University of Texas and Lon Kruger from Kansas State. Abe's humor and sharp wit followed him wherever he went. He was clever and was always making us laugh. However, some of his humor made more headlines than any headlines for his victories. Unfortunately, he sometimes directed the subject of his humor at the Valley and at Hispanics. Abe was not prejudiced, but used the contrast of the cultures in the Valley in ways that many "Valley people" did not think were funny! Kruger, on the positive side, brought law and order back to the basketball program. He was a super recruiter and coach, who brought the "wins" back to the basketball program. However, after a short stay, Coach Kruger moved to Florida University, Illinois, NBA Hawks, UNLV and then to Oklahoma University (2014).

Coach Kruger continued donating financial support to UTPA each year. He still has a true love for the Valley and for Pan American University.

Ashford Elementary School

After my residency at UH, my first job in my new non-athletic career began. It was teaching at Ashford Elementary School in Houston ISD.

I was finally comfortable! I had found my true niche in life; it was teaching and working with young children! I understood that they, in their own ways, could become whoever they desired to be! My job was to assist them achieve their goals and become successful to the highest level of their abilities. For the first time I truly felt like "Coach Rockwell" as I developed a program, that with my guidance and training, the students soon began to internalize and run by themselves, with only minimal guidance from me.

At Ashford Elementary, I thanked God for this unique physical education program that motivated children and even their families into becoming healthy and fit. I was finding out that it did not make a difference what sport, game, or activity I was teaching; my greatest strength was being able to "flat out" motivate children!

My Gymnastic coaching Career begins!

I remember trying to start an after school program in boys basketball. Title IX and girls' sports had not become a policy yet, so at that time the program was directed only at the boys. However, many of the boys were outside after school playing football on my fields, and my small school gym remained vacant after school. Each day, as I watched several elementary teams practicing football, I always had girls hanging around the gym jumping rope, hula hooping, and just having fun. They were looking for something to do athletically, but I was not sure what program I should develop for them! I finally took the initiative and asked the girls what activity or program would they want. They told me they wanted to learn gymnastics, like Olga Korbut, the popular Russian gymnast. Little did I know at the time, but my life would take a major step toward coaching again, but it would not be basketball!

I knew nothing at all about gymnastics, but I had promised my students that I would look into this for them. I had two to three student teachers sent to me from the surrounding universities each semester. I called these universities and requested student teachers for this coming semester who knew something about gymnastics... and my gymnastics focus began.

We began an after-school program one day a week that soon expanded to five days a week, Monday through Friday after school. The following year, the students had improved so much that we also opened classes before school for the primary grades! My student teachers and I were not able to teach all of the students so we trained student leaders to assist us. It was fun, and above all, everyone progressed, including me!

I taught at Ashford for five years (1975-1978) and the program received a lot of attention from the media. Our entire program was led by music, dance (beginning with aerobics from Jackie Sorenson's era) and of course gymnastics. I certainly needed help with the dance. I was not a dancer, unless it was slow. Interestingly enough, I danced each day with my students during our musical exercises without thinking about it. I had lost my inhibitions with them! Close the gym doors and I became one of the kids.

*Ashford Elementary students,
learning as we go!*

My program was exploding and I needed more teachers. I brought in my own children's teacher from day care, Chris Smith, as an assistant. She was brilliant with movement to music. I even brought in Deanna's brother, Charlie, who assisted with these classes. He gave me another strong back to "spot" the hundreds of gymnasts we had. Physically, it was killing me, but thanks to the principal, Dr. Clyde Blackman, who could tell the wear and tear it had on me, helped find extra funds for the additional staff.

We invited the community to join
their children once a month on the
outdoor playground for "Aerobics".
(New sensation in exercise).

Before long, we had routines to music, all of my favorite
music, all day long! Chris and Ms. Garrett, a parent of
one of my gymnasts, made the program a showcase for
what kids could do at an early age! The kids became
mini superstars within the school and in the Houston
area.

Super kids assisted me with teaching and performing in the major venues in the Houston area! My brother in-law, Charlie Powell, is standing next to me as he overlooks the students he helped in their development.

After our second year, we were very fortunate to be asked to warm-up and tumble with none other than Olga Korbut and the Russian gymnastics' team in the Houston Astrodome. The Russian team came to the United States on a "Good Will Tour" since their gymnastics team was so well accepted and admired in the United States.

Ludmilla Tourischcheva (on left) was the All-Around Champion for the Russian team. Cindy Vento (Student pictured on far right) was one of the Ashford students who participated in this memorable event.

Photo from the *Houston Chronicle, March 10, 1972*

*Olga Korbut (Far right) was the gymnast who
seemed to ignite the sport of gymnastics in the
United States. The Ashford students watched her
every move!*

At that time, our program seemed to appear in the papers on a weekly basis. The 5th grade class leaders in the gym were celebrities among their peers as well as among junior high students at the schools they would soon be attending. We even had high school students visiting our program to learn from these young students who were fast becoming well-trained teachers. Our after-school program expanded, allowing both junior and senior high students to attend if they had an interest in helping teach.

Our "Ashford Group" was invited to perform at the TAHPERD State Convention, which was to be held at the Shamrock Hotel in Houston. We were invited in April and the performance was going to be in December of the next school year, giving us eight months to prepare for a super demonstration. We already knew that our featured performance of the 90-minute show was going to be our routine of "Live and Let Die". It featured the leaders in an awesome cross tumbling routine consisting of twenty girls and Greg Peters, our super, tumbling sixth grader. We had already refined our presentation and had even presented the program at the half time of the Houston Rockets game on several occasions and each time to standing ovations!

I wanted to show all phases of our program, not only with the best athletes, but also from all our other children. From those who could just execute a forward roll to those who had achieved the more advanced skills. My goal was to utilize gymnastics to improve children's self-esteem and to allow each child to appreciate and accept each other and all children, from the advanced to those who were willing to work hard and take a chance by trying.

In fact, I will never forget a little kindergarten child who was attending her physical education class asking me if she could join. Her name was Diana Anglin. I had learned her name, not only because she had one arm and wore prosthesis for her other arm, but I had observed and recognized her desire to participate when she was in my P.E. classes. Without explaining, I asked her to report to practice the next morning. She was as skilled as she was beautiful: No limitations at all. In fact, she was a very fast learner and a wonderful role model for her classmates, our program, and our entire school.

Now we had a real dilemma on our hands. We had four hundred students in K-6 participating in our program. How were we to select those who would perform at the demonstration?

In May, before school let out for the summer, I placed a large poster on the wall in the gym. The hand drawn picture illustrated a stick figure performing an "L" on top of the photo of the Shamrock Hotel. At the bottom, it simply said, "Hold an "**L**" for five seconds, and make the traveling squad.

The students had several months to become stronger if they truly wanted to be a part of this festivity. Holding up the "L" position was the entry skill the students needed to become a "leader". At that time, there were only ten students at our school who could perform the "L".

An "L" is when a student can sit on the floor with straight legs out in front, with both hands flat on the floor on the inside of the legs, and then push down with both hands, raising the entire body off of the floor, and holding themselves up entirely with only their hands. Each participant had to hold this "L" position off the floor for at least five seconds.

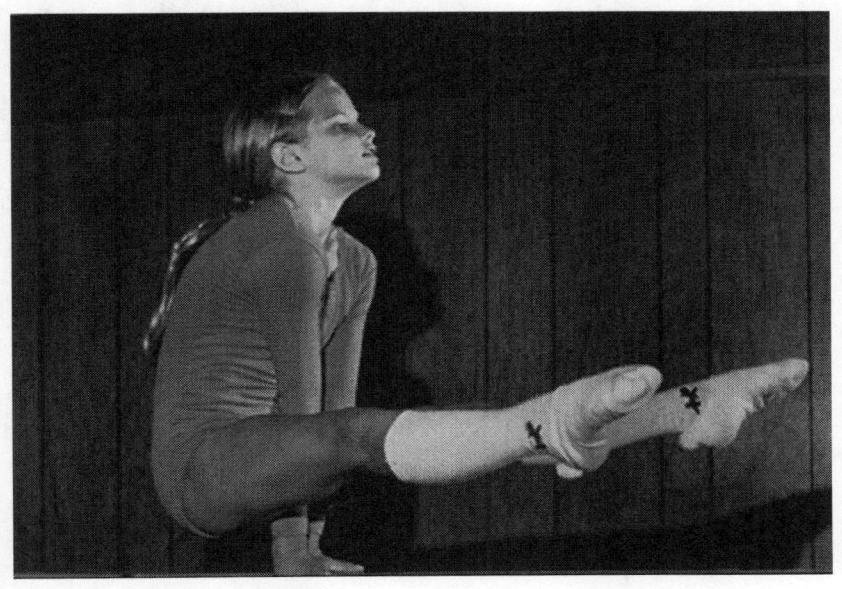

Peggy Collins performs a variation of an "L".

I always had high expectations for children, but I was taken by surprise with their intense, unrelenting desire to achieve this goal. On my way home each afternoon,

I saw children in front of their homes practicing their "L's". At school, we conducted tryouts each day for those who were ready to be tested. If successful, we wrote the child's name on a file folder that hung next to the Shamrock poster. It seemed that each week, we had to add more file folders as the number of names continued to grow! As the students kept improving and their numbers increased, the students started even a higher level of the "L." Now, they held contests to see who could hold that position the longest.

Our leaders used their bodies to spell out the acronym for the state association (TAHPER)

By the time school began in late August, the numbers for the demonstration had certainly grown. By December, we had to order six buses to transport the gymnasts to the Shamrock Hotel. The buses carried an astonishing 324 students to the Shamrock Ballroom in Houston. To the sounds of the Olympic Anthem, our boys and girls marched in separate lines through each one of the openings leading into the ballroom! All of the girls were wearing their orange leotards, and the boys wore blue shorts and white shirts with their various patches, which indicated their earned skill levels. With their chests out, their arms were straight and swinging to the beat, and each student flawlessly found his or her spot on the carpeted floor.

It was a sight that was shared by the over 800 teachers from all over Texas, who were packing the ballroom. Right in front of the teachers was my mentor, Dr. Garland O' Quinn. We were ready to rock the place!

With no introduction, the music began and 324 children all at the exact same time, performed the "L" for the opening of the song, "Jesus Christ Superstar!" Through my tears, I could not see if others were crying, but I was told that there was not a dry eye in attendance.

By the time we hit the finale of our "Live and Let Die" routine, and had completed it perfectly, the audience was standing in awe and the kids were signing autographs on the way to the buses! Since then my expectations for children has grown even more. I expect a lot but the children always give even more of themselves than I ask. I knew that I had grown from this experience, but it was the students themselves who had learned an even better lesson by seeing the success from all of their hard work. Many have told me that they have continued to carry that memory with them throughout their lives.

During that same year, the convention for AAHPERD, the National Association for Health, Physical Education, and Dance came to Houston. As part of their convention, AAHPERD offered a bus tour for teachers who wanted to take the thirty-minute trip to our school, Ashford Elementary. Not for routines, nor shows or demonstrations, but to just observe children participating in our daily physical education program and those participating in our gymnastics clubs before and after school. The tours began at 8:00 am and the last tour left our school at 5:00 pm each day, Monday through Thursday. The student leaders met each bus of teachers, brought them to the gym, and then the student leaders talked to the teachers about our classes, demonstrated their class routine, and answered the teachers' questions. The kids, about sixty in each class, knew exactly what to do each day when they entered their gym class. They followed the music for their warm-ups and executed their circuit training events for fitness one day, and then they followed with their circuit training skills the next day.

That year was very special to all of us and capping things off, Ashford Elementary earned the "Demonstration School of Texas" award, which was presented by the Texas Education Agency. We were all so proud of that blue banner, and the principal had it hanging in the front lobby of our school.

I am still friendly with many of the leaders and students who attended Ashford thirty years ago. We all developed deep feelings of respect for each other. Together we achieved heights that not many students or schools could even dream of attaining.

A few of the many student leaders from our Ashford program were: the Tourneur sisters, Kerri, Shauna, Kim and Cheryl, and also Brandi Lani, Cathy Massey, Peggy and Colleen Collins, Debbie Daniels, cousins Greg Peters and Louis Dozell, Jolene Gibson, Karen Marshall, Cindy Vento, Krista Bodine, Antoinette Gonzales, Diana Anglin, Gretchen Eck, Lisa Zulpulsky, Amy Rader, Mary Manning, Dallas Hollingsworth, Lynn Rodriguez, Julie Merrimen, Caroline Cummings, Susie Clair, Dixie Nagle, Janice Scott and Suzanne "Pru" Pruitt.

Among the many of those now "grown children" who I have recently visited, are Suzanne "Pru" Pruitt and her family, and Debbie Daniels. Below are a few letters, comments, and notes sent to me throughout the years from some of the participants or their parents, expressing their thoughts and personal feelings concerning the experiences of their *Ashford Elementary School* days.

The Impact You Had On My Daughter:

Every time Suzanne and I have any discussions and shared memories about her time at Ashford, they always include the difference that you and your gymnastics program had on her. As one of the first group of students at the newest "Open Concept" school, she seemed initially to be somewhat overwhelmed by the lack of structure and discipline throughout the school. Her quiet nature and reticence to volunteer any information or ask questions did not seem suited for her to excel in her new environment. The one highlight of her day was Marty Urand's P.E. class. It was your positive, individual approach to each student that really touched her and "made her day". When you introduced the class to gymnastics, she was so encouraged by her progress in performing the various tricks, which you constantly reinforced. She and her friends would carry that enthusiasm home and spend hours in our backyard (and sometimes in our house!) doing flip-flops, etc.

When you made her one of your "student gymnastic leaders", that opened a whole new vista for her. Her thrill and excitement at being so recognized carried over into her other classes as well. She became much more confident and extroverted.

Bob and I were honored to be chaperones on some of the bus trips to the various exhibitions. We both remember commenting how relaxed the girls were about their upcoming performances and how they were so excited about being able to participate. We felt their total positive approach, and lack of any nervousness, directly reflected your encouraging attitude.

As further indication of how lasting an impact you had on her life, she has remained fit as an adult and has happily shared some of her gymnastic moves when playing with her nieces. She now has taught these same moves to her own two preschoolers and joins them as they do these amazing tricks on their trampoline.

It all goes back to you and the efforts you made to have the children enjoy their activities and feel good about themselves. Your individual encouragement had a lifelong impact on their self-esteem. Thank you.

From Suzanne "Pru" Pruitt

It was just not only in gymnastics that you were a great teacher, but in fitness as well. You taught us about the 3 domains of learning: cognitive, psychomotor, and affective. You encouraged us for the president physical fitness achievement awards/percentiles. I still remember holding on to the chinning bar just a bit longer to reach a higher percentile with your encouragement. Field days were great fun, running the 50-yard dash and getting a ribbon, so much fun was associated with fitness, exercise, staying fit and healthy. Great stuff!

I CAN DO AN L-SEAT!!! I was so excited . . .I'd been practicing and practicing, and before long I was holding the L-seat and for more than 5 seconds . . .all this practicing had paid off . . .yippee. I was ecstatic!!! I also practiced in the bathtub . . .man was I in shock when I got out of the bathtub and tried again . . .my first experience with buoyancy I guess, I laugh now. At the time I realized I had lots more practicing to do, and yes, thank goodness I was able to do an L-seat be it in the bathtub or not . . a real L-seat . . .I was on my way to the Shamrock!

I remember when you took us all camping on a weekend trip . . . .we were able to do gymnastics from sun up to sundown, it was great fun . . .do you remember when poor Karen broke her arm? The trip was still great fun for all of us☺

Choosing me as one of the gymnastic leaders had planted leadership seeds in me which lead to running and serving on the student council during my junior and senior high school years . . .I ran for an office twice, I did not win . . .I tried . . .I showed up and I smiled. Thank you again, Marty Urand.

With tears of appreciation in my eyes now, as I reflect back, I appreciate Marty, aka. Mr. Urand. And realize my growth wasn't in the mastery of skills, rather it was in the trying, which became a lifelong skill!

Taken from Face book (9/20/11) From Krista Bodine Snuggs:

--

When I was a kid, I was sick a lot. I missed enough school that I frequently felt distant from the other kids. They had experienced things I hadn't, and from time to time, I felt left behind. It wasn't something conscious, it just was. When I was seven, I joined our school's gymnastics team. I was extremely excited about it and thought our coach was the cat's pajamas. Marty Urand was so healthy and strong and I wanted to be like that. Soon, there were tryouts for an upcoming event. Whoever could do, among other things, an L-sit for 7 seconds would get to do an awesome demonstration to the song "Jazzman" at the old Shamrock Hilton in downtown Houston.

A HUGE DEAL! The L-sit was really hard for me even for 1 second. You sit with your legs stretched out in front of you and hold yourself up by only your arms. I practiced a lot and never made it to 7 seconds. I tried out anyway, hoping, praying, but knowing I wouldn't make it. The big day came. I passed all the other requirements but knew it was all going to go downhill when I had to do the L-sit. One after another of my peers did it with no problems and I was sweating.

But then a miracle happened..., Coach Urand speed-counted SO FAST I got in!!!!! It was INCREDULOUS!

Did he know this seemingly small thing he did for me would inspire me? Probably not. I'll bet he's done something similar for many people. I have often thought about him, and this, and what it did for me in the long run. Barring a few hiccups, all of my life I have purposely surrounded myself with beautiful friends who support me, encourage me, and inspire me to be a better person. I want to be like Marty Urand, who sees something greater than the prize or the performance and cheers others on to their dreams. Through small acts of kindness, we can change the world one act at a time.

Each of us has the power to inspire someone in some way. I'd love to hear your story, so feel free to post and share. And, thank someone who inspired you today!

*Ashford Elementary was a favorite
at the Houston Rockets NBA games
performing at half time each season.*

Learning from My Students!

I speak of an experience that occurred at Ashford at most of my presentations to physical education teachers. I share this story with teachers to bring home the point that we should not be too proud that we cannot learn from students as well.

The story goes something like this; I was teaching a third grade class how to perform a cartwheel. Since I could not perform a cartwheel myself, I called on Greg to demonstrate one. Greg had earned a reward in his classroom to come and peer-teach in the gym with me. It was an incentive program to motivate students to do well in their classes. I really worked hard to make my domain, which I called, "Education through the Physical", the hub of the school.

After asking Greg to demonstrate a cartwheel, inadvertently he went on to embarrass the heck out of me. His reply was, "Which kind of cartwheel do you want me to do, coach?" When he saw that I was puzzled, he said that there were five types of cartwheels: there was a cartwheel in, a cartwheel out, a side cartwheel, an aerial cartwheel, and a dive cartwheel. I was shocked to say the least; I was at a loss for words! So

I kind of covered my mouth and said, "Greg just do a regular one."

After that class was over and Greg headed back to his class, I had a fifth grade class coming in. I could see that I had several of my leaders in this class and had plenty of demonstrators that I could call on. Therefore, with all the confidence in the world, I held up my hand signaling five fingers as I said, "Boys and girls, there are five kinds of cartwheels, and then I named all five!" The point being that at that moment, I had just learned that there was more than one kind of cartwheel... from my student.

I was hungry for more of the knowledge that Greg had learned from his private gymnastic school, Biron Gymnastics. Within that year, I began teaching (and learning) at that private club and really took advantage of the knowledge and skills of their students and teachers. I stayed late each night watching the coaches work with the teams, as they prepared the students for high-level competition. My mantra was that if I could learn the skill, then I would be able to teach it as well as or better than anyone else could!

Within two years, I became partners (in name only) with Beau Biron. He was an educator himself and wanted the best for his students. He now called his club, "Biron, Collins, and Urand" while Eugene and I were working there. Eugene Collins had just retired from the Houston Ballet Company and was excellent in teaching and training the girls how to perform and maintain perfect bodylines as they executed their gymnastics and dance routines. Biron is not only an outstanding coach and excellent businessman, but he also is a talented pianist. At gymnastic meets throughout the state, most other clubs bring tapes of their gymnasts' floor music, while Beau played his gymnasts' music live, on his piano. As he observed the gymnasts performing, he kept them to the beat by altering the speed of his playing to adapt to the gymnast's rhythm if needed. It was truly a great experience, and I am honored to have learned, taught, and coached at Biron Gymnastics Club.

In 1978, I was promoted to Assistant Director of Physical Education for Houston in ISD. My thought was to improve the physical education program in the other 265 elementary schools in HISD by modeling them after the physical education program I had developed at Ashford Elementary. It was a great plan and I was honored and enthusiastic to have this opportunity, but suddenly, the state created a "freeze" on all additional hiring and any new spending within school districts. With this freeze, my job offer was also frozen, which prevented me from beginning in this new position at the HISD Administration Building. Before the freeze, I had begun training a close friend, Ashley Glass, to take over my old position teaching physical education at Ashford Elementary. We both had spent several weeks and then months, waiting for the state to issue a "thawing out of the freeze" so I could move into my new office where all of my books and materials had already been sent, and Ashley could take over my job at Ashford Elementary. Nevertheless, the freeze continued and I was given a different assignment.

After four months, with jobs still frozen, Ashley was ready to begin his assignment at Ashford Elementary, and I was sent to Crockett Elementary on the Ship Channel to assist a new teacher, Ernie Weatherford. Ernie had a daughter in gymnastics, and he and his daughter were excited about adding gymnastics to his program.

After a year on the Ship Channel and going home reeking of malt and hops from the beer brewery, which was just a few blocks from the school, Ernie was ready to begin a new program to focus on preparing his students to focus on Gymnastic skills and I was ready to proceed to my next assignment.

With the hiring freeze still in effect, I asked to be reassigned to my own school. A transfer came, but I was sent to split teach at two different schools, teaching three days at Garden Oaks Elementary and two days at Benbrook Elementary in Houston ISD. Working part time at two schools was unique, and it was also positive because I learned a great deal from each of these assignments.

The students at each of the schools were very appreciative to have a "teacher-coach" at their school. Once again, at both schools I trained students to assist with my classes and become student leaders. When I arrived at Garden Oaks Elementary in the mornings, I always had students who met me when I pulled into the parking lot! Little Kelly Bankcroft was my main assistant and each morning she set up the small classroom that I used for my physical education classes.

I introduced gymnastics at both schools and continued with my points programs. he students who earned the most points at each of my schools earned spots to participate in an overnight campout I had planned at Stephen F. Austin State Park in Sealy, about sixty miles from the schools. I intended to run the camp with the help of student helpers, Deanna, and several parents assisting me as chaperones. One of the highlights of the camp was the gymnastics' meet that took place on Saturday morning during the camp. The events in the competition at camp were tumbling events and vaulting. Parents assisted with setting up tents, bringing equipment, serving the food, judging the competitions, and helping in many other ways as needed.

On this particular trip, we loaded all of the gymnastic equipment on one parent's truck while Deanna and I rode the bus with the 30 students and a few other parents who were our chaperones. We arrived at the campsite on a Friday evening in April at 5:30 pm. Our first order of business was to pitch the tents before dark and prepare for dinner. After dinner, we enjoyed some good stories, ate s'mores over the campfire, and then we were all off to bed.

I awoke at my usual time of 4:45 a.m. and headed to the restroom to get ready to begin the day before the students awoke, and to enjoy a cup of coffee in this setting. But man, was I off in my planning, because when I opened the bathroom door, one of our boys was under the sink trying to catch something in a bottle. When I realized that it was a copperhead snake, I called his name. He glanced at me just as the snake moved and bit him. I immediately grabbed the boy and yelled for his dad. John's dad came running grabbing his son from me as I rapidly gave him the details and told him to get his truck and rush his son to the hospital in Sealy. After he sped off, I realized that our gymnastics' equipment for the camp activities was still tightly tied in the back of his pickup truck..., which was on the way to the hospital.

However, we "ad-libbed", as teachers often do, and shifted our focus onto activities that did not require equipment. Other than that scary incident with John and the snake, we all had a great time competing in sprints, relays, handstand contests, games and in a giant game of kickball. We were all relieved when we got word that John would be fine and would fully recover. However, his finger remained discolored for over a year after the incident.

West Memorial Elementary
1979-1982

At the end of that school year, I resigned from Houston ISD, and I accepted an elementary position at West Memorial Elementary School with Katy ISD. This was only ten miles west from Ashford Elementary and Biron's Gymnastics.

Beau later became my silent partner and assisted me in opening and getting Katy "Kips" Gymnastics Club started in a shopping center on Mason Road and I-10 in Katy, Texas. Without Beau's guidance, help, and support, I would never have had the chance to own my own gymnastics' club. I will always be grateful for his unselfishness in providing a foundation for me to go out and start this gymnastics club, Kips Gymnastics! Beau guided me through the trials and tribulations of beginning a new club and provided me backing throughout the beginning stages of the business. I could not have been more thrilled as we created, built, and motivated gymnasts, forming our own "brand" and loyalty among our parents and gymnasts. The gym was very small as gyms go, but that was all we needed at the beginning. Beau gave me some equipment to help the program get started and we were in the gymnastics business! Deanna, who had previously resigned from her teaching job, was working the desk. Our daughters, Marti and Jacqui were now 6 and 7 years old and taking classes there.

In 1978 we sold our first home on Pine Lake Drive in Spring Branch, a suburb of Houston, and bought and moved into a newly constructed two story home in the new, fast growing neighborhood of Memorial Parkway, in Katy, Texas; and life was really looking up. Our house was near our new gym and close to the schools that Marti and Jacqui would be attending. Houses and schools could not be built fast enough to accommodate the growth in the area! For the first time, Marti and Jacqui had their own bedrooms upstairs with a den/ workroom in between their rooms. A railed balcony ran from the door of Jacqui's bedroom all the way to Marti's bedroom door. In the open hallway, they could look over the hallway rail down into the living room below. For a parent, this was good because everyone was always in sight. I am not sure what the girls' viewpoints were about this open-concept living, but I think Marti and Jacqui were used to it being that way, and never gave it a second thought.

Marti and Jacqui began attending Ashford Elementary and West Memorial Middle Schools after leaving St. Cecilia's Catholic School in Spring Branch. Around this time, our daughter Marti came to us and said she had decided she wanted to be baptized. We talked to Pastor Lester Collins, who was the pastor of First Baptist Church in Spring Branch. He was a warm, dynamic person who had befriended us when Marti was searching for her connection with religion through her Catholic school and religion through our Baptist church. Marti and Jacqui wanted us all to be baptized together, and after many talks with Lester Collins, he arranged to baptize us as a family at Tallowood Baptist Church, in the Spring Branch area of Houston.

During that time, I was having severe back problems from all the spotting that I was doing in gymnastics. Pastor Collins introduced me to his chiropractor, Dr. Jack Christie, who not only adjusted my spine but also adjusted my life throughout the next twenty years!

Dr. Christie is a laid back, soft-spoken, articulate person. He is also on the conservative side of things, and when he pulled up to his office in an orange Corvette, I was surprised. His personalized plates read, "Be Fit", which was a perfect "fit" for him.

Dr. Christie was a great role model, politically involved, and served on the Spring Branch School Board. I went to him each week for several months to receive back treatments and then once a month for the next five years whether my back needed it or not. The "visits" were therapeutic, enjoyable, and educational. It seemed that Dr. Christie was in tune to all phases of education. It was a win-win visit for me. I learned the latest in education within Texas, and best of all, my back became nearly as good as new!

Our new home in Katy played a larger role in our family than we had expected! We lived in our house on Park Downe Lane for thirteen years. During that time, I do not think I would be exaggerating if I said that our family often "hosted" temporary "house guests" who were waiting on housing or just in need of a temporary place to stay. As much as people helped us all through the years, it was instinctive that we reciprocate.

Our family routine was simple: I would bring the girls to the elementary school in West Memorial, in Katy, Texas, where I was teaching. After school, I picked the girls up from class and brought them to our gymnastics' club where they did their homework until Deanna, who at that time was still teaching in Spring Branch ISD, came home from school.

Jacqui and Marti grew up in
the gym throughout
Elementary and Secondary school

Deanna then usually took the kids to dinner and worked with them on homework while I taught classes.

At six o' clock, the team kids would come to the gym for their three-hour workout and Marti and Jacqui would return to the gym and join them while Deanna worked at the front desk for a few hours. At approximately 9:30 pm, I brought the girls home and Dee would rush them into the study to complete any homework and then get them into their beds. It was a hectic schedule, but Marti and Jacqui thrived on it. Knowing they had to focus on schoolwork in order to come to gymnastics' classes gave them great self-motivation. The fact this full schedule didn't give them much time for getting in trouble was also a plus for us.

It was a wonderful life being surrounded by great kids at school, having a business that was prospering more each month, and having my own children with me at home and at the gym. The negative phase of my life at that time was that my doctorate degree suffered from the demands of coaching and running a new business. My courses went well, but my Orals at the University of Houston did not! Until this very day, I regret not fighting one of my close-minded, hard-nosed professors and the politics that developed from a couple of egocentric professors who were born to bust balls!

My other professors fought for me, but to no avail. Therefore, after 76 hours above a Master's Degree, I left UH. Looking back at that very costly error, one professor stood out as a positive educator and befriended me during that period. His name is Dr. Joel Bloom and was relatively new to UH. His students loved him as he brought the component of pedagogy to the department. "Doc" as the students referred to him, soon became a favorite among perspective teachers. He brought professionalism to the field of physical education as well as tutoring his athletes utilizing his biomechanics background.

Dr. Bloom retired in 2013 as "Professor Emeritus" after a brilliant forty-four year career on the UH campus.

"Doc" and I worked together through the years in preparing teachers. He gave his life to UH and the students that he placed in many school districts.

As for my Doctorate debacle, I was upset, but I had a business to run and a school program that was honored again by the Texas Education Agency, and I realized I had to get over this and get on with my life.

Once again, Phil Hendrix evaluated the program at my school, West Memorial Elementary, and two weeks later, we received the Demonstration School of the Year banner, which we proudly displayed in our mini gymnasium.

Demonstration School Flag presented by
Fil Hendrix (Texas Education Agency),
Marty Urand, Marcella Porter
(Past TAHPERD President),
Senator Jane Nelson, and Fil Hendrix. (2002)

We had an exceptional staff in physical education at West Memorial Elementary and we all worked together at Kips Gymnastics. Our gymnastics' school was a large school in a fast growing community in Katy, Texas. At Katy Kips, we had three full time teachers who were also physical education teachers, and one teacher's aide who worked in Katy ISD. I was also able to bring my student teachers from the Ship Channel, John Alger, and Cherri Daigle into Katy as coaches at Katy Kips. Pat Unruh, another physical education teacher at West Memorial Elementary, replaced Cherri at the end of the year, and Steve Vonderharr was then hired by the school district as one of my aides. Our staff was superior. We were all very close, and we had a great program as well as a great time at school and at Kips.

West Memorial Elementary Staff (1978)
John Alger, Cherri Daigle, and Marty Urand

We all worked vigorously at our jobs, and the gymnastics club was growing so quickly that we had little room for growth. We needed a new facility that would allow for larger classes, as well as meeting our teams' needs for more room and more equipment for advanced training. Our teams needed more practice time without wasting time waiting for their turns on equipment.

Nevertheless, even in that small storefront space, our coaches and gymnasts trained and worked hard before and after school to win the Class IV Houston City and Texas State Gymnastic championships.

*Katy Kips wins the Houston City
and State Championships.
Katy Times, 1980.*

Must have been a good vision

Texas State Optical, the store on one side of our gym on Mason Road, made me an offer that I could not refuse, and I accepted their proposal to buy my gym space. Using that payment, we began building a five thousand square foot gym in downtown Katy, which was only a couple of miles further west of Mason Road

We had over five hundred students and under the direction of Ron Hanna, John and Gay Alger, Steve Vonderharr, Pat Unruh and me, and our teams had won all they could at this level. Now that we had room for growth, I hired a young woman, Jody Trncak, to handle the dance phase of competition (beam and floor), while Ron and I coached the un-even bars and vaulting. Jody worked miracles as she matched music to personalities and created routines specific to each gymnast's skills, music, and personality. And we won our first State Championship at the beginning level of competition! The kids were ready to move up, but none of the coaches, including me, had enough knowledge or skills in every area to move our teams forward without some help.

Jodie and I went to Los Angles, California to attend a gymnastic symposium and to recruit another coach who could help lead us up to the next level. In our search, we found a young married couple who we knew could fit into our program perfectly. Louie and Lynn Morales were a perfect fit. They were very knowledgeable, talented coaches from California who were on the rise among young coaches in the United States. So after visiting with us, and guest coaching at our gym in Katy, Texas, Louie and Lynn accepted our coaching offer! We were ecstatic and gave them several months to leave Los Angeles, California and move to Katy, Texas, to coach at our Katy Gymnastics Club. The timing could not have been any better since my sister, Enid and her daughter, Meena, who had been living with us, were moving into their new house. Enid and her husband Andy ("Sweet Smoke" base player) had bought a house in the Katy area, and their house was now ready for them. With my mission to get my entire family to Texas, the first of four were under way.

Grand Opening of the new
Katy Kips in Katy, Texas
Jacqui Urand, Marti Urand, Marty Urand,
Mike Follette, and Kim Childs

My contract with Louie and Lynn was to allow them to stay at my house for six months, which would allow them to save their money for a down payment so they could buy themselves a new home. At that time, we had offered to provide them with some furniture for the house once they made the purchase. These are incentives we wanted to do in order to recruit and get these, highly qualified people to move from California to coach for us. They were well worth all of our efforts and more!!

My poor wife and daughters had someone living in our home through most of the girls' elementary, junior high, and part of their high school years. Deanna and the girls never complained! I am sure they had justification to, but they were happy with their lives and took it all in stride. We were focused on having a high quality business, being able to provide Marti and Jacqui with opportunities we could now afford, and we were ready to do what was needed for us as a family. We were lucky that our "house guests" were usually good, thoughtful people. The one or two who were not, didn't last long.

*Our new gym opened (1982) and our
teams reached new heights!*

The newly assembled staff was ready for the challenge. The new gym provided the extra space, and the athletes waiting in long lines for a turn to work their routines became a thing of the past. With four sets of uneven bars, eight balance beams, a spring loaded floor, and a regulation vaulting runway with a foam filled "pit", and a loyal, talented staff... there was no excuse for us not to do well!

Our Katy Kips gymnastics' teams were preparing for the Texas State Gymnastics' Championship, which was being held at the Dallas Gymnastic Center. We had a large team thanks to our great coaches, who had worked thoroughly to prepare our competing gymnasts to qualify individually. By the time everyone competed, we had 27 girls who qualified to make the trip to Dallas. We were loaded and our staff was hoping we would take the overall title, and possibly, that the 9-11 age group would win their age division championship. We had two other age groups who were also competing, and if they all hit their routines, we had a chance to win in both the 11-12 age group and possibly the 13-15 age group as well.

The Kips Staff

Karen Vogel, Rick Baker, Ron Hanna, Lynn and Louie Morales, Marty Urand and Jody Trncak

Our coaches prepared our athletes
to perfection, filling the award
stands with our precious kids!

At the 1980 State Championship, Katy Kips made history. The Kips set a state record, winning all three age groups and taking the Over-All title with a new high point record With 170 points! We needed a separate car to bring home all of the hardware safely! Each trophy was massive and the Over-All trophy was enormous!

Katy, Texas was now on the map for gymnastics! This little town that was growing so quickly, opened its arms and welcomed the newly crowned State Gymnastics Champions back home. Several years later, we added another storefront gym on Fry Road, which was only two miles east of our main gym, toward Houston for beginning gymnastic lessons

In May of 1982, Dee and I decided to put a pool in our backyard for our enjoyment, but the next year we added another job to our lives and family and during the summer months, when Kips enrollment was usually low, we began a summer program and taught swim lessons in our backyard pool.

Marti, Jacqui, and I taught swim lessons for over ten years at our house in Memorial Parkway, Katy, TX. Each of us had a job to do with the young children. Our daughter's boyfriend was hired to drive the Katy Kips van to pick up and drop off twelve students each of the five hours that we taught the lessons. It seemed like we taught practically everyone in the small town of Katy how to swim.

Swimming and gymnastics became the sports that really brought me even closer to kids! My swim "coaching" kicked in when I was given the duty to fire the swim coach at our subdivision because he usually just sat back and "watched" practice as he sat on the diving board and smoked! Replacing that coach was not as easy as we all thought, and I ended up being hired to take over the coaching of the swim team at Memorial Parkway Subdivision. Once again, I lacked enough knowledge, so I attended other swim clubs' practices, getting advice from their coaches. I learned some techniques and developed plans to make our team better. So using my background knowledge, I took advice from others, studied videos and read books on swimming techniques. My life as a neighborhood, swim team coach began.

During the next twenty-five years I coached seven other neighborhood swim teams overall. I usually stayed at each community between 3 to 5 years, when I would begin to feel the need to move on. If I decided to leave any swim club, it was usually because the parents seemed to be getting to me. I believed that my teaching and training techniques were between the coach and the athlete. However, many parents were too soft with their children (my athletes) - and continually argued and interfered with our coaching decisions.

Parents sometimes use tactics to "promote" their children in ways that are not fair to the others on the team. The first few years as a coach was like a honeymoon. We were all happy with each other! However, the years that followed became more difficult. My goals and methods with children are to teach them to be self-thinkers and responsible for their athletic performances. They need to believe in themselves and the key to this is to gain confidence and self-esteem. I teach children that success is doing their very best and is not based on what place they finish in competition. I understand that many parents find it difficult to let go of their babies! For the most part, it is usually just a very few who made it difficult. In parent meetings, I explained my rules and policies involving expectations and policies involving me as a coach, and the children as part of my team. I explained my rationale about them not talking with me during or after practices, but meeting with me at a different time. I explained my thinking, the boundaries as to where parents needed to stay during practices and meets, and above all, that they needed to stay away from their children, my athlete, while practices or competition is going on.

I remember often speaking to large groups of coaches and remarking to them how I admired them for putting up with parents and spending such long hours coaching. I often concluded with the comment that in my second life, if I ever think about coaching again, it would only be in an orphanage!

In gymnastics, it was a little different. One of the tactics I utilized was to bring parents of team members to the gym before the day of competition to have them watch their children's routines in a dress rehearsal setting. One purpose was to help relieve the gymnasts' fears and pressures when performing in front of their parents and other spectators. I asked the parents to sit two feet from the balance beam and had the gymnasts perform their routines. I also encouraged the parents to talk to their children while the gymnasts performed on the beam. The purpose was for the gymnasts to perform their routines and block out any distractions around them. The students' goals were to work on their routines while blocking out the noise and their parents, while focusing solely on their gymnastic routines.

It usually doesn't make a difference if parents have prior experience in a sport, but parents frequently believe they know it all. (And I put myself in that category as well..... although I try to hold back those thoughts).

I had parents who brought their five and six year olds to the gym to try out for advanced classes. Everything would be going fine until the magic word was uttered, "Olympics". They would continue saying things like, "My child is very advanced because he/she practices all the time in our house," or they state that their child needs to work out with the older advanced classes or they asked how long until they their child will be in an Olympics level. I certainly did not want that pressure on me, let alone the poor child who has to grow up with this thought of the parental pressure on his/her back at this beginning stage of gymnastics.

Therefore, as soon as I hear the magic word, Olympics, I stop the tryout and bring the parent into the office to explain my reasoning and to advise them to back off the pressure. If that did not change the attitude, I usually gave the parents a map to Bela Karolyi's gym, an Olympic training gym, which was forty miles from Katy. I would pat the parent on the back and tell them that if they were right, then Karolyi's was the place for them! Interestingly, when highest-level competitive gymnasts make Karolyi's team, they have to move out of home and live in a dormitory that he has on his gymnastic ranch! Bela was brilliant, and I really looked up to him. He knew that to reach their goals, these elite, high level gymnasts would need to leave their homes and get tough as they devoted a large part of each day to training!

At our gym we were running a purely, educational program with competition included once the children progressed. The coaches all had the same philosophy and we all taught with the same lead-ups, goals, and techniques. We had high teaching goals, training, character, and therefore would not even take a team member currently competing at another club. We never wanted to hear that, "My last coach taught this to me this way".

In the parents' defense, where would Renee O'Connor, Renee Zellweger, and other children with exceptional talent be without their parents' high expectations, and their willingness to let them follow their dreams? Both had been gymnasts at Kips. I usually get bent when I receive excuse notes from competitive team level parents wanting to take their children out of practice to attend theater classes, rehearsals, readings, and tryouts. In both of these girls' cases, it was frustrating, but also exciting; making us especially proud with O'Connor, who used her gymnastics skills to help her become the side kick of *Xenia: Warrior Princess*.

When I first began teaching in Katy, I taught at West Memorial Elementary School in Katy for five years. My students had many positive experiences that affected their lives and mine as well. However, one event that has affected me for my entire life was not a positive one. With all going so well for my family, and my excitement in teaching and coaching at Kips, one event destroyed my pleasure in all of it!

I worked closely with classroom teachers, counselors, and the librarian at our school to improve, inspire and to integrate instruction through students' gymnasium time. In an attempt to motivate children to read, the librarian offered an incentive to children to read ten books that dealt with "feats of strength". If they attained this goal, they were rewarded with a special class in the gym. The special class included activities that tested their personal strengths.

Since our school had been built in the middle of rice fields, there were no trees for children to climb. In an effort to improve their upper body strength, I purchased a tug of war rope and hung it over the brackets that held the basketball goals to the wall. The intention was to have students climb on both sides so they could become stronger. However, the children were not successful in their endeavors. It was simply too difficult for them! The solution of course was to place knots along the rope as I had seen in many activity books and at workshops. The theory was that this would help so the students could get a footing while they reached higher on the rope to pull themselves up. Our students were having success, and became stronger while building their self-esteem in the process.

At this special event for promoting and encouraging reading, one of the most popular activities was the tug of war contest. This activity, thought of as "American Pie", became a liability because of the lack of education on my part and on the part of others at higher levels concerning the dangers and risks of rope activities.

In preparation for teaching, only a few issues were listed as topics concerning the safety rules for the activity of tug of war. It was, of course, common sense that taught us not to allow any students to place the rope around their bodies, especially their necks. In addition, we taught them never to stand in the loops at the end of each side of the rope was another caution we recognized and addressed. I wish we had all recognized other possible dangers, and had received some guidance or more intensive instruction about more of the safety precautions of tug of war! Surely as popular as this activity is among groups, more incidences of injuries had surfaced, "flagging" physical educators and others of the dire consequences that could occur through this activity. Training for possible dangers and injuries were never addressed in my schooling as I became a teacher, and at that time possible dangers had not been addressed in the general public either. Our view of "tug-of-war" mainly came from seeing it in movies, and hearing and talking about times many of has had participated in it ourselves. Movies even had tug of war activities showing fun, laughter, and excitement. Unfortunately, other dangers had not been taught to most teachers and we, as instructors, were unaware of the other devastations that could occur.

With sixty children on each side of the rope, and of course no children in the loops, I primed the class over the microphone. Pointing to one side and saying, "Is this side ready?" and then while looking up and down the rope for improper positioning, And being confident that it was safe, I called for the tug of war to begin asking the other side, "Is this side ready?", "Pull!"

With my eyes scanning both sides as they pulled, rather than watching to see the result of who was winning, the laughing, and noise in the gym went silent in my mind, as I caught a frantic look on a child's face that brought me immediately to attention! It was a third grader, April, one of my favorite students, trying to pry her hand from the rope! I could vividly see her elbow up in the air while trying to free her fingers. She was still pulling as I dropped the microphone and ran toward her. By the time I reached her, she had pulled her hand free, but in her visible anguish, she severed her finger from her hand. I reached down and picked her finger up off the gym floor and immediately picked April up with her head pressed to my neck and her injured hand held high, and raced to the office. Halfway down the hall I heard the contest end, with no real thought as to what transpired. All I could think of was April!

I gave the finger to the nurse, and placed April on the nurses table. She never cried, just kept asking me, "Coach what happened?" I lifted her again when the ambulance arrived and placed her inside. That is all that I remembered from the incident. That night I woke up moaning and crying in my bed very much as I had the night my brother, Jeffrey had died.

As expected, the family sued me for liability and was seeking a large amount of money for the child's injury. As much as I understood her parents' pain, I had no savings or money to give. I wanted to do anything for April and her family that I could, but I did not have the money they were seeking. I knew that the funds would have to come from other sources than what I could provide.

Although I was very concerned and devastated for April, I was advised to find someone who I had confidence in who could represent me in case I needed legal help. I asked one of my gymnast's dad, who was a lawyer, to assist me because I wanted someone who knew me and my passion for children and for their safety. Chausey Leebron was also a gymnast on my team, and she was a friend of my daughter, Jacqui. I knew her dad well. He was an attorney and a wonderful person. Therefore, I asked Mike Leebron if he would represent me in this tragedy. I still could not believe that this had happened to one of my students. In fact, it was only later that I found out that there was another student, Nicole, who at the same time, had the tip of her thumb severed as well! To say that I was not thinking clearly after this devastating tragedy would be an understatement!

I stayed home from school and from Kips for over a week because I could not bear to face my students. I was distraught and just wanted to go away. I wanted to disappear. My daughters went to school and had to answer all of the questions that I was avoiding. Of course, the big question they were asked was if their dad had been fired?

Nothing was the same for me nor the little girls and their families! Parents simply do not send a child to school to have them return home injured.

All I can remember through the legal mess was that Mike Leebron walked with me for an hour in the tunnels beneath downtown Houston, trying to get me to relax for the deposition hearing. I could not think or speak about the injury without crying. When I did manage to talk, I made no sense whatsoever. Having dealt with people traumatized before in his work as a lawyer, Mike finally settled me down enough to take me into the courtroom.

Among other things, I remember sitting in the courtroom while the prosecuting attorney made me feel like an inadequate moron!

"Mr. Urand, with over sixty hours toward your Doctorate degree, did you not know the hazards of rope-related activities?" Before I could reply, another question was aggressively directed to me.

"Mr. Urand, are you not aware that tug of war has been banned in several states?" Once again I was not given time to reply!

"Mr. Urand, are you aware of the amount (holding 50 case folders) of life threatening injuries that have been caused by this activity?"

I sat quietly, not even attempting to answer as he kept going without stopping.

The prosecutor then explained to me, as well as the judge, how the injury occurred. They had confiscated the rope and determined that it was the knots in the rope that had traveled (moved) under the pressure exerted by so many students pulling in different directions.

Throughout the trial, I questioned why I had not been aware of these facts! Broken necks, backs, and rope burns caused by this "All-American" activity were listed one after another! And as far as I know, there is still no mention in teacher preparation programs of the devastating results that can occur from this dangerous activity. However, for some reason, God chose me, at the awful expense of April and Nicole, to alert others to the dangers of this perilous activity. Both of these girls moved from Houston, but I received a newspaper clipping from Chicago several years later, with a photo of April announcing her engagement. It thrilled me, but it broke my heart again, thinking she could not wear her engagement ring on her ring finger. There was no letter or address with the clipping and that was the last time I heard from or about either family.

During the entire third quarter of my life, I used every speaking engagement (over 250) nationwide, to teach and warn of the hidden dangers of the activity of tug-of-war. My goal in speaking out was to make other teachers aware of the dangers. The teachers immediately eliminated the tug of war activities in their districts, saving many children from possible injuries through tug of war. I continued spreading the information about the dangers of tug-of-war through word of mouth and through my teaching, my lectures, my workshops and through my training in my professional organizations. I always begin the story of tug of war by saying, "Once you hear this story, you will have received the knowledge that now makes you liable in a court of law."

I conclude by saying, "Now, it is your choice as to whether or not you include this *deadly* activity into your yearly lesson plans: you are now liable!" The stories of the dangers of tug-of-war reached sporting goods companies and manufactures, and they are now producing ropes specifically designed for tug of war. No loops at the end, and every six inches has a strong loop sewn onto the main rope so each child has his or her own safe grasp. Even with the safety measures, I personally will never be involved with any tug of war activities again. My stories always end by me apologizing to April and Nicole, (even though they are not in the audience) for my not having had the necessary knowledge to have protected them! I then simply end my warning with, "Now teachers, because of this catastrophic story, you should never have to make this kind of apology to any of your students!"

Mike Leebron, a dear friend, lawyer, and an exceptional educator in his own way, passed away suddenly in 2013, years before the publishing of this book. It was his friendship as much as his psychological mentoring that helped keep me sane throughout this ordeal. I still have a sinking feeling whenever the mention of tug of war comes up. Moreover, no matter what was said in the courtroom, I will always have a heavy heart about this tug-of-war activity causing such a violent injury under my watch! I will always have a special place in my heart for the girls involved and my wonderful friend, Mike.

Friendship: Uncle Lenny

My sister Ilene finally decided to leave her husband, "Wild" Bob in New York, and to start her life over with her two children, Christopher (9), and Danielle (12), in Texas. My mission of getting my family to move to Texas was almost complete, now I just needed to talk my parents into coming on down to Texas also. When my sister decided to make the escape from NY, we had a rare vacancy in our home! Ilene decided they would come to Texas after the school year was complete, which gave me the opportunity to help my buddy Lenny Kravitz, not to be confused with the famous musician, by letting Lenny stay with us while he looked for a job in Houston. Lenny had been the Houston Baptist University assistant gymnastics' coach before the HBU program went "south", as it was discontinued because of a serious injury to a gymnast at the college.

My family all called him "Uncle Lenny". He is a unique and talented person! Lenny was studying dance, acting, and helping with our gymnastics classes and teams at Kips. He looked like a tall Groucho Marx, with a very large mustache and an exceptionally full head of hair. Lenny had several small parts in theater productions in downtown, Houston Theater. Since he helped train our gymnasts, some of the team kids and my family attended some of his plays and watched as his small roles unveiled even more of his talent. His theater parts usually had tumbling sequences, like in a fight, or in comedies as a tumbling salesman. Uncle Lenny was as frugal as they come. At that time, other than his clothes, a motorcycle was all that he owned. To boost his income, he built balance beams in our garage and sold and delivered them for Christmas. Lenny was like a part of our family and a very trusted friend. He was a magnet to children; they all loved him.

Lenny marched to his own drum! He basically did what he wanted and went where and when he wanted. I guess I would have to say that when he traded his motorcycle in for a Chevy van, he was beginning to settle down. However, do not get me wrong, we still never knew where or when he was going to go or what he was going to do next!

Friendship: Barbara & Bill Voight

At that time, great friends of ours lived across the street from us. Bill and Barbara Voight were the first friends we met when we moved into the Katy area. Bill Voight had been a 6'7" All-American basketball player at Southern Methodist University in Dallas. We bonded, partly because we both possessed a sense of humor that comes with our having been athletes and from each of us hanging around basketball locker rooms.

Bill was a geologist with Enron and was in the Philippines when Uncle Lenny moved in with us. Bill had come home and met Uncle Lenny for the first time when there was an electric shutdown on our street. We all came out of our steaming, hot homes and visited on the street while waiting for the electricity to be turned back on. Meanwhile, Uncle Lenny, getting bored, decided to practice his ballet pirouettes and other dancing skills down the sidewalk. I was talking with Bill and had never had the chance to introduce Bill to Uncle Lenny before Lenny began dancing!

In a heartbeat, Bill had everyone cracking up as he directed everyone's attention to poor Uncle Lenny. Things got considerably worse when he found out that this dancing free spirit was living in my home! I don't think I ever lived that one down with my neighbors, who probably had reservations about the Urand family as well! But once they got to know "Uncle Lenny" better, they also appreciated this true free spirit, with nothing but good in his heart.

I was not too close with anyone on our street except for Bill. We had so much in common, Bill and I played on the same basketball team along with my brother-in law, Charlie when we played at the YMCA for a couple of seasons. He traveled extensively around the world in his job and missed half of our games, but he was great when he did participate. When Bill was in the country, our team never lost any basketball games! He was dominant, a banger who loved rebounding and jamming over everyone. Bill was by far the best white jumper I have seen.

Bill introduced Deanna and me to scuba diving, and we went on several trips together. In many cases, he would fly his plane and we would meet him in Cozumel. It was not that I didn't trust him; I was always worried because of my airsickness problems. I even have a hard time sitting on a hammock! In fact, many times I had to put on my scuba gear in the water rather than on the diving boat that was rolling and reeking from Pemex gasoline fumes. Fortunately, Deanna did not have these problems.

Bill was six years younger than I was, but I always looked up to him because he was both exceptionally intelligent and intuitive. There was not a project that he hesitated to take on. Whether it was building the only brick mailbox on the street or adding a second story to his garage. He was a man's man and I could ask him anything because of his vast knowledge base. He towered over Barbara, his wife and college sweetheart. They had one child, Jason, a super athlete who was just like his dad, quiet, thoughtful, intelligent, and athletic.

Bill and Barbara were always arguing about something. They both possessed unique, strong personalities and it was hard to know when they were being serious or joking with each other. Bill referred to Barbara

MARTY URAND

as "Wonder", and she just laughed it off. She pretty much thought she could control him because he was so quiet and a man of few words. But, when he had enough, he had enough! However, no matter what, they rebounded and always came back stronger.

One night I went over to Bill's house to bust his balls about Rudy Tomjonavich having a great game for the Houston Rockets. I was so excited because Bill hated Rudy T, and it was my turn to rag on him. After entering their house, Barbara took me into the backyard, I was shocked when I saw Bill at the bottom of the pool in his scuba gear lying perfectly still, and every so often I could observe small amounts of his air bubbles being released, bubbling up to the top of the pool.

I asked how long he had been down there, and she replied a little over an hour! I asked if he did this very often and in one of her serious moments, she stated that, "He does this when he doesn't want to argue with me anymore! This is his alone time"

The Last shot of my life!

With teaching (WME), coaching (Kips), and spending time at home with houseguests and family, I had little time for other activities. However, on Sundays, I made time to devote to my favorite sport, basketball.

My Sunday YMCA games played a big role in me being active playing basketball with some of my basketball friends. In a game similar to one played in Boston for the National Championship, my basketball career came to an abrupt end!

With the YMCA basketball championship on the line, game tied and five seconds remaining, I dribbled to half court with the idea of jumping into someone, hoping a foul would be called against that player, or if not, that I'd get the ball near the rim for Bill to stick it in. However, while in the air, my man undoubtedly figured my plan out and moved away leaving no options other than to give it everything that I had and let the ball fly! God was kind and "my last shot" went swish and my head swelled, but so did the vertebras in my back when I crashed into the ground!

And there I went....back to see Dr. Christie once again!

Will my Teaching take a new turn?

With the school year ending, I decided to interview for a position which would take me away from public school teaching. The position was for the Director of Health and Physical Education with the neighboring school district, Spring Branch ISD. I had mixed emotions about moving away from directly teaching children and going to work directly with teachers. From my own experience, I had always had a difficult time working with the administrators who would visit my teaching programs from time to time, and then, after a quick look, made recommendations to change either my teaching style or my program. Seldom were reasons or explanations given. The administrator usually just read his written statement and then left to go on to his next assignment. I knew if I were offered the position in Spring Branch, I would have to make major changes to this process.

This would be a unique experience for me, to say the least. Dr. Joan Whitten was the search committee chair from Spring Branch ISD, as well as the Executive Director of Elementary Schools. I breezed through the interview and was offered the position. Dee and

I celebrated with a great steak from Steak and Ale, only to receive a telephone call when we arrived home, asking me to come back in to visit with the committee again the next morning.

At that meeting, they indicated that they wanted to combine the elementary and secondary positions, which would streamline their budget. I was taken by surprise and I guess my reaction was very telling. The committee was uncomfortable with my reaction and starting digging into the cause. Being young and inexperienced with interviews, I told the truth about my debatable feelings about supervising secondary teachers who were also coaching!

I knew from personal experience that for them, coaching was first and teaching was second! It seemed like my whole life passed in front of me and I remembered Dr. Billy Tidwell at Sam Houston saying, "You never want to be categorized as a coach." He always believed that we should be teachers first and coaches second, and because teacher/coaches' salaries were 95% for teaching and 5% for coaching; the energy of a teacher/ coach should follow these same percentages.

I balked because I believed the same as Billy Tidwell about dealing with the coaches; all I could see was one argument after another with them! The meeting ended and I left with a bad feeling about this job. And as I had feared, I received a call from the hiring committee when I arrived home, and they told me that I was not what they had in mind for the job after all, and we parted ways. Although I was disappointed, it was probably best for all of us.

In September, I returned to my teaching assignment at West Memorial Elementary in Katy, Tx, and felt great because I knew the decision to return had been the right one for me. It was a year later, January of 1982, and a mystery of life revealed itself! Sports Illustrated ran an article about Clair Bee, "A Hero for All Times". It was several pages long and one of the pages truly shocked me as I saw the 23 small books in their colorful jackets staring me in the face. The memories of Clair Bee and his books cycled through my head and into my heart as my breathing picked up considerably.

These were the same books that I had first begun reading as a child, when I had needed to rely on the book jackets for understanding. It was about Coach Bee, who I have always strived to emulate when working with children. And of all people to have authored the series, it was "Clair Bee", the person who had not given me the time of day when I had talked about how I had felt out there in the boat. There was something telling me that I knew him better than I thought. I could have asked him a million questions about the stories if I had realized he was the author. It was his stories: each one of them that had helped mold my life. I believe that Clair Bee and his philosophies were some of the main reasons our basketball team did so well at Pan Am!

I scooped up the magazine I had received and ran down to Cami Jones, Jacqui's kindergarten teacher, to tell her the long story about the "Chip Hilton Series". Between Cami, my wife, and a few other friends, it had taken fifteen years to collect the 23 books in the series!

What would Mac and Arthur, my public school custodians, have thought?

Vacancy on Park Downe Lane

My home life was beginning to feel somewhat normal; no one was living with us now, the kids had their rooms back, and it felt great. We literally had five months without a guest, and the kids brought this up on many occasions. After enjoying a brief time of "just family" life', Mike Spiller called me from Switzerland asking if I could possibly help him out. Mike was one of the leaders in Houston gymnastics and was always trying to learn more about the sport. He had decided to go to Europe and learn from the countries that were leading in the gymnastics field. Mike had gone to Switzerland, and began working with the Swiss National gymnastics team. A family he had become friends with asked him to help their daughter obtain experience working in gymnastics in the United States. In fact it was a requirement of that Sport University that their students work in the U.S. at a sports facility to expand their learning experience.

Mike Spiller, Karen Vogel, and Marty Urand

Three days later, a Swiss beauty arrived in Houston! Karen Vogel was a stunning 18 year old who was in great shape. Not so much for gymnastics' competition, but more for a beauty contest! She had a seductive accent and looks that went with it, but that was all! She did many things that tended to piss people off! She worked at our gymnastics' club as part of the arrangement for us to provide her free room and board at our house. It had been pre-arranged that Karen would help by teaching and training our gymnastics classes and teams at Katy Kips. However, she was lazy and self-centered. She never wanted to demonstrate her skills to our team kids. It was as if she felt like she was too good. Karen had a big chip on her shoulder, talking negatively about most things. I could never figure her out. We all tried hard to make her feel welcome, but she never had appreciation of our hospitality. She let it be known how much she disliked the United States, compared to her own country through her actions and her direct comments. It was frustrating not to be able to work together and make things work. It made life miserable, as we felt uneasy around our house, listening to her negative comments about American food, American people, etc. etc. Karen did bake bread that was delicious, but her social graces did not go along with the opportunity to figuratively "break bread together". Deanna, Marti, and Jacqui were ready for her to go home.

We could not wait for her Visa to expire so she would leave. We were so tired of hearing how bad the United States was compared to "her country". While still staying with us, Karen went skiing in Colorado with some people she had met and later called to say that she had received a job on the slopes and would not return to Texas. I gladly shipped her belongings to her and told Mike that her beauty did not go deep. We were thrilled to get her out of our house...and no more favors from me! There were also shouts of happiness and relief from Deanna and our daughters.

The next time I saw Mike Spiller was not until ten years later when he was presenting a workshop on "Games of the World" for physical education teachers at the TAHPERD Convention in San Antonio. We had many laughs about the young beauty. I went into the details about some of the incidents that had made her stay go so sour during her time with us. I also told him that Deanna and I celebrated with our daughters once our negative boarder was gone. In this case, we certainly had not been able to judge the "book by the cover:"

Summer Fun and Camp

Katy Kips seemed to be on top of the gymnastics world! However, contending with the yearly pitfalls with the slowdown of summer business was always a nightmare. Although we had a few hundred students, families felt like it was vacation time from school and I guess from gymnastics as well.

My swim lessons, swim team income, and coaching helped our family during the summer, but I had to worry about our full time employees as well. Camp was a natural for me because of the years I had attended in Pennsylvania, at Camp Cherokee, so I decided to recreate that summer experience for our gymnasts and their friends in Katy. I rented a camp-like facility that provided a great environment and their staff even provided hot meals for our campers. The "J Bar J Ranch" camp was located in Sealy, Texas, which was only 15 miles from Kips. We offered an opportunity, at a reasonable price, for children to sign up for one or more two-week overnight sessions at our camp. We had a bus to take the campers to Katy Kips gym for dance and gymnastics, which we scheduled in daily. This was a complete camp, which also included swimming, games, contests, and included sleeping in the cabins at camp.

At one of our camps, as a drawing card, we brought in Trace Talavera who had been a member of the Olympic Team in 1980 and 1984. This was a great highlight in the lives of the campers and team members attending camp that year. This camp came to be a summer tradition for us, and it was a very positive experience for all of us.

Coach Rick Baker and the campers who gave him "Pie in the Eye!"

Tracee Talavera loved our camp and our kids loved her! Color War was a great highlight during the camp as we competed in everything other than in peeing contests! As I said, we kept everything first class and above board.

Another new career begins for me

In 1982, I received a surprising call from Dr. Joan Whitten, who at this point in her career was Executive Director for Elementary in Spring Branch ISD, promising me that If I was still interested, I could have that director's job and it would be limited to only the elementary level. I promise," said Joan."

I was all over it! I resigned from West Memorial Elementary and began my new job in Spring Branch ISD, which, at that time, was a much larger district than Katy. SBISD had 23 elementary schools, 7 middle schools, and 5 high schools.

What a transition: not teaching on a daily basis and not teaching the same gym classes in the same school each day, every hour of the day. Now I had the opportunity to research, to provide training and guidance to teachers, and to develop plans to upgrade the teaching of physical education in this district. Spring Branch I.S.D was a unique and diverse community. Interstate 10 cuts through the bottom half of the district. At that time, a few of the Houston Rockets and some Astros players, along with soon to be Boston Red Sox pitcher, Roger Clemens, lived on the south side of SBISD.

Deanna taught Roger's oldest son, who is now with the Astros' farm team, computer literacy in middle school. She loves to say, "I knew him when...."

On the eastside of the district is a large cemetery that always brought me moments of sorrow when I passed it as I was traveling around to the schools. Marvin Blumenthal, the person responsible for getting me to Texas, had died about five years before I began working for SBISD, and Marvin was buried at that beautiful cemetery.

After Marvin's death, many of the great players who had played at the JCC began working out at Fonde Recreation Center in Houston. Consequently, the recreation basketball scene in Houston changed, and it was never quite the same for me!

I have visited Marvin's grave several times during the twenty years I was with the district. I always felt the need to thank him for the faith he had in me, a young punk from New York, coming all the way to Texas, aiming to prove he was right to have faith in me. Where would I be if it had not been for Marvin? Maybe a cop, or a detective in New York City? "God only knows!"

Fizz Ed

My life was in the midst of a change, but I did not realize just how much! During the last several years, we had once again opened our family to pet dogs. We enjoyed German Shepherds, and we had owned three German shepherds in a row during our time in Katy. Marti and Jacqui came up with great names that reflected my passion for my career. They named them "Fizz Ed I, the next dog, Fizz Ed II, and the third dog was Fizz Ed III".

We were still living in Katy, and I had worked in SBISD for three months when we had to put Fizz Ed III to sleep. Walking into work the next morning, I tried not to show my sadness when telling Bill Tucker, SBISD's Director of Science, about the loss of our dog. Bill was a true love of nature and everything that lived within it! It felt good to have shared my loss with a person who I knew felt my pain. In addition, shortly after that, Bill found just the remedy.

After lunch a few months later, I went back to my office and my face lit up! Bill walked in and brought me a six-week-old "Red" Great Dane with a black mask, a beautiful face, and whose body had every muscular feature that defines a Great Dane. There was, however, a large scar on the hind leg which had once been broken when she was mistreated by a previous owner. It seems that Bill rescued and raised Great Danes, nurturing them to health, and he then put them up for adoption. When Deanna and the girls saw the Great Dane, it was love at first sight for all of us! "Babe" grew up big and strong and when possible I took her everywhere with me. She attended all "dog friendly" outdoor conferences with me as well as attending our Kips Summer Camps.

Bill Tucker and I worked for ten years together, and "Babe" was a subject we discussed each day. I thank Bill T. for his humanity, his friendship, and for becoming a part of my life. In addition, of course, I thank him for Babe!

Dad Sunsets "Stick-Up"

In 1984, Dee and I finally convinced my parents to move to Texas. Naturally, they moved in with us for a while. We gave them our room, and we made the den into a bedroom upstairs for us. The move was dependent on my dad selling his taxicab and its medallion (the silver badge on the hood that is required for every legitimate yellow cab) which he did very quickly. I could not believe my dad was willing to give up New York City" and move to Texas!"

My mother was the instigator of this move and we all had a ball together for about two months! My mom and dad then bought a house in a neighborhood near us, and my dad kicked back. But eventually my mom became bored. She wanted to go back East, but this time alone!

My dad bought himself a car and found an apartment when she left. He also did odd jobs, and even took on a paper route. He seemed perfectly content with everything. What a change in thinking by our Dad. If it were anyone we thought would have wanted to go back to his or her roots, we were convinced it would have been my dad.

However, I am not going to pretend that Texas cured him of his quick temper or poor driving habits. He still was a "cabby" deep down, and that meant no one was safe crossing the street, especially if he was making a right hand turn!

My dad finally had the time to visit with his daughters and their children without my mom always hassling him to hurry, as she had done in New York. Marti and Jacqui were getting to know him better as well. The only extended family our girls had really known up until now was Deanna's family.

There were many things my dad had to get used to while living in Texas that were certainly different from N.Y. Even though Houston is the third largest city in the U.S., we have water drainage problems that are still far from being solved. With any healthy downpour, many parts of Houston flood, making my parents quite nervous. In New York City, there were sewers that drained the water and sent it out into the ocean and bays. In rural cities such as Katy, drainage ditches were used to catch the overflow of water. Nevertheless, once the ditches filled, we again had the flooding to deal with until the water eventually drained into the ditches, dirt, and grassy areas.

The lesson in "drainage" is necessary, to explain why as a cab driver, my dad was unable to transfer his New York driving style and driving shortcuts, to Texas. While driving in Katy, Texas, during a heavy rainstorm, my dad took a sharp right hand turn too quickly, and crashed his car into a large, deep ditch. He slammed his head hard during the wreck, which resulted in a brain aneurism.

My mother immediately came back to Texas to help care for my dad, but it was not long before my father died and we went back to New York to have my dad's funeral in Elmont, New York. My dad is buried in the same cemetery where my brother, Jeffrey is buried. My dad's gravesite faces Belmont Race Track, which I am sure would have pleased him: to have the vibrations of the horse's hooves shaking through the cemetery during each race! Shortly after my father's death, my mom moved back to Texas and into an apartment in Katy, across the street from a bar that was similar to the bar in the TV series "Cheers". "Her" neighborhood bar had bar-b-ques, bands, and special activities for their customers. The owners and regular customers sort of "adopted" my mother. Having friends and a place to go helped my mother adapt to my father's death and to living alone.

Poor mom received very little from dad's estate, even though my dad had continued collecting stamps for as long as I could remember. I often thought about his fascination with stamps and even remember watching dad get into fistfights at the malt shop during an argument about the value of a set of stamps. At home, I must have heard my mom say a hundred times, "Jack, put down those damn stamps and pay attention to your family!"

Dad also had the stamps that "Horsey" had contributed to my father's collection before Horsey had mysteriously vanished! However, I also knew that many of his exotic stamps were "hot" and could not be displayed or sold. My father told me to be very careful if my mother ever tried to sell Horsey's six volumes of stamps, he felt that she would get into trouble.

My dad had believed the collection would be worth several hundred thousand dollars, but I figured that high of a price was only for the black market value. And I wanted no part of that. I went with mom to various stamp shops to see if we could sell the albums. I wanted to be sure that she was not ripped off!

Every owner that evaluated the collection was impressed with the immaculate collection. The proprietor's usually asked if he could examine the collection overnight, or asked to take it to the back room to analyze the value by looking through high-powered magnifying glasses. I knew never to let the collection leave our sight.

We spent six weeks trying to market the collection. We had several calls from various shops but their offers were nowhere near my dad's expectations. I contemplated going to New York to dump the collection, but frankly, I was afraid of landing up like "Horsey" or placed in jail!

We found one buyer who was willing to take a chance and we felt comfortable with his offer. We took the stamps back to him, met the buyer in his bank, and he gave my mother cash. We never gave our full names, address, or phone numbers. The shop owner did ask where we were from, and when I replied, "New York", he said, "I should have known! Some of these stamps have been missing from some well-known collections for years!" He then ushered us out the door and we went to our car. When we got into our car, I said to my mother, "Jesus, I bet dad is "up there" biting his knuckles just about now!"

We had finally settled for only fifty-five hundred dollars for the collection, and never looked back! We were happy to get those stamps out of our possession and to come home with some money and without any major problems!

Marcella Porter

Over the next few years, I gave much of my life to my job and the school district. Kips became secondary to me, as public school teachers and the school children became the focal point of my professional life. Since I had so much faith in the Kips Staff, I felt comfortable shifting my focus and assisting teachers had now become my center of attention. I traveled everywhere in Texas to monitor teachers in districts that had directors of physical education and school districts similar to us.

There were approximately 15 other districts that had specialized administrators for health and physical education, and TAHPERD had a section designed for these leaders who were over-seeing these programs within the state.

It was during this time that I met Marcella Porter, who had a position in Irving, TX, that was similar to my position and program in Spring Branch ISD.

We worked well together, both striving for teacher excellence and exemplary physical education programs within our respective districts. Marcella was the Physical Education Administrator in Irving ISD. She had held that position for many years and had accomplished a great deal toward raising the standards of physical education and in helping children of Irving, Texas to become healthy and fit. Her focus was to have all of her physical education teachers providing excellent programs for all children. She worked closely with her local school board, the physical education teachers, administrators, and the students. As her district grew, she and the administration had second elementary school gymnasiums built so instruction would not have to suffer because of an overload of students in cramped facilities.

As a new administrator, I used Marcella and her program as role models for what I wanted to accomplish in Spring Branch ISD. I was pushing for the same quality outcomes for our children and our programs in SBID as Marcella was reaching and still accomplishing in Irving ISD She had the experience and success within her program that I was working to achieve by building a similar high quality program in SBISD.

I knew Marcella was a diligent planner, always doing her homework, digging deeply and methodically through the pros and cons of each change before taking any actions. Beyond that, Marcella, strong, decisive, and creative, is always willing to open her mind to the questions, suggestions, and opinions of other professionals before she re-analyzes any possible changes even more... until she is absolutely confident. Bouncing some of our ideas back and forth always invigorated us to strive to improve our programs. It was the beginning of a lasting friendship between Marcella and me: And thirty years later, it is still as strong as ever.

Spring Branch Becomes a Family

By the end of my first year in The district, the physical education teachers in Spring Branch decided to organize their own local association for having a local collective voice for physical education. We became a miniature TAHPERD as far as structure and even as far as policy. One of the first policies our association accomplished in our district was to change the name of physical education in our district from PE (physical education) to Health Fitness. We all believed that what we were teaching the children had a much broader scope than just the physical aspects of "PE". We wanted the community to realize that what we were teaching their children was more valuable than what all of us had been offered, back when we were younger and in "P.E." We were now teaching about the healthy benefits of physical activity and including knowledge along with teaching safe and healthy guidelines as well as physical activities.

Another change occurred because of the terrible tug of war accident that had happened at my elementary school in Katy. Many of the teachers had knowledge of the tug-of-war accident that had occurred and overwhelmingly agreed that we ban tug-of-war activities from our curriculums.

Spring Branch ISD Health Fitness Association hosted the Second Annual TAHPERD Summer Conference and from there our reputations took off to even loftier heights! We were a young, dedicated group, who loved being active and held activities in one of our school gyms one night per week. We brought members of our families, participated in a variety of activities, and played together while getting to know each other and our families better. We were just enjoying each other's company and ideas. Our coaches backed this program and were easy to work with for scheduling etc. A gym was set up for our group activities, while the coaches worked with their teams in a second gym. This change occurred during the beginning of my second year as SBISD Health Fitness Coordinator, when the district expanded my job to include the teachers and their programs in both elementary and secondary schools.

We had such a great nucleus of teachers in all age levels of our schools. Most of us traveled together to educational training, and improved our knowledge together at conventions, workshops, and presentations throughout the state. Spring Branch always had a number of people presenting at the workshops. The audiences usually followed any presenters from SBISD listed in the programs, and could pack the auditoriums as many as 600 to 800 teachers!

We were the hottest ticket in town. As a result, many college graduates applied to teach in **Spring Branch ISD!**

Spring Branch ISD, Health Fitness Staff (2005)

This popularity gave us a worthy identity, with a great reputation and a large academic following which SBISD Superintendent Dr. Hal Guthrie noticed. He supported us in every way possible. It was unique having the top dog of the district showing strong support for the physical education program. At that time, few districts went out of their way to assist their PE teachers. It also helped us that the SBISD local School Board President was none other than Dr. Jack Christie! Together, Hal Guthrie and Dr. Jack Christie set high standards academically and physically for the 32,000 students in SBISD.

Haunted by My First Job Interview!

Fil Hendrix (Texas Education Agency) hosted a conference for teachers to come together, share ideas, and participate in activities and games in a small gym under the bleachers of the Darrell Royal Football Stadium at the University of Texas. Teachers from all over Texas came to attend this workshop, in Austin, Texas.

I was especially excited to be bringing sixteen of our Spring Branch teachers to meet the new U.T. football coach. It seems that Fred Akers, who had hired me as a teacher/coach when I was coaching high school in Edinburg, TX, had left from Wyoming University, and had now moved on up to the big time at UT!

It was perfect timing to have our staff meet Coach Akers, who coached at The University of Texas. He had helped me get back into the good graces of our teachers from a poor driving decision. On an earlier trip, when driving several of them home from our State Leadership Conference, I had driven down a large hill outside of Comfort, Texas, and the teachers were griping about my driving speed... just before I was stopped by a State Trooper for driving over the speed limit and I received a speeding ticket. There were twenty-four teachers on my speeding school bus! It had been poor judgment on my part to be speeding. The thoughts of what "could have been" still haunt me.

However, to divert the focus from my lack of judgment, I called Coach Akers and set up a time for the teachers and me to meet with him in his office overlooking the UT football field and stadium. We were all excited as we took the elevator to the top floor to meet him. I knocked on the door expecting his secretary to answer and show us in, but the door flew open and Coach Akers stood in the doorway pointing his finger at me, as the teachers stood behind me. As I reached out to shake his hand, he did not reciprocate so I uncomfortably pulled my hand back in. He kept pointing at me and finally said, "I have waited many years to tell you that you did not fool me a bit at your job interview for the football job at Edinburg High School. You obviously did not know anything about football! He then said, "And I hired you because the superintendent in Edinburg told me to make *sure that I did hire you!*"

We both laughed so hard that it brought tears to my eyes. Coach Akers had a great career at University of Texas, and I have always admired him.

Spring Branch School District was still on the move, and growing in popularity within the field of health and physical education. One of our innovative activities was to host a district banquet at the end of each school year presenting honors to deserving health fitness teachers, administrators, student teachers, programs and other special guests who had major effects on our program and the health fitness discipline. Teachers, principals, district administrators, many members of our local School Board and special guests, both inside and outside of our district, attended our banquets. The Superintendent's attendance helped build the morale of the teachers, and it kept everyone updated on our programs through various health organizations such as American Heart Association, American Lung, and Cancer Fighting Associations for Lymphocytic and Leukemia. We had many teachers who advocated for an assortment of health organizations. This event served us well in so many different areas.

For our first banquet, I chose Walter Yates to be our guest speaker. Walter was an advocate for athletics, health, and physical education. Walter was on his way toward earning a spot in the Texas Coaches Hall of Fame. Usually called "Trim", he had been the third highest ranked high school coach with a record of 892 wins. Later in his career, Trim was selected for several Hall of Fame awards from his high school (Wheatley), and college (U.T–Pan American). Walter was an outstanding athlete, teacher, and administrator during his career.

*Walter "Trim" Yates came to support my efforts
at our first Banquet. Trim brought greetings
from the Texas Coaches Hall of Fame.*

As my years in education mounted, many stories have
surfaced, but none quite like the staffing dilemmas
that occur at the end of each year. At the close of the
school year, staffing is altered, due to changes in the
student population caused by apartment closings
and openings, or the dreaded moving of a district's
boundaries.

It was also the time of the year when teachers could
ask for transfers to move from their current school to
teach at a different school in or outside of the district.
One of the problems I was experiencing in my first
year as Director of Health Fitness was that secondary
health fitness programs were diminishing because of
the number of families who had moved from Spring

Branch into Katy, Texas, and were attending school in Katy School District.

Because of this, we were overstaffed at one of our high schools, and the softball coach from that school no longer had a job there. There were no other vacancies in the high schools or middle schools so she applied for a vacancy as an elementary physical education teacher.

I was very opposed to this type of transfer. I went to Barbara Hunt, the principal, and pleaded with her to take a teacher, not a coach, to work with the elementary age children. I was worried that a coach would be too focused on her "team", and that her class lessons would take a back seat to coaching. She told me that she would try to protect the position until I could hire a trained elementary teacher from the University of Houston. Thanks to Dr. Joel (Doc) Bloom (U of H), I began teaching at University of Houston part time in the evenings as an Adjunct Faculty member. Through this teaching, I was privy to outstanding students who were training under "Doc." Throughout this time, Dr. Bloom assigned many of his prospective student teachers to Spring Branch because of the high quality of our programs. That was the start of the rewarding teaching connection between the University of Houston and SBISD!

The fact that the Director of Physical Education was blocking the teaching part of this assignment must have gotten to the softball coach who was applying for the elementary physical education position. She went to the principal and showed her some of the lesson plans she had developed and assured her she would follow them and would be a great elementary school teacher if she were given the chance to prove herself! Fortunately, against my wishes, Anne Daily, the past secondary coach, was hired as the Health Fitness teacher at that elementary school. And to my absolute delight, she was and still is a fantastic teacher! During her first ten years at this elementary school, Anne became Teacher of the Year at her school and then Teacher of the Year in our district. Anne was and still is an innovative and motivational leader for her students and for her profession.

Ann has also been elected to many leadership positions in TAHEPRD, our state professional organization. I admitted to Anne, that if she had not been hired, it would have been one of the worst mistakes in my career. Anne later humbled me again, by inviting Deanna and me to be her guests when she was presented with the TAHPERD Honor Award in Dallas, during our state convention. We were delighted to see Anne honored for all she has done for children and continues doing for our profession. I was filled with pride and respect once again, when Anne was elected as the Vice President of TAHPERD! Anne had become my right-hand person in running our school district, and I consider her a close friend, twenty years later!

Anne Daily served as my right-hand assistant all through my presidency (2002)

Reunited with Uncle Lenny

From time to time, I still received postcards from "Uncle" Lenny, so I knew he was alive and making it. He had gone into the camp business in Massachusetts and during the winter months, he made a name for himself in the exercise world by producing exercise videos and exercise books.

In April, Lenny called, very excited about having me assist at gymnastics' camp in Massachusetts. The owner of the camp, after hearing about my "Color War" events, told Uncle Lenny to get me up there to conduct the "color war" at his camp that coming summer. Deanna and I planned a vacation to Massachusetts for the two weeks, and lived, worked, and played at the camp. Although younger than the other campers, both of our daughters attended this well-known camp with outstanding gymnastics' coaches and with better camp facilities than we had ever seen before. Some of the older campers watched out for them, but also let them participate in the training at Marti and Jacqui's skill levels. It was as if they were their "mascots". I learned so much from Abe Grossfield and Muriel Grossfield (Olympic gymnastics' coaches) during that camp! The "Color War" went off great, and I have heard they still carry on this event.

The highlight of the trip was when my family and I went to visit the Basketball Hall of Fame in Springfield, Mass. My daughters were six and eight when we visited, but unfortunately, they do not remember sitting in the Basketball Hall of Fame and seeing the film of me playing with the Pan American College team in the video stored at the *Hall of Fame* facility. This film had probably been at the highest point of my basketball career! What a shame! But who knows, maybe they will go to Springfield with their families someday and see the film again with their children!!!

We noticed several traces of Pan American College as we toured the Hall of Fame. Pictures of Luke Jackson hung in several areas of the Hall of Fame, and a picture of our National Championship Team was on the wall. However, it was downstairs in the auditorium where my socks were literally knocked off! As we walked into the auditorium, a man asked us if we had a preference to which year's basketball championship we would like to view. I replied "1963", thinking that he would say, I am sorry but we don't go back that far! However, to my shock and absolute delight, he said, "I'll set it up. Have a seat and it will begin in a few minutes".

"Wow"! My family and I sat through basketball championships that included the Armed Forces, AAU, and finally, the N.A.I.A. championship game. Marty Glickman was the announcer calling the plays. To hear him just say the name of our college sent goose bumps up my spine! He went through the tournament game that to me seemed to pass in just seconds. The announcer finally came down to the big men of the tourney, Willis Reed and Luke Jackson. Jack received most of the airtime, but Glickman remembered me from Brooklyn and commented, "Marty likes the horses in Texas better than the horses on the merry-go-round in Coney Island!" It was a dream come true and it is definitely a goal of mine to bring Marti's and Jacqui's children to the "Hall" before the fourth quarter ends!

The All-American Physical Education Class

The Texas Education Agency, located in Austin, Texas, has twenty "Educational Service Centers" throughout the state that serve as arms of the agency. In Houston, The Region IV service center is located off highway 290 and Tidwell. It is a large building, serving 52 school districts within the Houston area.

Molly Berger was the spark plug for health and physical education at the Houston Educational Service Center while I was at Spring Branch ISD. She spent much of her time visiting schools in her area and presenting on a variety of student focused health topics. Children loved her because she dressed in costume to gear up the children's interests. Molly used humor to teach her lessons and looked like a mixture of Mary Poppins and of a circus clown, as Molly always delivers her messages while wearing an inner tube around her waist as she makes her "health" points. Molly began her lessons by telling the students she was there to save their lives through the information that she was going to share with them. She had great strategies to communicate her points for the children so they would remember them. Molly had them laughing and listening throughout her hilarious, but factual presentation. Molly often offered monthly workshops for nurses, health and physical education teachers, and for their students.

Molly was a great supporter of my program and of Spring Branch School District. She gave me the opportunity to host an after school T.V. show, "The All-American Health Fitness Class", on the Region IV Educational Center Channel.

The All-American Health Fitness class
aired once a month. Visiting teachers were
(L) Sylvia Beatty, TAHPERD Elementary
Teacher of the Year and Nancy Miller,
outstanding middle school teacher.

The class featured a cross-section of SBISD students in upper level elementary, and middle schools, and these students were the regulars on our monthly program. I invited a variety of teachers from our district and sometimes from other school districts to lead the TV class in exercises, games, stretching, or lead-up activities for sports activities.

Teachers who watched the show after school could call in while the program was airing and ask direct questions to the students or to the presenting teachers. I scheduled the teachers, the students who participated, and I produced the program as well. It was a great way to teach new methods without requiring teachers or other viewers to travel after a long school day to attend a workshop. Staying at their own schools, sometimes with their students, gave them the benefit of a workshop via television without the need to travel. At the time, it was the only such program in the state or nation that I know of, and Molly was the brainchild of this concept. My greatest satisfaction with this program was having had the opportunity to help develop material that could empower teachers to present and to be a part of their own professional growth as teachers. I consider this program to have been one of the highlights of my career.

Another high spot of my career was being invited to join Dr. O'Quinn on a writing team in Chicago, to work on educational materials for teachers and children to use for the upcoming Olympics.

Katy resident named to olympic committee

A Katy area resident has been named to the K-3 Curriculum Committee by the United States Olympic Committee, according to Olympic Committee officials.

Marty Urand is one of seven members of the K-3 Curriculum Advisory Subcommittee of the Education Committee for the United States Olympics, officials have announced, expected to develop a kindergarten through third-grade curriculum based upon "Olympic Day in the Schools."

Urand, who is employed as coordinator for Health and Physical Education at Spring Branch Independent School District, is to attend committee meetings in Chicago, Ill., April 28-29, officials said.

Also named to the committee were Dr. Garland O'Quinn Jr. of Austin, TX., Thomas Reigner of Brookhaven, PA.,

Marty Urand

Dennis Snyder of Ft. Myers, FL., Karen Thompson of Olathe, KS., Dr. Richard Vrable of Brunswick, Ohio, and olympian Lucinda Williams Adams of Dayton, Ohio.

Urand, a Memorial Parkway resident, has been active in the Katy area as a swim-team coach for a number of years.

The Career Move-"Westward Ho"

Things were going really well for me in SBISD during my ten years with Spring Branch, when Dr. Christie called me to his office and told me that he was going to run for the State Board of Education, which in Texas is an elected position. The State Board is the most powerful educational organization within the state of Texas and the State Board works closely with the Texas Governor.

Dr. Christie asked to meet with me to see if I might be interested in applying for the position of Director for Health and Physical Education at the Texas Education Agency in Austin. Dr. Christie felt confident he could be elected and was setting "his ducks up in a row" to strive "for a healthy Texas". He strongly believed in promoting and providing programs for children's health, and he wanted to see other school districts offer programs such as the model used in Spring Branch ISD.

Therefore, after 28 years of teaching in Texas, I applied for a position at The Texas Education Agency in Austin, Texas, to support our state leaders in their quest to raise Texas Education and Physical Education to new heights. With a few kind words from Dr. Christie, I was packing for the trip west! Saying good-bye to Spring Branch was difficult, but the timing was too good to pass up! Both my daughters were now attending college. Marti was at Texas A&M learning how to be an "Aggie", and Jacqui was dancing her way through school at none other than Sam Houston State!

As for the family, things were starting to settle down! My sister Ilene met a "True" Texan, Dave Quinney, and she and Dave got married. I could not have been any happier for her. Dave was a very down to earth man who also happened to love sports, so he was ok with me. When I said, he was a "Texan" I meant it! He was right out of the mold of John Wayne! He was also a Vietnam survivor with all the nightmares that came with serving there.

I would have to say that Dave was an opinionated sort, and loved the USA. A funny story comes to mind when I think of him and his quick dry humor. Dave was not a person to hold back from saying what he thought. Once, when he and Ilene were on an elevator, the door opened and a young man with pierced rings all over his face entered. It was not thirty seconds before Dave asked this man if he had fallen while in Home Depot, and fortunately this "ringed" man found the comment amusing. Dave never hesitated in saying what he thought.

Ilene's daughter, Danielle, was divorced, but when Danielle's son Billy was ten, Danielle fell in love and married Bill Steele, from England. He is a "Hoot"!

With Bill's great sense of humor, and pronounced accent, his jokes become even funnier! He turned out to be a down-home kind of man. A few years later Danielle and Bill had a daughter, Jenna! They live in a nice house in a country-like setting in the Katy, Texas area. Danielle must have had some of my dad's genes. She began a business she named "Katy Cab Service". Danielle eventually sold her company and has since been involved in many other endeavors. Like my Dad, she was born to be an entrepreneur.

Ilene's other child, Chris, ("Bubba"), finished his tour of duty with the Marines, and began working at the Intercontinental airport in Houston. Unfortunately, things were not working out at home so he eventually went through a divorce and was looking to begin anew. Eventually he found Sarah, whom he married, and he began his second family. Sarah's dad is a former Marine, which gives them *two* "common bonds".

My youngest sister, Enid, had finished her nursing degree from UT and settled down in Doylestown, PA. I cannot believe I had to watch her move away from Texas! However, Enid's daughter, Meena, had moved to Doylestown and fallen in love. After Meena's engagement and wedding in Pennsylvania, Enid knew Meena would be living up north instead of in Texas. So to Meena's delight, Enid decided to move to Pennsylvania to be closer to her daughter. Once in Pennsylvania, Enid finished her graduate studies and received her Nurse Practitioner's degree from LaSalle, in Philadelphia.

With everything in place, Dee, Babe, and I moved 151 miles west to the beautiful city of Austin, Texas. Since we were moving, we had decided to sell our gymnastic school, the Katy Kips. We kept our word to our long time coaches, Louie and Lynn, who had originally come to us from California, and gave them first option to buy the gym. We were thrilled to go to Austin, but sad to leave Katy Kips. The Kips had really served our family well by fulfilling our dreams to own and run our own gym, with our overall goal being to provide safe, high quality training for children. Our coaches, the families we met, and all of the children who had trained with us had enriched our lives as well as our children's lives.

This fulfilling adventure had not only been the pride of our lives, it had also helped fund our children's education, had provided us with a good down payment for a home in Austin, and had provided memories and friends that will never be forgotten and are priceless.

Once Deanna and I moved to Austin with our girls and dog, we found a neat small home on Lake Austin near Mansfield Damn. We purchased a boat, a couple of jet skis, and we were ready to party!

The lake water was clear, but very, very cold... even in the summer! There was not a day in the summer that we did not wake up to someone who had fallen while water skiing, shrieking as they were thrown into the ice, cold water! We could not help but laugh as we heard their comments once they hit that frigid water...

MARTY URAND

Our house was unique in that it was one of three houses located on land that had once been part of Selma Hughes City Park, located at the bottom of the Steiner's Ranch in Austin. In order to arrive at Selma Hughes Park, we had to travel four miles down from the main road, Hwy 620. This intersection is just one mile past the famous Oasis Restaurant, which has at least 20 decks overlooking Lake Travis (which looks toward the other side of the dam). Our drive, when we turned off of Hwy 620, was a short seven-minute drive through winding roads through the ranch, which led to the small park and to Lake Austin. Each mile of the trip had cattle guards, which are in-ground metal gratings that the cattle are afraid to cross. The ranch had a couple of hundred head of cattle roaming freely from cattle guard to cattle guard.

There was a fork in the road before we came to the lake. A left turn took us toward a small city park and our house, but going straight took us down the road that ended at the entrance of a very fancy "Fat Farm!" I am sure it has another name, because it was exceptionally nice, but that was what we, along with our neighbors, called it. All I had heard was that it cost around "a grand a day" to stay and participate in the services of this health spa. It was a first class establishment. It was amusing to travel our rustic roads, only to have been slowed down by a car or two trying to locate the "fat farm"!

It did not take long to fall in love with the beautiful lake and our home! The job at the agency, on the other hand, was very political. There were unwritten rules and policies that I needed to learn on the do's and don'ts of how to operate around the Capital. Somehow, I also had to learn whom I could speak with and whom I could not!

My first day at the office was different from any working experience I'd had. I drove to downtown Austin, to my office, which was located in the Travis Building. Floors 1-9 belonged to T.E.A. and 10-12 was for the Texas Railroad Commission. My office was very tiny, but had a window facing the Capitol Building where Governor Ann Richards had her office. My desktop was stacked with books and policies, and I was told to read these before I could even answer the phone!

I spent the first month on the job reading and taking a Governmental course about the "Quality Professional System" for all new employees. The reading was the worst reading of my life! It seemed that all the employees talked in numbers rather than words. It was all about policies and the numbers that they represented. There were several volumes of State Board policies that I had to read and learn, because basically, I worked directly for the Governor and for the State Board of Education.

One week a month, several hundred employees were confined to our offices prior to and during the State Board of Education Meeting. The meeting usually lasted two days and we, the staff, needed to be on hand to immediately perform research and provide

MARTY URAND

in depth information to be used by members of the State Board prior to their next discussions on that particular topic.

These meetings were the most enjoyable parts of the month for me. Each district sent their "movers and shakers" to attend the meetings from beginning to end. During the day the Board separated into various committees, and each of us who were staff members, sat in the galleries listening to the conversations in the meetings where our particular disciplines were discussed. We were in the gallery so that during the meetings, if a question arose regarding our educational focus, we could be summoned from the "staff gallery" to answer questions if needed, or to give additional details or more background about any given topic relating to our fields.

During the day it was all business, but at night, the parties begin! Austin is known for its music and food, and these clubs and stores are brightly lit all along Sixth Street. A very eclectic crowd forms each night of the week, and especially on the weekends. Sixth street was often closed off to motor vehicles so pedestrians could safely walk from club to club, filling both the sidewalks and the streets. What a town!

The favorite place Deanna and l love is Esther's Follies, on Sixth Street. The theatre is very different in that there is a very large glass plate picture window facing Sixth Street from behind the Esther Follies stage. The people passing by often look in, not realizing that the audience is looking out at the pedestrians, and the comedians/actors are usually cracking jokes about those very pedestrians themselves. The laughs never stop.

With Austin being such a liberal town, the entertainment, jokes and skits at Esther's Follies ranged from juggling, singing, magic acts, and of course skits using political satire focusing on Texas, The Texas Capitol, 6th Street, and nationally all the way to Washington, D.C. No politician, political party, or political situation is immune from Esther's Follies skits. Any current, relevant politics in Austin, Texas, or elsewhere, is humorously torn apart and made fun of in their skits. The skits were very timely, and most skits changed weekly, or in some instances by the day! During their performances, the actors will turn any funny or unusual people and their activities seen through the windowed wall into the act. Their ad-libs are as funny as the planned sketches.

Dee and I usually get there early to get seats in the middle, several rows up from the stage. Once Dee and I made the mistake of sitting too close up front, and I was picked to be involved in a skit on stage! We learned quickly, and decided it was more fun for us to sit back from the stage and laugh at others rather than being chosen from the audience and included in the skits. So early meant arriving 45 minutes to an hour before the show begins, choosing seats further up from the stage and while waiting we entertained ourselves by watching the people on 6th Street walk by and look in, unaware that we were all being entertained by watching them as they carried on in the street. Across the street from Esther's Follies was a bar that always caught my eye because of its unusual name. It was "The Alternative Lounge". The police sirens and lights were a common sight at that lounge, and the police entered that club several times during the evening. I did not know, and do not want to know, what the "alternative" refers to.

When Monday came, I was back at work, gathering the materials I had prepared for the day's meetings, and I returned to my "post" in the Board Room. It was an interesting time as each of the directors worked behind the scenes trying to push through policy changes that would positively affect each of our particular fields of interest. Many times, I heard testimonies from my TAHPERD friends or sometimes even from the Executive Director, Quentin Christian, as he tried to convince the School Board to either consider or reconsider a policy that we felt would benefit the health and lives of students.

Sometimes I felt like a spy when I had to ask my friends to testify at a hearing, because even though I was working for my field of Health and Physical Education, I was also working for the Board! It was fun to see if my colleagues become nervous during their presentations, or if after they delivered a good point and questions were asked of them, how they responded if they did not fully know how to answer:

then the fun began. Occasionally I was called to the podium to clarify a point or two about an item that had been submitted, and my colleague was "figuratively" holding his breath, hoping I could substantiate the information and give a solid answer to support his agenda!

Of course, when this happened, the jokes and winks from the other directors were part of the game. As I made my way back to my seat from any follow up, it was always a major risk to communicate with testifiers, and I guess that was what made it so exciting. If it were considered a real "sting", a director would find funny things on the office desk the next day or even receive prank calls from friends, who would say they were from the Governor's Office and pretend they had complaints.

As I said before, it was like living two different lives. In one life, I had meetings with the agency on how they wanted me to function, as well as meetings on general budget issues that I hoped would not affect the areas I represented. Of course, the budgets for my field were considerably lower than the budgets for the "Main courses of study"!

I maintained my friendships with my colleagues in various school districts, as well as with Dr. Christian from the TAHPERD Organization. Through my many years of belonging to my State Association (TAHPERD), I have developed many quality friendships. Members often refer to our association as their "second family". It was evident to teachers, principals and others within a school, the closeness of the physical educators with each other and with their state association. There is a passion, energy and an observable family bond exhibited by the four thousand members in Texas.

It is a support group like no other! Each of the letters of the acronym (TAHPERD) represents the Texas Association of Health, Physical Education, Recreation, and Dance. TAHPERD has summer and winter conferences, leadership symposiums, as well as dozens of workshops throughout the cities, districts, and schools throughout the state of Texas.

Austin is the "Capitol" of politics, and over each hill and grassy slope, new state agencies make it their business to have representation for each of the school subject areas. Fine Arts had a beautiful building nearby with scouts from their discipline meeting frequently, sometimes on a daily basis with the Agency Director in their fields, making sure everything remained status quo or better!

My friends were happy for me! Happy that I was in this leadership position, and they felt "hopeful" and confident that I would continue to support their agendas. My view was to act as a "Watch Dog" for physical education and to be an advocate for the children and the teachers in our field.

In other words, they all supported me fully, assuming that if I had an idea that was different from the way things were currently being done, I would check with all State Associations first! If it were construed that "we" were not heading in the same direction, the Association's loyalty would be quickly withdrawn.

The Three Amigos

Roger Rodriguez   Marty Urand   Adolf Yanez
"The Mayor"   "The Commissioner"   "The Senator"

After thirty years, the "Three Amigos" unite on December 8, 2012, at Roger's daughter's (Elizabeth & Javi) wedding in Castroville, Texas.

I have two friends who served their school districts in the same position that I held when I was with Spring Branch, and we have been friends for over 30 years. The three of us had nicknames for each other and rarely used our real names when we were together. We referred to Adolf Yanez, from Dallas ISD as the "Senator". Adolf was a track star in his youth in Corpus

Christi and was the oldest of the trio. He was a great leader, runner, and politician!

The "Mayor", Roger Rodriguez, was a director of physical education for San Antonio ISD. He received his title as "The Mayor" after he bumped into Henry Cisneros, who was the Mayor of San Antonio and the keynote speaker at our state convention. While Mayor Cisneros was still holding his name tag, - Roger went over and asked if he could have the mayor's name tag for a souvenir. The mayor said, "Sure", gave the name tag to Roger, and ever since then, Roger has worn the San Antonio Mayor's name tag instead of his own at all TAHPERD functions.

Since I was with the State Department and under the direction of Dr. Meno, the Commissioner of Education, it was natural I was given the nickname by this group as the "Commissioner".

They were two of my closest male friends, and we usually believed in the same goals, and because of this meeting of the minds, they would back me up, and even "testify at State Board of Education meetings if I called on them!" During the four and a half years with the Agency, I called upon them several times. They were each good at testifying for beliefs we all held dearly, and they gave sound explanations, solid facts, and relevant examples, while keeping the attention of the school board members.

Quentin is someone I look up to as a great leader, and who, with the help of our members, led and guided our TAHPERD organization to develop and prosper. Under his leadership and mentoring, our members grew into a strong and respected state organization. He is a quality person whom I have strongly supported. Quentin is a man of high character, and most of us felt we could turn to him for advice and honest criticism whenever needed. He certainly wasn't a "yes" man, and he would think about our suggestions or questions and always explain why he thought our ideas would work or why they couldn't. The "mayor" and "senator", knowing Dr. Christian was from Mississippi, laughingly referred to him as "Mississippi Burning.

The "mayor" and "the senator" are dynamic individuals with superior leadership qualities, and they promote their districts toward developing superior, quality programs. The three of us are always willing to help when needed. I am proud to call them my friends.

A True New Yorker

If a meeting was particularly rough, Commissioner Meno sometimes called me and I would head down to his office where he would cut loose with a couple of swear words. Cussing is a native matter of pride to most New Yorkers, and outsiders could not keep up. Because of New Yorkers' accents and our colloquial vocabulary, we seem to have a special knack for spewing out and enhancing our cuss words! I was just his "vent" partner, and he would get it out of his system and return to his calm, professional self.

After a contentious meeting, Commissioner Meno sometimes put on shorts, tennis shoes, his Yale T-shirt, and started running down Congress Avenue right past the Capitol. He was in great shape, and his running seemed to help release his pent up frustrations, while mentally and emotionally cooling down his emotions.

He believed in health and wellness, and he demonstrated his passion for health, physical activity, and his belief in his overall wellness actions daily.

The Longest Four and a half Years of my Life!

As much as I admired Dr. Christie, who was now State Board Chairperson, I could tell he was fighting an uphill battle. He was idealistic and committed to health and healthy lifestyles, but he had some battles with a number of politicians. It was hard for him to deal with this day in and out! One of Dr. Christi's first efforts as Chair was to show his concern for being healthy in Texas. He knew the Commissioner of Education was a runner like himself, and felt that if he could get Dr. Meno's ear, he might listen to some ideas that would benefit the health of children.

After researching the finances of how the State of Texas received funds, one of Dr. Christi's first motions as the Chairman, was to prohibit accepting funds from the tobacco industry! The budget reflected that the highest percentage of funds came from the tobacco industry, but Dr. Christi did not want to utilize funds from drugs, as he put it. Unfortunately, he lost that vote, 14-1!

During my years with the Texas Education Agency as Director of Health and Physical Education, Dr. Christie opened the door for me and my objective of trying to abolish the activity of "tug of war" in schools in Texas. The Board just could not support the proposal against a Texas activity that they felt was an "apple pie" type of activity. Unfortunately, the vote was once again against 14 to 1! I could not believe the result, and unfortunately, I could do nothing but shake my head.

I spoke to the State School Board during the Board's monthly meetings as much, or more often, than any previous Physical Education Director had. I pushed strongly for things my colleagues and I considered vital for children, and I too often got my hand slapped when I came on vigorously during my presentations to the Board.

In one of my presentations, after presenting a point in the five minutes allotted to me, I closed with the statement, "Members of the Board, Commissioner Meno, I have never known of anyone who has died because they could not read or write! By their expressions, you would have thought that I told them to kiss my ass! Well, in so many words, I guess I had! After that comment, Meno immediately bent under the table to tie his "loafers", I assume so he would not be seen holding back his laughter. Dr. Meno also knew I had ripped my drawers on that one! One does not mess with the other sacred subjects or disciplines when you are in the field of physical education: which many still think of as the old typical P.E. exercise classes!

I always did my homework for State Board Meetings, and I contacted Dr. Christie and some of the other board members prior to the meetings to give them a question or two to ask me if they felt it was pertinent after my presentation or the comment time opened. If there were no questions or comments and just the sound of "crickets", I knew I was finished! The Board Chair would say, "Marty, thanks for your insight; we will consider your motion in our chambers". My time was done, stopped! All that research, preparation, and work.... and in five minutes, it ended!

Success came if the Board internalized the issues I was presenting. I had learned that it was crucial to hit on an issue that hit close to home for them, and then they sometimes allowed me additional time to make my points. I tried to make my concerns or suggestions relevant to health issues close to home; which might also include their own concerns for those of their children or grandchildren; then I might receive the nod to continue. If I could gain eye-to-eye connections with the Board members who were listening, while half were reading the next agenda item, I powered forward thinking there was still time to make that last point to "rev" up enough interest to continue or re-address the current issue.

It was delicate working with the School Board, but in thinking back, it was the most enjoyable phase and challenge of my position. I took great pride in preparing for the meetings when Physical Education was listed on the agenda. It was where the "Rubber met the Road" and what an opportunity it presented for our field. It did not take long during my career to realize, again and again, that physical education was on the bottom of the totem pole! There were too many academic problems to be dealt with, so we were frequently pushed to the bottom or "reset" to continue at the "next meeting". Therefore, having the Board's "ear" for even five minutes was exciting. Of course, when a topic on physical education was extended for whatever reason, it was celebration time!

The opportunity for positive changes was always an on-going goal for me. Education was in the midst of some major changes, and I hoped that our discipline of health and physical education would be considered as important as the other courses of study, and that we would be moved up the ladder of importance.

The Texas Education Reform

The State of Texas was in it's second year of an educational reform, and Ross Perrot was championing it. The shaping of education and the requirements being mandated for high school graduation were the bottom lines of the reform!

So, "turning off" the State Board Of Education was not a particularly smart move on any account! It took me several weeks to become familiar with the terms and actions of the SBOE. One term that was often used during these meetings, made a huge impression on me: The term was to "Sunset". It is such a beautiful term, especially in Austin, which is well known for their magnificent sunsets. However, the term did not in any way paint the true picture of what it implied in this educational setting. Here it simply meant ended, done away with, never to be seen or rise again! I knew that I did not want to be sitting on top of a program (physical education) that might be scheduled for a sunset!

Career heads South (The Three Strike Rule was in Affect)

Overall, there were three situations that helped send things south for me.

The Governor of Texas, Ann Richards, was a super person, and I loved observing her working with groups. Our building was across the street from the State Capitol and my office window, along with the office windows of several other directors' offices, faced the Texas Capitol building. It was a standard joke among the TEA employees that you should not be walking to the Capitol to discuss our particular issues there. It was a no-no to the first degree! With that in mind, Commissioner Meno called me and gave me permission to attend a meeting he had set up with the Governor.

My walk to her complex was fun as I looked back and waved to the fourth floor directors holding up signs in their windows indicating that they were going to tell! The meeting was about her re-election strategies for the upcoming year. Her question for me was, "How could she gain support from the "fitness" population?" My answer followed suit with Dr. Christian's battle to have a Governor's Commission on Physical Fitness and Sports. Therefore, between TAHPERD and the Governor, we came up with a plan to bring in Arnold Schwarzenegger, who at the time, was serving as Chair of the President's Council on Physical Fitness and Sports. Ultimately, Arnold came to Texas to kick-off the Governor's Commission on Physical Fitness and Sports. He was gracious with his time and consented to talk to thousands of school aged-children at Palmer Auditorium in Austin. I was thrilled to be able to serve as the emcee/filler to the sometimes out of control children until he came on stage. After only five minutes, the children were screaming and creating turmoil as we prepared to greet, *"ARNOLD SWARTZENEGGER"!!!*

After the tenth time, using the microphone, I yelled, to the screaming kids, **"Are you ready to meet Arnold!!?"** I could tell he was approaching the stage as the noise level kept growing and growing, reaching such a high piercing pitch that I could not even hear myself as I yelled into the microphone! As Arnold came on stage in the midst of the pandemonium of screaming children he had me hold his President's Council jacket. I had thoughts of making off with that jacket, which was the focal point of the press conference that was to follow. However, Arnold Schwarzenegger took the jacket back from me and held it out to Governor Richards, who was standing next to him. Then standing tall, looking down at Governor Richards, he held the jacket up to her chest and turned and looked at the audience, and said, "I don't want any of you thinking that this is going to be the start of *Twins II*!" Referring to the movie in which Danny DeVito had played his twin brother.

Even the children must have found it funny because everyone was laughing and yelling when Governor Richards put on the jacket, accenting the difference in the size between the two of them. Arnold Scharzenegger, having a great sense of humor, was down to earth with all of us.

I held his jacket backstage behind the curtain as I watched him leading the thousands of children in exercises. One of the exercises I remember the most was when he asked the children to stand and follow him. Arnold stood straight wearing a knit, short sleeve shirt and khaki pants. When he extended his arms out to the side, I saw his triceps hanging down, which immediately reminded me of my grandmother. I had always kidded her when she was cooking spaghetti that she had the biggest triceps in the world! With every stir of the spaghetti, her triceps flapped from side to side as she stirred with her large wooden spoon! However, Arnold's triceps were not flapping at all.

His triceps bulged with muscles and just hung down because of gravity! They would reappear once he bent his arms up as he motioned to the children to stand. It was unbelievable to see his arms so huge without him even trying to pump them up.

I had first met Arnold Schwarzenegger with the Texas governor for breakfast, and we were all looking him over as we greeted him. We all had the same thoughts, "Is this really him?" His face was exactly what each of us had pictured, but it was his body that did not fit with our memories. We expected enormously, monstrously large biceps with veins standing out at all times! When we saw him, he looked fantastically fit with large, strong muscles, do not get me wrong, but he was missing his familiar "pumped-up look". He still had the strongest body that any of us had seen, but not as over the top as we had thought.

During the exercise with the children, as light as the exercises were, he began to gain that pumped up "look". His arms became shiny with sweat, his veins were popping-up everywhere, and his accent became even more pronounced, while his muscles became more visible as we worked. Even his voice pitch gained more deepness and volume as he intensified each of his movements and exercise! By the time he finished demonstrating the push-ups, he had gained that massive "hulk" look right in front of our eyes. Arnold "flat out" "bulked out" and accomplished his mission! Everyone in the audience was animated and energized, the Governor was overjoyed, and the state took a major "healthy" step forward!

The following day I learned that I had been appointed as the Executive Director of the Governor's Commission on Physical Fitness and Sports. I was thrilled and felt honored. After accepting and thinking about the positive ramifications this could have, I met with Governor Richards in the Governor's Office to be officially welcomed and to discuss her thoughts and my thoughts on the direction we wanted to go. We discussed the need for me to select a committee to get things started.

Governor Richards maintained a low profile, but reiterated the fact that time was of the essence! I was to work with the publicity department to inform the media of the emphasis on fitness, health, recreation, and sports that she was pursuing for the youth of the state of Texas.

Willie Nelson gets me fired!

One of our first fitness promotions was with Willie Nelson who lived just outside of Austin. We filmed him first singing at a concert and turning to the camera and saying, "This is what I do to make a living". Then we filmed him again when he played golf. After making a putt, he turned again to the camera and said, "And this is what I do to live!" It was perfect, and three months later, just before production, I received another call from Commissioner Meno informing me that I will no longer be the Executive Director. No questions asked, no reasons given and it was over! I had a strange feeling that it was about elephants and mules!

Just when I thought Governor Ann Richards had written me off, I received a phone call asking that I meet her at a local gym. Being that I ultimately was working for her, I knew I needed to show up and present a positive attitude. I was still upset about being "canned" for the Willie Nelson outing! Governor Richards wanted me to assist her by giving her exercises that would strengthen her legs and ankles. I was hesitant to ask why, but I asked anyway! It seems that she had been given a Harley Davidson motorcycle, and although she did not want to drive it, she wanted to take a picture sitting on it and have the power to hold it up with her legs. We met a few times and she did see some improvement. However, I did not hear from her about it again. After she took the picture, the bike fell on her leg and it broke her ankle!

The rest was history as they say, and George W. Bush won the next election for Governor. Later I found out that Governor Bush and Dr. Christie were friends, and that the two of them would work together and I could again promote health fitness for children statewide at the very least. When George W. became President, I hoped that he might even appoint Dr. Christie to his cabinet, maybe as Surgeon General or even on the President's Council. However, that was just wishful thinking. …. No such luck!

At that point, my job was becoming frustrating. Any attempts continuing the pursuit of upgrading health and fitness for school children were put on the back burner. My pursuit of academic success was still ongoing, but the connection between exercise and health fitness to academics was now put somewhere in the back of the line.

For whatever reason, our health and fitness progress was just lost in the educational focus and I could tell that I was in a difficult situation. The process of having physical education or health fitness strengthened within the schools seemed to have become unimportant or irrelevant. Some of the disciplines saw us as the "Bad Guys" trying to intrude on their territory. Moreover, my passion and enthusiasm in demonstrating the success in uniting academics and health through physical activities were ignored.

The leaders at TEA did an about turn and I felt like I was on the wrong side of play! The funny thing was that all of these health enthusiasts, runners, Frisbee golfers, and hikers in Austin surrounded me, but the program focusing on exercise, health, and healthy lifestyles for children was still not getting anything in the way of support from the regime at the agency!

I was searching for something to help me to get out of my rut. It seemed that everything I was involved with was crumbling around me! I needed something to get my "teeth" into and relieve me of my "funk".

While eating lunch one day, I met a person from the Textbook Division of TEA. He told me that his daughter was a cheerleader in Dripping Springs, a short distance from Austin, and their squad needed assistance with their tumbling skills. He asked if I would be willing to work with the cheerleaders in Dripping Springs. Consequently, I began teaching and training these girls two evenings a week in an effort to upgrade their tumbling skills. At that time, many students in small towns did not have the opportunity to receive training from established gymnastics clubs like those available in Houston, and in other larger communities.

I had a feeling this was the "lift" I needed. I felt more alive, motivated to give the squads an opportunity to conquer their aspirations to perform a higher level of tumbling. This was the bright spot that I was missing in my professional life. Dripping Springs was proud of their athletic teams, especially the women's teams. The women's teams had just won a second State Championship in basketball and were very competitive in volleyball as well.

The front of their State Championship T-shirts read, "Dripping Springs, where men are men"... and on the back, it simply said. "And women are Champions!"

I worked with their girls' team during the last two years I was at the Agency. It was a short drive from where we lived, and the girls improved quickly in the short amount of time that we were practicing. However, more than that, it provided me peace of mind to be working directly with kids again!

Aussie and Babe

Therefore, with two strikes and nothing going well in the office, I decided that the remedy was to stay at home more. Then Dee and I decided to get a companion for our Great Dane, Babe, and we found a breeder of Danes in Austin, and fell in love with an off-white, blue eyed, Great Dane puppy, with a very light gray mask. We named our new Dane, Aussie. She was gorgeous and we almost brought home her sisters also, but thought about the food bill and that discouraged us. The two dogs, Aussie and Babe, played and got along well with each other, and they had plenty of room to gallop and chase animals. Babe loved to hunt, not to kill anything, but just the thrill of hunting and "playing" with whatever she could catch. A couple of times Abbie caught armadillos and brought them home for approval. Each time she carried one home in her mouth, the armadillo's legs dangled to the beat of Abbie's excited prance. She was so proud of her catches! We were not so dazzled, and I separated Babe from her "prize" immediately.

As the two Danes grew closer in affection and in size, they seemed to give each other more confidence. Danes for the most part are not especially brave. Each night when we let them out, they would first stick their heads and necks out the door to look all around, checking things out in the darkened evening. We never knew if they would charge out looking for excitement, or if they would get behind us, wanting us to go out first. They had such great personalities, and although very adventurous, they were always gentle with our daughters. Marti and Jacqui loved Abbie and Babe as much as we did.

The dogs range for exploring kept growing each day. We tried many methods of fencing them in, but the call of the wild was just too demanding, and they often found creative ways to get out and wander. Other than the three homes by the park, there was nothing for miles near us, except rocky hills and rangeland along with the cows, deer, and I didn't want to think about what other animals might be out there.

When Abbie and Babe saw either of our cars coming down the winding road, they sprinted to the gate, running and jumping, searching for any openings in our fence hoping they could get to us sooner. While Abbie and Babe were in this state of anticipation and exhilaration, they were hard to control. Therefore, when we did open the gate, we had to first lean against a car to keep the dogs from accidentally knocking us down as we calmed them down. Nevertheless, once Aussie and Babe received their desired attention, and had been petted and "loved", they relaxed and were just happy to be around us.

When Dee and I took walks with Aussie and Babe, they ran ahead to "hunt and discover", and then ran back to take us to inspect their findings. The dogs left their discoveries in various places along the trail, and as soon as we said, "Good Aussie-Babe", they would sprint off to explore for some new "treasures" to bring us.

L to R: Aussie, Marti, Dee,
Jacqui, Babe, and me.

Aussie and Babe knew the forest and trails well, and we sometimes traveled for a couple of hours through streams and large boulders that I am sure few people explored or knew about but us.

We always had a fear, which those not familiar with deer hunting might not understand, when we heard the three words: "Deer Hunting Season!" We worried that from a distance, our Danes could be mistaken for deer. While we were at work during "the hunting season", our Danes were large enough to mistakenly get the attention of overly excited hunters and we were concerned that some hunter might shoot before taking a better look to notice that our dogs were not deer. Our back yard was adjacent to the open hills and tree covered areas. We tried to be sure Aussie and Babe, were safe and put up a wire fence around an area next to our house. They still looked similar to deer in coloring and size, but we hoped with the fence, the hunters would stop and recognized them as pet dogs and not wild deer to be shot for food or trophies. We tried to contain Aussie and Babe during the hunting season by placing large orange collars and neckties on them so the hunters would identify as "pets" more easily.

During this time, Marti was working at a physical therapy clinic in Austin, and sometimes she took extended lunch hours during the hunting season to drive to our house to check on the dogs. Jacqui was still at Sam Houston State, and Dee worked in Bastrop, an hour and 30 minutes away, so Marti took it upon herself to help keep the dogs safe.

Our drive to and from work could sometimes be hazardous. Driving in the dark was an adventure as we tried to follow the twists, turns, cows, deer, and hills, which only got us up to FM 2222. Then we still had our drive twisting up and down hills to actually go to work. After we reached the main road to Austin, we carefully maneuvered another thirty minutes down the dark, twisting roads to reach Austin itself. On a good day, we were in Austin an hour after leaving our house. We tried taking one car when possible, and Deanna would drop me off downtown at Gold's Gym early in the mornings and then she'd take the car and drive the additional thirty miles for her teaching job in Bastrop. As for me, I was close enough to walk to work from Gold's Gym. But no matter how rough the travel, it was worth the drive.

Deanna worked in an alternative school, which had been set up to assist the junior high and high school students who were having behavioral difficulties in their regular schools or had been in trouble with the law. "Difficulties" was a mild term for some of the students who had been to the judge for their unlawful or unsuitable behaviors. A few were awaiting a judge's decision as to their final destination, with the possibility of going to jail, depending on an improvement in behavior and an improvement in their academic work. Nevertheless, because of the small classes, and the close-knit faculty and administrators, the atmosphere was positive, and a close bond formed between faculty, staff, and students. Deanna said it was a win-win experience and her favorite teaching assignment.

Marti and Jacqui,
Christmas on Lake Austin (1998)

Strike Three Was on its Way!

Halfway through the four years working for the Texas Education Agency, things really picked up! "A dream come true", you might say.

In one of my better sessions with Commissioner Meno, he asked me what I thought would be the best thing for the children that could happen in your area of physical education and health?"

My reply was immediate: I answered, "Both physical education and health need assessments in our fields like the other disciplines".

His reply was simple and expected. "You mean you want to test these kids to see how fast they are and how high they can jump?" I told him that I was hoping to broaden the scope that he had in his mind, and asked for time for me to explain my thoughts and goals.

We discussed many possibilities for several days and finally came up with a super plan: a Wellness Assessment that would focus on health and knowledge. Where students could prescribe and initiate their own individual exercise and healthy food plans for maintaining a healthy lifestyles.

I spent several months meeting with both health and physical education teachers so we could all work together to make our programs accountable. I found one thing out for sure; the two groups disliked each other! They each were afraid that they would have to give up too much of their own turfs and did not want to work together! I knew this was going to be a hard sell if both disciplines did not come to a common understanding about wellness. They seemed to be years apart to say the least! I remember the defensiveness of some of the teachers when I showed a transparency that simply said, "If you are not teaching health in physical education, then what are you teaching?" At that time, many of the teachers were teaching games and sports with no concern for the health issues and outcomes that accompany these activities! We hashed and rehashed our roles as educators and about what we *should be* teaching our students.

We had meeting after meeting and received input, as well as a buy-in to the new term of Wellness, which encompassed what the "physical education" teachers did. Once we had something together, and many teachers liked and agreed with the change of focus, I traveled to each of the twenty Regional Service Centers located throughout Texas to explain and promote the changes. It was simple, giving a definition to what Wellness was, and how students should become accountable. Interestingly, the teachers were not the only ones attending these meetings; some of the school administrators attended as well. School districts were becoming interested, but also concerned that their teachers in the areas of physical education and health should be accountable like other teachers and their subject areas. If this was to be the trend, the school administrators wanted to be sure their physical education teachers were ahead of the pack.

However, as with all changes, these were not received well by everyone, to say the least! Some teachers were hollering that I was putting an end to physical education. I had a very difficult time getting through to some of them, that this was not the case. Our discipline would be adding a cognitive component to our discipline. We could do this with tests and measurements, and we just had never done it this particular way! I emphasized that this would add credibility to the importance of our field.

The next year, I traveled once again to each of the Regional Centers, and this time had many physical education teachers at each center develop actual questions that could be used to assess the knowledge and understanding of our students relating to their physical and health-related information and skills. These questions were then submitted to and ultimately voted on by a group of teachers who met in Austin several times to read, discuss, and study the suggestions and comments we collected at the different Regional Centers in Texas. After analyzing and discussing the questions and information that would give the best overall picture of what we should be teaching and how our students could use that knowledge to benefit their physical and mental health. It was finally a way to assess and have concrete evidence to show the significance and usefulness of our classes to all students. This could give us ammunition to present concrete evidence of the benefits of Physical Education and Health, and really felt excited that this was heading in a positive direction. However, I guessed wrong!

The teachers who were close to me for many years and had been supporting the idea began to call and complain. They were all having too many within their districts balking at the idea. Everyone, the health teachers, and the physical education teachers were afraid of losing their teaching discipline to the other. The territorial lines were being drawn. My two "Amigos", who were supporters of the change, were also being pushed by their districts' teachers to stop this movement. As we were now losing supporters, many of the teachers wavered and began balking because of what they thought was the preservation of their physical education programs. However, there were still teachers supporting the idea, but none more so than Marcella Porter from Irving ISD. She was consistently on my side with this issue and believed strongly that the implementation of this new program was the right move for the children and that it would benefit our profession. She had to be careful however, because as active as she was with TAHPERD, we were not getting the majority support from them either. Christian, the director of TAHPERD, was representing and acting on behalf of his members and although the elementary teachers out-numbered the college and other members, the secondary teachers and colleges were calling the punches.

My best friends were calling me and letting me know that I was putting a dagger into their hearts! The bottom line was simple; a Mason-Dixon Line had formed between the Health Departments and Physical Education Departments. Each group did not want, in any way, to work with each other. End of that story!

I was circling the drain and trying my hardest to find some avenues that would permit this assessment or something along this line to take hold. It never happened! I received the big call from Meno, asking that the funding for this project be stopped. Sunsetted! He said, "Sorry, I have to pull the funding before we both get fired!"

A N.Y. Mom dies

When I thought things could not possibly get worse, my sister Ilene's husband, Dave, called to say that my mom had died in her sleep. She had died at the age of 70!

She had been having respiratory problems for several years, but had continued to smoke anyway. On the top of that, only two years earlier, she discovered that she was not her father's child. Her father of Irish descent had passed away when she was four years old and when her mother remarried; her mother's husband became my mother's "father". Can you believe living with two other sisters. and for 68 years never knowing that you were a step-sister! This, in my opinion, is the kind of thing that probably happens more often in New York and other large cities than in smaller cities or towns!

My mom was the oldest of the three sisters. Connie, the middle sister, had died fifteen years earlier. Rozy, her youngest was still alive, but Rozy and my mother had had a huge falling out and had not seen eye to eye for several years. My mom had made us promise that if anything ever happened to her, my sisters and I were, at her request, to NEVER notify Rozy, who still lived in New York. We have never contacted Rozy nor heard from her again!

The cemetery that we chose for mom was in Katy, where we all lived at that time, and it was a half-mile from Kips Gymnastic Club. Her grave sat a few hundred feet from the Katy water tower. On her head stone it reads, *A "N.Y." Mom.*

Time For a Change!

It was definitely time for a change! All I could think about was getting out of Austin. My "professional" family (TAHPERD) and my Amigos were not too happy with me. Both my parents were gone and I felt like the world was caving in on me. If it were not for Deanna, our kids, and Aussie and Babe, it would have been lights out! At this point, I felt like Marcella and Dr. Jack Watson were my staunchest friends within my TAHPERD family, and they had a very calming effect on me. During this time, I spoke with both on almost a daily basis for support!

Dr. Watson, a retired professor from North Texas State University, was a past TAHPERD President (1983-84). He was one of the oldest living presidents to serve us and he had a superior memory for dates and facts concerning the earlier days of our associations.

Dr. Jack Watson and I shared rooms at various conferences over a twenty-year period, and we became good friends. Each night after the conferences, we watched one basketball game after another on T.V. Jack and I both loved sports and playing "handball!" Jack continued playing handball until his mid-seventies. He was a walking sports encyclopedia when it came to

Kansas University. He had quite a background in the mid-west as well as the east, where he had received his Doctorate at Columbia University.

Through the grapevine, I heard that my good friend, Tom Hubble, had decided to go full time with continuing education, and was leaving his part time position as Health Fitness Coordinator in Spring Branch ISD. I called the Superintendent, Dr. Guthrie, and asked if the story was true? He confirmed it, and then followed with a question: "And how soon can you get here?"

Therefore, just prior to Christmas of 1995, I gave my two-week notice in Austin, to what only four and half years earlier, I had considered this position to be my dream job. Two weeks after my conversation with Dr. Guthrie, I slapped an 8x10 picture of me walking into the "sunset" on my office door in Austin, and happily closed the door of my office! I was done! So much for being a leader at a state level, "Change is what it is cracked up to be: difficult...and no one wants it!"

The bottom line, as I look back, is that I realize that I did approach some things the wrong way. I understand that the failure in my attempt at change had more to do with the way that I delivered the concept of this change that caused the failure. I consider much of it due to my lack of education in politics, and in my trying to lead the charge singly rather than educating and enlisting more teachers, so we could tackle it as a large group.

Second, (my thinking, fifteen years later) is that maybe I could have made the changes mentioned above, but I had become frustrated, and I gave up too early. Or was I too idealistic and dogmatic with an all or nothing attitude, unwilling to accept partial success? Dee wasn't happy with my decision to leave out of frustration. She thought I should have stayed until a conclusion was officially reached.

When I left for Spring Branch ISD, Dee stayed and finished out the semester in Bastrop and sold our palace on the lake. She cried when we sold the house, but reluctantly agreed that it had to be done. At this point there was no way I wanted to stay in Austin. I reported to Spring Branch to a standing ovation at the first district wide administrators' meeting. This gave me the lift I really needed to regain my motivation. I was glad to be home among friends who had fought the wars for change, regarding physical education, wellness, and for the "health" of children. At that moment, I knew my decision to "come home" was the right choice. Deanna still has second thoughts, but as usual she supported my decision once I'd committed to it.

It was almost like picking up where I had left off four and a half years earlier. SBISD, for the most part, had everyone on board the wellness movement, and that was a delight to me! The only thing different was that I had an empty feeling concerning some of the conflicts that had occurred while I was in the TEA position and with some of the negative situations I had incurred with some groups or members within the state association (TAHPERD). I was still hurt about our relationship and needed time to mend. Quentin and I remained good friends throughout the fiasco of that proposed paradigm shift in physical education and health. I realize that good and bad happens in all things and that TAHPERD had done so much that is good, I couldn't abandon the association; it meant too much to me! Although the days with the agency had been difficult and placed many of my friends and associates in a difficult position, TAHPERD stands tall in my mind!

The Staff was Great, but the Job was Difficult!

I was thrilled to be back at Spring Branch ISD, I always enjoyed working with teachers, both experienced and new. These initial learners (new teachers) were always a positive experience, fresh, excited, and open to new challenges. Their thrill just to be there was a joy and contagious to me and appreciated by the experienced teachers as well.

Sylvia Beatty, always a joy to work with, was one of the great teachers in our district and had been honored as the Elementary Teacher of the Year in Texas. She had been at Hunter's Creek Elementary for ten years, and I recommended that she move to the middle school for a change of pace. The school I had in mind was a Charter School called Westchester Academy for International Studies. Sylvia, rejuvenated, established a dance team which became popular not only at her school, but within the district. This was a perfect teaching position for her and her innovative ideas. She worked to have a health club located on the campus and then opened the "club" so the district employees could utilize it as well as students. I contacted the local

Bally's Fitness Club and they donated over fifty pieces of equipment for the use of our students and teachers.

It was exciting and re-energizing to work with teachers who were excited to share their ideas, and who were motivated and appreciative of the opportunity to test out innovative ideas and develop them with and for the students. We were united in our desire to improve the instruction and increase the interest of our children in their physical well-being. We had discussions with all those involved on how to increase the interest from the students in each of our programs. It was always win-win! The teachers were rejuvenated and the beneficiaries, of course, were the children. Over time, I came to the realization that the younger teachers were more amenable to change! They had not had the time to form poor habits or become set in their ways, and they seemed to enjoy novel and innovative ways of doing things.

One Spring Branch teacher, Joan Schrader, who was very close to retiring, excitedly embraced this new movement and developed pioneering ideas to enrich her Health Fitness classes. Her students loved participating in her classes, and within two years, Joan became Elementary Teacher of the Year! She is a wonderful educator who definitely thought and taught "out of the box". Joan developed a type of square dancing that elementary children loved; it was called "Dancing without Partners." Most children disliked holding hands with each other while square dancing. But without the hand holding, the children had fun and loved the dancing without being intimidated by needing to "touch" their partners.

Most of the teachers in Texas were seeking Joan out, inviting her to come teach this new dance method to them and their students. Joan traveled to other schools in our district and to outside districts to share this creative activity. I also loved when Joan was gone sharing with others, because I would get to sub for her and hang with her students.

The district is blessed with many exemplary teachers who care for children. These teachers were very professional, were members of TAHPERD, and quickly became leaders at the state and local conferences. When SBISD appeared in a conference program, there could be six to seven hundred teachers attending a "Spring Branch School District" session. TAHPERD scheduled the largest rooms for our presentations. We had a superior cast of teachers who presented quality workshops at conferences each year.

Another dynamic teacher who I encountered through the years was Connie Thrower. She was an outstanding teacher who children absolutely loved! She had them on an enthusiastic "high" 99% of the time. She wasn't one to necessarily perform on stage with us at our sessions, but she always attended and shared her ideas, and the other teachers were free to present them, which they usually did. Connie was also a master at getting donations for whatever holiday season we were in, and then she used the money to enhance her program for her students.

Connie taught at Meadow Wood Elementary for several years. She taught and trained her students how to walk on their hands, and by the time her students reached the fifth grade, they were walking on their hands up and down the stairs that led to her temporary "Gym" buildings. We all used these "temp" buildings prior to the new gyms that were eventually built.

A good lesson I learned working with teachers was that at some levels, a person with a good personality can go pretty far in teaching. But in working with elementary students, a teacher needs much more than just some knowledge and a friendly smile!

The Summer Coaching was Always a Highlight for Me! ROSA to the Rescue!

By the end of April, I was still choosing and seeking positive situations to get into. Maureen Madden, one of the elementary health fitness teachers contacted me to let me know about a swim team coaching vacancy at the local community swim pool. I contacted ROSA (Royal Oaks Swimming Association), I settled on a contract for the summer, and I was itching to start teaching again.

ROSA was a great community that has been around for a long time. When I was coaching in Katy, years earlier, ROSA was winning the Meet of Champions year in and year out. However, that had been quite a few years ago, and many of those swimmers were now in college. Fortunately, several of their younger sisters and brothers were still here and they were bright spots to build around.

I inherited a good older group of swimmers along with the non-experienced swimmers at the lower end of the age groups. I needed to teach many little ones to swim so they could be on the team and compete in the six and under category. One of my major challenges was a little girl, Sara, who was the younger sister of two of my stud swimmers (Jack and Ryan). She was a handful because of her fear! Her two brothers were record setters, but Sara was very apprehensive in the water... at the beginning!

Royal Oaks Swimming Association (2001)

Looking back, this was a great bunch of kids with whom I became very close. Color War found its place at Royal Oaks for four summers, and Color War allowed the swimmers to have a ball! There were always a few pranks that occurred during the three day festivities! Josh, a thirteen year old on the team, was my "right-hand" helper. Lane ropes were a chore each day for me and putting them out and rolling them up was not my cup of tea! Nevertheless, Josh loved it, and he organized the younger swimmers to complete this tactical task of getting the ropes rolled onto the giant rope spool before the pool could open.

Josh rode his bike to the pool every day, arriving at the same time each morning, almost to the second. He was a good helper, but he was also easy to rile if he got out of his organizational pattern. I depended on Josh, and he knew it and loved it! Early each morning I arrived with a cup of coffee and several donuts for anyone who happened to show up early to help out. I realized long ago that I was a water person, pool or beach, and I enjoyed kicking back and looking at the water, thinking about the day's workout and maybe a thought or two about little Sara and her fear of the water.

We started a Breakfast Club that met each weekday morning, thirty minutes prior to the beginning of practice. Josh and a handful of children who showed up early, always came and sat next to me as we listened to each of the Breakfast Club members' stories. We all cherished the half-hour or so of relaxation and comradeship, and at the end we all headed out to accomplish the tasks that I had assigned them.

At the pool, the highlight at the end of summer was Color War. Our entire team was divided into two halves (Orange team and Blue team) and then all Hell broke loose as each of the two teams began their challenges to earn points. Nothing was too far-fetched to be counted as points for or against a team. The pool became a war zone! The pool was always smoking due to frozen ice, floating candles, and balloons representing each team's colors! Points were also given for tricks played on either team.

The Blue team earned some points when Josh, who was on the Red team, came to the pool, crying that his bicycle had been stolen! Everyone was busting at the seams when we looked up and saw Josh's bike now painted all blue, standing on the roof top of the dressing rooms! He was mad and no one wanted to claim the points for that prank!

Two current school board members had children on the swim team. Josh's dad, Bill, was one of them. I had a feeling that Bill may have enjoyed the bicycle prank the most.

The other school board member was a mother of two of the best swimmers, who were really neat kids. All the girls loved them, and they were both born leaders. Beau was 16, and his brother Blake was 13.

This particular summer, we happened to have five boys competing for the four spots on the free style relay team. There was Gabe, Matt, Billy, Beau, and Jack. Jack was a baseball player who played at a high level. At the beginning of the summer, I told his parents that his absences would take a toll on his swimming participation, but I agreed to take a backseat to the baseball schedule, even though Jack did miss a lot. But he was such a hard worker and a great athlete that it didn't take much for him to keep up with the other swimmers in his group.

There was no problem when he was absent, because the four remaining senior boys would fill in for the relay teams and they'd still blow out the other teams. The problem arose when Jack was at the meet, because it sometimes caused confusion as to who was supposed to be swimming. So we all made a pact that by the end of the season, regardless of absences, the four fastest times would swim in the league championships. As one might guess, the school board's child had the 5th fastest time, but probably had the best attendance record! Beau wasn't happy, but he knew our rules, had agreed on them, and was a good sport about it. The policy had been set by the boys and me, so Beau was out! His mom was not too happy, but she played by the rules also! I can think of better things that could have occurred than to mess with a school board member! Over the years, we became closer, but I am sure it was never completely forgiven.

The senior boys and I were close, and we had a super relationship. The "Breakfast Club" and swimming lessons created a wonderful environment. ROSA was as close to actually attending summer camp as a person could get, and I loved it! We all had a great time for the four years that the pool remained open.

The neighborhood began to grow and apartments were being built nearby. I thought it might increase the size of our team, but I was wrong. The cost was too much for the tenants to join the pool. For those who did join, their children had not had any previous experience in swimming, and therefore, the experience did not turn out positive for them and they eventually quit.

Within two years of closing, the ROSA pool became a neighborhood park with the pool being filled in with dirt and grass! It was a loss for the team, their families, and the neighborhood.

My two "Buddies"

I was once again having my usual teaching withdrawals, and tried teaching gymnastics again, but found that my age was preventing me from spotting tumbling as well as I'd like. I brought in two super spotters and tumblers who were just starting out in college, who certainly helped me and the program.

My friend, John, was still cheering at a junior college. He certainly knew how to tumble, and he also had a good understanding of the higher levels of spotting. "Jay boy" was strong as a mule and he had the strong back that I was lacking. Both of the guys steadily improved and quickly became excellent spotters. John Neiser and Jay Cutler stayed with me as my right and left hands, and I am still in touch with them. I love them both like they were my own sons!

John Neiser

Michaelina and John Neiser

Both Jay and John found wonderful girls and each couple got married. I was asked to be in both of their weddings, which was quite an honor for me. At John's wedding to Mikki, the president of the college from which John had graduated attended the wedding.

I guess I stood out, being the oldest by a long shot, in John's bridal party, and the college President asked me how I knew John. With a straight face, I answered, "I was his parole officer!" I walked away and someone who overheard the comment explained to him that I was just kidding.

MARTY URAND

Aeson Neiser (2014)

My son-in-law, Chad, hired John to work at Cotton Restoration. Mikki, John's wife, graduated from UH in architecture and went to work for a builder. Their son Aeson, their pride and joy, came along shortly thereafter.

John and Mikki both loved our great Danes and decided to get two black male Danes that were both "Huge!" Watching Aeson playing with his 150-pound pets was something else!

John and Jay assisted me with tumbling, mainly for girls who wanted to be cheerleaders, until I retired from Spring Branch ISD. John had the most experience with cheerleading stunts, and I added tumbling know-how for Jay and John. We trained the girls mainly for middle and high school cheerleading.

John brought Rachel Pendray, who had already graduated from Spring Woods H.S., to our gym. Rachel had good tumbling skills from her high school days, and she was trying to make the Sam Houston State University cheer squad. Rachel needed a full twisting back flip to qualify for the collegiate squad and she asked John to help her prepare her for SHSU try-outs.

Since Rachel and John had both cheered for Spring Woods and were from the same neighborhood, John picked Rachel up and brought her to our gym to work with him on obtaining the higher cheerleading and tumbling skills for her upcoming try out at the college she was attending.

John worked diligently, and after six months, Rachel was throwing her "full". It was celebration time in the gym, for Rachel. She went back up to "Sam Houston State" and made the squad at the end of her freshman year. We were all so proud of her and her desire and motivation.

However, soon after the summer ended, I received a call from John. It was very much like the time he had called, telling me his dad had passed away on a flight to Hawaii. I could tell by the tone of his voice, that this call was bad news as well. He read me the news in the paper: It was unbelievable!

News

Sam Houston State cheerleader killed in apparent murder-suicide

Monday, December 04, 2006
By Elissa Rivas (12/04/06 - HUNTSVILLE, TX) (KTRK)

-- A college student from the Houston area has been struck down in the prime of her life. The Sam Houston State University cheerleader was killed in what police are calling a murder-suicide. Police say a male friend shot her, and then turned the gun on himself.

From Houston, but attending school at Sam Houston State University, Rachel Pendray was shot to death by a male acquaintance in an apparent murder-suicide at the apartment she shared with friends in Huntsville.

Rachel was a sophomore, a cheerleader, and pre-nursing major. She graduated from Spring Woods High School in Houston, where she had also been a cheerleader.

John attended the funeral and I knew the impact it had on him and the family and friends of Rachel. We hear of disasters that cost the lives of people on a daily basis, but it certainly makes you think when it comes to a person that you know so well!

Jay Cutler

Chrissy and Jay Cutler

Jay is from Boston of all places, and we had running arguments, since I was a Yankee fan. His wife to be introduced us while he was working at Home Depot. I could tell from his outgoing personality and his love for children, proved that we needed to be working together! We worked for years in swimming and gymnastics. During this same time, I was able to hire him as a physical education aide at the elementary level where he found his love for teaching.

He was firm with his Boston accent, and loved to laugh! Children loved him! It was at this point in his life that he began college and obtained his teaching degree from UH.

At their wedding, I felt like I was in the cast from the movie, "The Departed", with all the New England accents echoing in my ears! Many of his Southside Bostonians came down for this blowout! Jay married my assistant swim coach at ROSA (Chrissie, a gem of a person!) who is also the music teacher at an elementary school in the Spring Branch School District. Her talent did not stop there; she was also Director of the Boys Choir and travels throughout the nation performing.

After graduation, Jay took a job teaching third grade at an elementary school within the Houston ISD. Chrissy and Jay love children and adopted three in one haul! It was without a doubt, a "Win-Win, made in heaven for all parties involved!"

The Cutler Family Christmas, (2013)
Jay-boy, Rainey, Chrissie
Stormy and Dusty

For the past eight years, Jay, John, and I have reunited for the "Camp Lawrenz" fundraiser. The three of us, along with Jay's son Rainey, and several of my students from both colleges, joined other teachers from SBISD to work the camp. This camp provides many activities, but we went to teach the gymnastics sessions. We have so much fun working with about 150 students during the camp. We divided the participants into three groups of fifty elementary students who rotated through each of the three activities during the three hours of the camp. The three of us have remained good friends, having bonded through the sport of swimming and gymnastics!

My daughters decide to get married!

Chad Weigman and Jacqui had gone to different high schools, but they had met each other at a baseball game in high school. It was bottom of the ninth, bases loaded, and down by 2. Chad was at bat against Taylor's pitcher, Robby. One swing later, the game ended with a grand slam! While the teams were preparing to load up their gear, Jacqui brought the home run ball over to Chad. That was it, no hearts and flowers or hugs, they just met and went on their separate ways!

However, they met again at Sam Houston State University and began dating in college. Chad was on a football scholarship at "Sam" and played middle linebacker. Dee and I went to one of his games with his parents and it was quite a show. He was fast, strong, aggressive and loved the game! The quarterback, Chad and another player decided to start a business together after they graduated. The name of the business is Cotton Restoration and has become very successful.

Unfortunately for Jacqui, during the game I watched a cheerleader being passed through the stands. I guess it was that little stunt that caused me to give a negative reply when Jacqui asked if she could tryout at the end of the year! She soon fell in love with the dance squad that Dee and I enjoyed on a safer note!

Once Chad and Jacqui decided to get married, Jacqui went to work for "Together" a dating company in Houston, and interviewed prospective clients. Jacqui soon led the nation in sales. It certainly helped with giving out the best cigars money could buy!

Chad Weigman and Jacqui
Urand, August 14, 2008.

Marti and Scott Fisher met at the elementary school where I was teaching in Katy. Scott was a super kid that excelled in sports. They dated off and on while he attended Texas Tech and Marti was at Texas A & M.

Marti was an "Aggie" and we attended many home games. Marti was involved with her sorority and received many honors during her four years.

They were married for five years and parted friends

Coaching in the Summer
"A sure mental pick-up"

After two years off from coaching swimming, some of the parents who were at ROSA, contacted me about a coaching vacancy at Spring Board Pool, which was a couple of miles down the road from ROSA. It was perfect for me, and again I was excited about getting the opportunity to work with many of my old kids! The team had always struggled getting funds for this pool. The pool had been around for many years. In fact, we bought our first house on Pine Lake Drive down the street from this pool, and Marti and Jacqui learned to swim at this very pool.

I took over the team with 57 children, and after four years, we had increased our numbers to 185 swimmers. Spring Board turned out to be the best team and coaching position that I had in my long career of coaching swimming.

Once again, I relied on my swim team to lift my spirits and assist me with the stress in my life! I knew I had, at the most, three years with Spring Board and pulled out all the stops, wanting to make the team as good as it could be. I held swim clinics and brought in Dr.

Joel Bloom from UH on two occasions during the year to help with technique. He is an aquatic genius and all the swimmers and staff really benefited from his tutelage.

I had a great staff working with me each of the summers I worked with the swim team at ROSA. Katie Loewen, Emily Hurstmann, Jennifer Edwards, and Sara Ruffing were all back at ROSA and the swimmers loved them. And the boys, Jason Harn, Nick Olsen, Ryan Giesler, Bullet, Grady, and the West brothers were great role models for the young kids as well

Every day was filled with fun while working with these focused teenagers and these diligent kids. I always preached to the staff that, "We don't teach fun, but fun is the product of good teaching!"

These children were from hard working families and they knew what work was! The team slogan was, "We work hard and party hard!"

Positive things were always happening at the pool. There was a tremendous amount of pride among the parents as they planned and worked diligently to prevent their pool from being turned into a park! The pumps and motors were held together with Band-Aids like "sutures" due to a low cash flow, but they were held together.

Many champions were developed while swimming at Spring Board Pool, and many swim records were broken by these boys and girls. I believe the parents' commitment to their children, and their hard work to provide them with opportunities, provided wonderful role models for the children. The children modeled themselves after many of those involved with the swim team, from swimmers, coaches, parents, and even other swim teamers. Our swimmers never gave up. These children did not have the attitude of "I can do it", but the attitude of "We can do it". They taught me a lot!

The Turner Family
Miles, Denise, Caroline, Claire, and Todd

Coach U-

It is so hard to express just what you mean to my family. Words cannot explain what I feel you have done for us and have given our children. Never did I think that our little neighborhood swim team would have such an impact on not only our children, but on Todd and me as well.

Soon after our first swim lesson, I quickly and quietly nicknamed you, 'The Baby Whisperer', and the name quickly caught on with the other moms joining our team. You have such a way with children that just seems unreal! None of us could understand just how you were able to get the kids to do what they were accomplishing . . .even when they started out scared to death to come near the water! Remember our first lesson ever: Miles, 4; Caroline, a month shy of 3; Claire, Miles was enrolled with two other kids and none of the three were all that interested in getting in the water. Every time you asked who wanted to come into the water next, Caroline would jump up from the sidelines (she was not even enrolled in the class) and yell, "I do, I do!" After a few unsuccessful attempts on her part, you finally relented and said, "Well, ok, come on Little Bit." In she went like a flash and never looked back. That was the beginning of a wonderful friendship. Three seasons later (at age 5), you coached her all the way to winning the Meet of Champs, 6 & Under with a 19.8! Unbelievable!

Your second season as our coach was the year you asked Miles to swim up with the 7/8 yr boys relay at the Meet of Champs. They were missing a relay member and would have to forfeit. I am sure you do not remember my reluctance. It took everything I had to hold it together while watching him on the starting block ...... he was so nervous ..... and so small! He did not want to let the 'older' boys down! I don't know what you told those older boys, but Parker, Preston and Grant, as disappointed as they were.. were so gracious and supportive of Miles . . .even after their 7th place finish! Miles, was on top of the world . . . he had his first medal... and a new found confidence! In one event, you managed to teach all involved parties life lessons: the older boys, patience and humility; Miles, confidence and perseverance; and me, pride and encouragement. Subsequently years yielded better results for him and I do believe it was because you showed him that you believed in him from the beginning.

By the time Claire was old enough for swim team, you had already moved on. I tried working with her on my own to no avail. It wasn't until you worked your magic that she flourished.

MARTY URAND

No one could believe that I would drive her 25 miles away during rush hour traffic for a swim lesson . . .until I told them who was teaching her! It worked like a charm, and she is now as confident as her siblings! I'm so thankful she didn't have to miss out!

Looking beyond your work with the little bitties, I have always been equally in awe of your relationship with the teenagers of the team. I'm so amazed that so many teenagers, both young and old, came voluntarily to the pool (freezing water and all!) daily to help run practice as Junior Coaches! I personally believe they all just wanted to hang out with you! Little *did you know that you were being given the opportunity to be the teacher! The biggest bummer of all is that my kids won't have the opportunity to 'coach' along side you!*

Five years have passed since our first meeting and I'm not sure who has learned more from you . . . our kids who have learned by being coached by you, or us(as parents) who have learned by watching you coach. Either way, it is certain; we have all 'won' from meeting you! Your impact on my children is immeasurable and everlasting. You laid the foundation for the confidence they achieved not a boastful confidence, but confidence with respect. *I am forever grateful that you were the 'first coach" in the lives of my children.*

Thank you — thank you —thank you,

Denise and Todd Turner

Another "Sunset was in Store"

1999 was a bad year for Deanna and me, as Aussie was diagnosed with cancer, and we had to put her to sleep. Within two months, Babe broke her hip and we had to put her to sleep as well. Deanna and I were devastated and decided to hold off from getting another dog.

The Retirement Home

We were living in Spring Branch on Parana, with a nice pool, but that water just did not take the place of Lake Austin! Then one Saturday we went water skiing with some friends and fell in love with a house on the San Jacinto River, east of Houston. Still not what we had in Austin, but at least we were able to go boating and water skiing again. In one month we were living in that house in the Rio Villa subdivision. The house is built on stilts in case of flooding, so the water can pass through under the home if needed.

The trip into Spring Branch from Rio Villa was a little hectic. Thirty miles in busy traffic was something we both had to get used to again, especially when the

Astros played an early game or the Rockets were in town, which immobilized the freeways!

"MarDee Beach" home on the
San Jacinto River, 1999

We had to drive right through the downtown area freeway and the travel time could escalate up to an hour and a half during those times.

Being down at the river and sitting on the dock without a pet felt sinful! My daughter Marti did the leg work and found a black and gray "Brindle Dane" that was up for adoption and called me about it.

At six weeks old, this puppy was taking on the look of a junkyard dog! However she was a sweetheart, and we all fell in love with her as we spent more time with

MARTY URAND

her.. She was still a puppy and full of mischief, and I worried about protecting her from falling into the river. We nearly did not have to worry about that after she ate the varnish off of the wood in our enclosed basement. It was three days in intensive care before we got her back.

Our daughter, Marti didn't have room in her apartment for her Great Dane, Daisy, and we were elated when she let us adopt Daisy. Now we were back to a two Dane family once again. Abbie (our junkyard looking Dane) had been given that name on behalf of Aussie-Babe (A-B), (therefore coming up with the name AB-ie! Daisy had a light cream colored coat and beautiful eyes. She was both beautiful and loveable.

Abbie, Daisy, and Conner on the
San Jacinto River (2002)

Never Underestimate the Power of Athletics

In 2000, a highlight from the past came true for our National Championship basketball team from Pan American College. Thirty-seven years after being crowned the N.A.I.A. National Basketball Champions, the members of that team all received emerald diamond studded rings with our names and numbers engraved on them. It was a closure for a wonderful experience.

What a blessing, seeing our old teammates from all over the country traveling to my home to receive our "Championship Rings". My daughter, Marti, had surprised us and had the event announced on Houston radio, and we played the announcement just before receiving the rings from the Athletic Director, Scott Street.

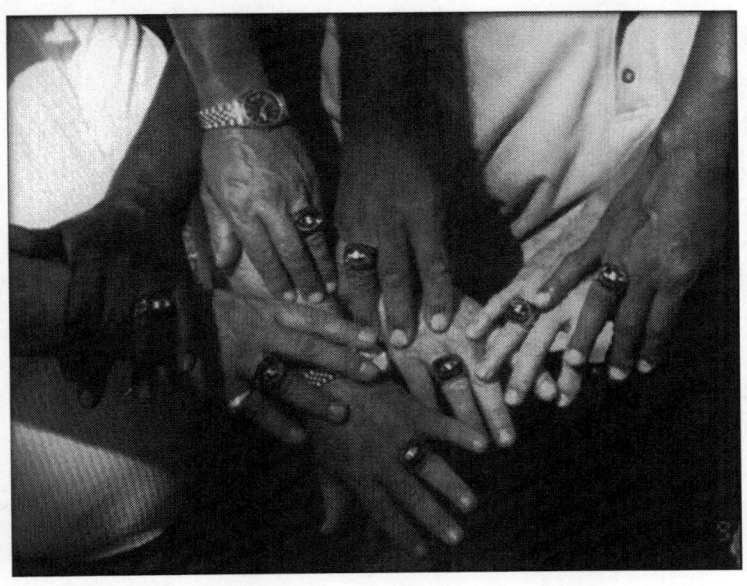

It was interesting, after all these years, how this even came about!

Back when our team was playing at Pan American, a young boy with exceptional leadership ability figured a way to get into our Pan Am games-free. I mentioned him and his friend earlier. He and his friend, David Garza, "visited" the orange grove just across the street from our gym. Then they brought some of the oranges they had "harvested" from these groves to the team, which became their tickets into our games! Both these kids loved being around athletes and having a "little" part of our nationally known team. Moreover, we cared about these boys as well.

Both boys grew up in the Valley and they became very successful men! David and his wife had twin boys who I later coached at Edinburg High School. David became a police officer and Gilbert is currently an Athletic Director for San Antonio ISD, with "the mayor," (Roger, the Director of Physical Education).

JJ. Avila built and owned successful health clubs around the Valley and JJ donated the funds for the championship rings to honor us, 37 years after we won the title! What a dream come true for all of us!!!

One of the principles that I share with my college students is that we never know how we may affect children and become motivational sources within their lives.

Getting back to TAHPERD

My school district work was both enjoyable and rewarding. We were like a big family and some of our teachers had even been students in a class I had taught at the University of Houston.

By my second year back at Spring Branch, I felt rejuvenated and was excited to again be working with my school district and TAHPERD.I had needed that brief break as I again began participating in the Leadership Conference, and conducting workshops in school districts within Texas.

By the year 2000, I had agreed to run for TAHPERD President and I was excited to be elected the following year. Becoming President was a goal that I had thought about for over twenty-five years. It actually meant more to me than the TEA work that had been a paying job!

Marcella Porter, a Past President,
had a greeting for me at Irving ISD
in the School Board Room (2001)

The Executive Committee, also known as the "EC", was made up of a President-Elect, President, Past-President, and the Executive Director.

Traveling during the three years on the committee was a major responsibility. Spring Branch had to give consent for the many absences that would be caused by the travel and help with financial support for my dual representation for our district. The lodging and room arrangements worked out well, since there were two females who could share one room and two males who shared the other.

I really enjoyed the workshops when I was rooming with the Executive Director, Dr. Quentin Christian,

MARTY URAND

because he was a wealth of knowledge as well as a very innovative thinker. Quentin was also a Past President and Executive Director of our National Association. He is without a doubt a very capable leader and someone that I admire and trust.

As President-elect, Quentin and I traveled extensively with the Executive Committee of TAHPERD. (Reston, VA., 2001)

Quentin Christian was the Executive Director of TAHPERD for only half of my term as President. He was a wonderful leader for the state of Texas. I felt blessed to have the opportunity to learn from him and his extraordinary career! He is a multi-talented individual! He is a talented artist who displayed his talent at each of our conventions. Our journal led the nation in overall quality and design. Quintin is a southern gentleman with a great sense of humor. A storyteller bar none!

But with all his good qualities, I felt like he was railroaded by a few past officers of TAHPERD and I am still somewhat bitter about the way he had been treated. It did not please me to see him ousted the way it panned out! Unfortunately, politics shows up everywhere! Quentin's classy handling of our association ranked him as the nation's outstanding administrator. Even with the backhand that he received, his attitude and gentle approach toward people raised him even higher in the opinion of many.

Planning is a major criterion for the backbone of our Association and everything is well thought-out several months prior to each event. I learned a great deal from the TAHPERD association, took the planning structures within TAHPERD, and utilized many of them within Spring Branch ISD.

The Polar Company donated one hundred heart monitors to be distributed as our committee saw best. Our committee awarded the monitors to be distributed to the "Major's Clubs among the colleges who had students attending. Partly because of this incentive, the Conference had the most college students attending our convention in the history of our association!

I never really reached a point within my presidency where I wished that my presidency had never occurred! But there are always frustrations in these situations, but "Lexapro" kept me in there, along with the help of Marcella and Jack!

While selecting a keynote speaker for the Second General Assembly, things went south in a hurry! In the history of TAHPERD, a President had never been denied his or her choice of a speaker. However, that is what happened to me. After several weeks of arguing, the by-laws stated that when an Executive Committee cannot come to a decision, then the Board of Directors would have to be called in to assist with the decision. Since the B.O.D. had already had their quarterly meeting, they would have to travel to Austin to hear the case. This would have cost the Association $26,000, which I did not think was fair. The new Executive Director, Dr. Diana Everett, came up with a solution. Why not bring in the Parliamentarian, Dr. Betty Myers, from Texas Women's University to facilitate the meeting. I agreed with their decision.

After hearing the case, Dr. Myers decided that the President should have the right to select his own speaker. My choice was Ms. Beth Kirkpatrick, a representative for Polar Inc. She was the salesperson for the heart monitors that were bringing accountability to the "playing field". She was a dynamic, aggressive, six-foot woman who presented to standing ovations all over America!

The objection to her speaking was that the executive board felt that she would utilize the stage for promoting her business rather than delivering a state of the art speech, motivating teachers to leave at the end of the conference vitalized, refreshed, and leaving with new ideas and building blocks to support and strengthen their teaching ideas. I had talked to the speaker about this issue and she said she understood the issue so I believed we should give her the chance to fulfill her contract with us.

I had heard her vibrant speaking sessions before and was looking forward to another dynamic, presentation. Unfortunately, I ended up owing an apology to the Executive Board, as they were partially correct in their thinking. Although she did give an excellent presentation, she did bring up and promote her product during her speech. Most of our general audience loved the presentation saying it was very well done and they were happy with the basics of her message and thought she was very good. Although some in the audience may have seen her presentation as advertising, it was evident to those of us who had selected her as presenter, that the edge towards promoting was a little more than we had expected. Other than "leaning" toward her product, Beth's speech was as powerful and well received as I had imagined! And I was correct in one area, it was nothing but a standing "O" for Beth!

My daughters Jacqui, Marti, and Wife Deanna

This conference had been a great experience and I learned so much by working with so many qualified professionals. The following are a few of my memorable experiences:

The Summer Conference was held at UT-Pan American in the Rio Grande Valley. I was delighted for my alma mater to be the host! In fact, *Sportime Inc.* financially supported a beach party on South Padre Island. Dwayne Puckett of *Sportime* brought in the "Teachers of the Year" from other states and these teachers taught many of their activities on the beach during the conference.

Sportime also provided each attendee at the Summer Conference with a basketball with the conference's logo. I had chosen to represent the conference as, *The Power of One*, printed on one side of each ball! I was so proud to be in a position to give basketballs to everyone who had attended this summer conference held at my alma mater, where I had played basketball. There were over five hundred attendees represented at our Summer Conference!

Another unique experience I planned with a longtime friend, Esther Lopez from Edinburg, also occurred at UTPA. We provided three buses to transport the teacher attendees to Progresso, Mexico for dinner on the first night of the conference. Again it could not have been done without the support from *Sportime* and TAHPERD!

The TAHPERD State Convention was held the first week of December in Ft. Worth. Many memorable experiences enriched my life and I hope enriched the lives of the attendees during my tenure as President of TAHPERD.

My Westchester Academy gymnastic team was the convention opening.

Performers: Bottom: L to R: Valerie Falerio, and Jessica Sornson, Middle Row: Kate Green and Jenny Sornson,

Back Row: Kate Sornson, Danny Dyer, and McKenzie Gillium

Fortunately, I was able to bring my gymnastics group to open the first General Session at TAHPERD to present a super performance! This group was from Westchester International School of Studies in Spring Branch ISD.

Our Presidential Suite was huge with three bedrooms and a massive living room. Dee and I had the master bedroom, Garland O' Quinn had one of the other bedrooms, and some of my male students from the University of Houston occupied the third bedroom. Not only did the students short sheet my bed, but each night Dee and I retired to our room to discover a new innocent, but funny prank for the evening.

My theme during my Presidency was *"Health is in your Hands: The Power of One."* This idea came to me when I was visiting with Dr. Christian on one of our trips. His theme when he was the National President was also "The Power of One!" and I wanted to take the idea of his national theme and bring it to Texas.

As the first of the three General Sessions began at my convention, thirty health fitness teachers were in the aisles, each wearing a white glove on one hand. They were performing a synchronized hand movement to "A Beautiful Noise", by Neil Diamond. The words to the music are so meaningful, especially to educators. The last lyric describes a beautiful noise coming from the street (cars, horns, and the sounds of children playing in the background), *"and it was coming into my room waiting for me to give it a tune!"*

When the people in the auditorium were seated, Garland O'Quinn did his "thing" that he does so well: to lead an audience in hand movements to rhythmic beats. Garland is so honest and sincere, and what he says is exactly what he means. Because of the pureness

MARTY URAND

in Garland's thoughts and actions, he is loved and admired by everyone (especially his students)! He has a smile that is contagious and a heart as big as Texas!

Garland O'Quinn my mentor for forty years!

I was so proud to have so many of my friends involved in the conference, as well as the teachers from Spring Branch leading and organizing the General Session. My Keynote speaker was Dr. Buddy Gilchrest from Baylor University. He is a person that mesmerizes not only me, but also all of his audiences with his stories. Through Dr. Gilchrest's description of his sights and experiences, he formed a pictorial of breath-taking scenes from his adventures of climbing mountains. If anyone ever heard God speak aloud to an audience, I am sure they would tell you that it sounded very similar to Buddy from Baylor University! I was on cloud nine as Buddy spoke from his heart and shared his love of nature.

After he finished his inspiring presentation, I was off the stage and standing in the back of the auditorium as the lights dimmed and the Power Point presentation began. Marcella Porter, Jack Watson, and I had been putting together the Power Point during the past year. A picture of each past TAHPERD President flashed on the huge screen, set to the music we had chosen from the era of that president's tenure, and my heart was beating faster. The attendees in the audience could be heard whispering, clapping, and cheering, especially when the faces of the familiar and more recent TAHPHERD presidents began appearing on screen to "their" music. The applause heightened with the change to each year's president, especially as it got closer to our more recent presidents. All members, cheering and honoring their memories, respectfully acknowledged the presidents who had passed away. During the twenty-minute presentation, I paced in the back, as tears filled my eyes and at times even having to try not to sob loudly. This was such a monumental moment for me, as I saw the faces of those who had meant so much to our profession, and had meant so much to me during my forty years working with them. And now, being able to honor their leadership meant everything to me.

A special feeling came over me when Marcella Porter's and Jack Watson's pictures appeared. They always motivate and inspire me through their supportive, sharing, and honest critiques, which always make me think deeply before making major decisions. I have such a high regard for these leaders, and so many other leaders at TAHPERD!

Quentin came in from California to attend this Conference. He had left Texas and now was in a three-year term as the Executive Director for CAHPERD, in California.

I was so happy to have him in attendance; he, with his wise leadership, also had inspired me through the years. During our rooming days when attending other conferences, we had shared so many dreams, and this conference was the culmination of all the ideas, planning, encouragement, advise, and history that had all came together, inspired by so many of the leaders and peers from TAHPERD. The video, the music, and past Presidents remind me of how far our profession has come and how we have advanced and grown under their leadership.

Dr. Jack Watson, Marcella Porter, and I supported President Dr. Mike Bobo (Texas Tech) at one of his last President's Luncheons. Mike and I had attended graduate school under the direction of Dr. Billy Tidwell at Sam Houston State University.

Spring Branch supported me!

It meant so much having the teachers from Spring Branch assisting me, leading, taking charge of assignments, and always carrying through on all the events professionally and with love. This group always kept going, above and beyond. I will never forget the creativeness of this group of teachers and the support, hard work, and ideas they gave to me, to our District, to TAHPERD, to Spring Branch ISD, to teachers from other districts, and more importantly to their students.... I still feel chills when I think back to all that was accomplished because of so many great people. Karen Fitzgerald, the Gifted and Talented Director at SBISD, attended the convention to support our goals, our teachers, and me. Karen and I became very close over the years, and we retired at the same time. During the same year I was President of TAHPERD, Karen was President of the Texas Association for the Gifted and Talented.

Texas Association Presidents
Craig Weller (Music), Karen Fitzgerald
(Gifted and Talented), Gloria McCoy
(Art) and myself (2002)

Spring Branch was a leader among Texas school districts. Gloria McCoy was President of the Art Association and Craig Weller was the President of the Music Association. It was special and highly unusual that all three of us would become presidents of our associations during the same year!

Although we each had differences of opinions on how our disciplines should line up with each other at our schools, and we fought against each other to keep or "add hours" for our particular disciplines, we eventually came back to the center and worked together as a unit for our district.

MARTY URAND

I guess, in our own ways, we each guarded our turf! Improving programs and strengthening these disciplines in SBISD is what we were each hired to do, what we each believed in, and fighting against each other for the children in "our" fields was basically what made each of our programs so strong.

Bond Election: "A Highpoint for Health Fitness!"

A Bond Election is a very important event in the life of a school district. It is when a district asks the community to assist them with their financial needs regarding new facilities or refurbishing the old ones. In SBID's bond election, our teachers lobbied to have gymnasiums built in the elementary schools. At a cost of approximately $1.6 million for each school, 27 elementary schools needed these new or upgraded facilities; Dr. Guthrie took the lead in pursuing and promoting this action. The community supported the massive Bond Election and within the next five years, gyms were built on each of the elementary campuses in SBISD.

Spring Branch School District was one of the last major districts around the Houston area to add gyms at the elementary level, so the teachers who had been around for a long time were ecstatic with the new air-conditioned venues for instruction. Of course, the children were euphoric as well!

Dr. Guthrie was a strong supporter of health fitness and believed in the importance of our discipline. He and I got along well, and I feel like I owe so much of my positive career in the schools to him, for his support of the importance of physical education for children. When Dr. Guthrie retired, I worried that a new Superintendent would not have the strong understanding of the importance and value of physical education. I had always hoped Guthrie would continue as superintendent until after I had retired! However, that was not the case. I was relieved and happy when we received the word that Dr. Guthrie, our superintendent who had retired, had been replaced with my wife's middle school principal, Dr. Duncan Klussman. Deanna had always told me what a great principal he had been at Spring Branch Middle School, and she was sorry to see him leave her school. I was blessed having had two excellent leaders who both cared about health fitness and the health of children.

With my presidency of TAHPERD almost finished, I began looking forward to the day I would retire. However, for now, I was excited about spending the end of my public school career working with the gym architects and watching the progress as our gyms were built. I was determined to do everything I could to be sure our teachers had the best, before the "Sunset" would once again cast a shadow over my office.

With a couple of years to go before retiring, McGraw Hill Publishing Company asked me to write up the *Health is in your Hands* activity book.

They wanted to utilize my idea of adding these cards with activities as a supplement for the new textbooks in physical education that they were promoting. They also asked if I would become a representative and conduct workshops throughout the state.

Health is in your Hands

I worked diligently each day promoting the supplement, and talking with groups to show them that we had the best educational package among the other publishing companies. Unfortunately, the textbook adoption "split" many of the educators in Texas, and we did not receive enough support from the adoption committees to achieve our objective of adopting what we felt would have been the best textbook for our state adoption.

"The bench strength grows"

With just two years remaining before my retirement, some good happenings occurred within the family. First Jacqui and Chad gave birth to a son, Conner Allen (Allen, my middle name as well!). In addition, my other daughter, Marti became engaged to marry Gene Johnson. Gene, a nice ex-jock from Oregon, is bright, loves my daughter, and we enjoy talking about sports.

He had two sons when they were married, Alex, 11, and Casey 9, and we spent some time enjoying the two boys as they grew up. The boys participated in sports, music, and other activities. Both of the boys played soccer and basketball in school as well as recreationally. At this time, both boys are now in college, one at Oregon State, and one at Texas Tech.

Marti and Gene thoughtfully worked around my swim season to have their engagement party in the Dominican Republic. Gene rented a villa overlooking the ocean and he invited his family, our family, and a few of his and Marti's friends. What a great time we had for five days! He was definitely good to Marti and a great person to add to the team!

It seemed that the family spirit was increasing and with that in mind, Cousin Mark, coincidentally called me after many years of us being out of touch. He informed me that Ruthie's husband, Murray, had passed away and when he was at Murray's funeral in New York, the family had inquired about me. Mark took it upon himself to reach out and get in touch with me and he reopened the connection between our families. With that one call, I began reconnecting with other members of my family as well. Deanna and I traveled to Florida to visit my favorite cousins, Ruthie and Delly. Sadly, during the year of making the plans for the road trip, Hy, Delly's husband, passed away. The trip was rewarding as I could share memories and my love for these two women, who my sisters and I had looked up to in our early years. We had all been very close when we were young and Jeffrey and our parents had all been alive.

Ilene, Dee, and I hit I-10 to Florida to meet with Mark and the cousins who were now up in age. Ruthie, 85, was bent and frail with a smile that never left her face. Her brown eyes, like all of my dad's family, took in everything. Delly was now 80 and still as beautiful and graceful as ever! It was a visit that I will always remember as we all shared stories involving various members of our families.

As we visited, all I could think of was that they had never ever met my daughters and their families. It was sad. I was so proud of my family, and none of my dad's family had ever met them.

Both of my cousins have wonderful children who are very loyal and loving to their parents. They had always been very close, and my sisters and I greatly admired that trait which seemed to be missing within my mother's side of the family. I will always remember Delly stating that on many occasions, when talking on the phone with her daughter, Jaci, who lived far away, that they would sometimes just listen to each other breathing even if no words were being said, because they were grateful to be together! These cousins never smoked or drank, but just lived for the companionship and love of their families!

The visit also made Ilene and I feel the loss of our parents even more. When we visited in Florida, Delly's son, Alan, was living close by and we were excited to get to visit with him also. Alan was one year younger than I was, and it amazed me how much he resembled my dad. I felt closer to him than I did to Ruthie's children, and we shared many stories of the past.

Alan brought up the time when he was playing basketball on the Island and challenged the local high school studs to a three-man game while his cousins (Mark and I) were in town. As was usual with Alan, he made a large sized bet on our game. We kicked their butts, Alan collected, and it was off to the delicatessen.

Two years later, my daughters and their families met us in Del Ray Beach, Florida, for a wonderful visit as my cousins met my family for the first time. This also included Jacqui and Chad's two-year-old daughter.

Marti and Gene also flew in and visited with my cousins!

L to R: Daughter Jacqui, Dee, Kylie,
Cousin Ruthie, Conner, Me, Cousin Alan,
and Cousin Delly in Fla.(2004)

It had to have been almost 50 years since I had visited with my dad's family. All those years being separated, and then with our very short visit, feeling like strangers at first, we had all been brought back together, regaining our connections, memories, and our love, because we were family!

Ironically, Del Ray Beach is where Vinnie Marino, the basketball player from Pan American, and his wife JoAnn had retired: They lived within three miles of my cousins!

Vinnie and I in Del Ray, Florida (2004)

I was able to see our cousins a year later in New York, when Ilene and I went to the cemetery to attend the "unveiling" of the grave of Deli's husband, Flash. At that time, we were able to become reacquainted with the relatives who are left of my family. All of Delly's kids (Jack, Spencer, Fred and Alan) and Ruthie's family, (Ira, Joanne, and Mona) and my sisters and I had a re-bonding with our relatives.

While we were in New York, it was also a time for Ilene and me to visit the graves of my dad and of my little brother. It had been 48 years since I had stood at my brother's gravesite. We still remembered exactly where Jeffrey's grave was. Ilene and I both remembered the headstone next to my brother's grave. That boy's graveside once had a picture on it, but half of the picture was missing. I guess the birds had pecked away at the porcelain picture. Looking at my brother's grave again, I sank deep into my sadness from the past. There is nothing worse than losing a family member, but when the person had only been four years old??? Even now, after all this time, I was again asking myself... Why? And I still have no answers. My response is still the same, "God only knows why?"

Paul Simon Comes to Houston

Throughout our lives, our daughters have always taken care of Dee and me. It seems that it is one surprise after another. This was one of those occasions where Jacqui heard on radio that the station was giving away tickets to a sold out performance by Paul Simon in the Woodlands, Texas. Jacqui called the station all day until finally, she was picked, and she "won" the tickets!

Dee and I attended the concert, and I hesitantly left my business card with the person who screened backstage visitations. We were told to check back after the concert to see if we were approved to visit with Paul afterwards. I loved hearing Simon sing, but honestly, I was thinking mainly about the fact that it sure would be easy for Paul to have forgotten me after all these years! Sounds like a lyric from one of his songs!

This was the first time to see Paul in all in these years... and singing at a concert! When we were young, we would sometimes harmonize, as young kids tend to do. This was obviously, before he hooked up with Art and went professional. Obviously Art easily beat me out in the singing department. It was also a time to confirm all the stories that I have told Dee through the years... if we made it backstage!

I am sure we all go through times when we wonder if we remembered it all. If in reminiscing, I questioned if I had anything wrong about one thing or another. I had the fear now, that Paul would not remember me, or maybe I was suffering from what Mark Twain once said, *"I have been through some terrible things in my life, some of which actually happened"*.

At the backstage entrance, after one wave of the attendant's arm, we entered backstage with my credibility on the line. Within minutes, Paul came out wearing his customary New York Yankee baseball cap, and a scarf around his neck to protect his vocal cords, and a thin leather jacket.

One look at him and it sent chills throughout my body. Tears came to him and to me as he came over and embraced me, and said, "You have not changed a bit!"

We both caught our breaths as I introduced him to Dee. I was so pleased, and of course relieved, that he would take the time to come out and say hi. I could have said so many things, but the next words that came out were, "Paul, I can't believe that you remembered me?" He placed one arm on mine, and held up my business card as he yelled to his manager, "Vaughn, what did I tell you when I showed you this card?" Vaughn replied, "Marty, Paul said he almost killed you with a softball when you were twelve years old!"

Paul said, "I thought I had killed you when
You were 12 years old!"

That was my validation! We probably did not spend more than 15 minutes with him, but Dee and I were impressed with his character and genuine emotion, as well as his great singing. We were practically speechless as we drove back to Houston; it affected us that much. Thanks, Jacqui, for your insight in persevering with your phone call to provide us this magnificent experience!

Retirement Party

In May of 2005, Anne Daily, Helen Wehring, who had been my long time secretary, Karen Fitzgerald, and Marianne Elias, my current secretary, hosted my "Sunset Party!" It was a great event held in the School Board Room, and I was very grateful that Marcella came down from Dallas to celebrate with me.

Conner also came and he may have been the hit of the party. While sitting in one of the Board members seats, he accidentally turned on the microphone and was having a great time, jabbering on the microphone's loudspeaker. He finally took time away from his "new toy" to give me a T-shirt that Jacqui had made, which had his picture on it with the words, "Now you have more time to play with me!"

It was now a new game for me. I had no work other than around the house, and I loved to build, especially with my power tools. The more time I spent at home, the more "MacArthur's" training and skills came out of me! The house and grounds began to look like a maintenance/janitor occupied our house!

Several of my friends were already retired, and reminded me to "stay healthy". I made it a goal not to fall into the trap of doing nothing and becoming unhealthy. I would listen to comments from others that began to sound identical, "This is great! Do nothing all week and then rest on the weekend!"

After 30 years, my swim coaching Gets sunsetted!

I kept up my coaching in the summer, knowing that it would have to come to a halt pretty soon! Beginning my last swim team season, our record was impressive. We had won the district championship three out of the four last seasons. Even when we finished second it was only three points that separated us from another championship!

Spring Board Swim Team

During the last year, knowing that all my high school coaches were going to be heading to college, and the next summer, they would need more funds for college and would probably need to work at "real" jobs, I decided to call it quits after thirty years of coaching. It was very difficult to say the least! The decision was based on Jay Boy doing so well as my assistant coach, and the kids knowing how to be winners that brought the "closure" to my swim coaching career to a satisfying end.

We had a nucleus of great swimmers, great parents, and a system in place to continue to win for many years to come. A winning team does not come without conflicts! Dealing with the daily problems in my opinion is about 90% of the job. Throughout my career, there was never just one way or approach to deal with children. Although I followed Lou Holz's (*Notre Dame, football coach and sports commentator*) mantra, "When players need love and understanding the most, it is usually when they deserve it the least!"

Funds were always a major problem with community recreation swimming. At the close of my last season, I asked the swim board for funds to get trophies for each athlete for their hard work in winning. I did not believe in awarding trophies unless they won the championship. The swimmers did not get trophies when we finished second. For each of the years that they won the championship, the trophies increased in size and of course cost! Now, this was going to be my last purchase of trophies for this swim team.

To my surprise, the Board said they had very little funds left and could not afford to buy the trophies because it was taking every penny just to keep the old pool running. Being a child at heart, and remembering the "Roller Skate" debacle, I would not accept awarding a smaller trophy than the previous years. If I know anything about kids and sports, the bigger the better as trophies go!

Therefore, I took what they had in the way of funds and ordered T-Shirts with a cool logo on the front and back. They were a hit as it raised the necessary funds to get the biggest trophies that the money could buy! The trophy's were gigantic and each swimmer was so proud of his trophy that many of them brought them to school for "show and tell" in September! I was never good at accepting "no" for an answer, especially when it came to children! That certainly could have been the reason for my short tenure in a few communities. My mantra was, When children "deserve, they should receive!"

Springboard Swordfish Swim Team 2006

Little Sara Ruffing, one of my swimmers, seemed to grow up right in front of my eyes! She went from a scared beginning swimmer to a top high school competitive swimmer, and then again competed as an advanced summer league swimmer with me. At the end of the summer season I was honored and surprised, when Sara showed me a copy of a writing requirement she had submitted along with her application to Texas A&M. I am so proud of her being accepted as a Texas Aggie, and this letter has a special place in my heart. Thank you, Sara.

The Chain of Caring
Sara Ruffing

Every person who comes into contact with you makes an impact on your life in some shape or form, so it is difficult to choose one person who has impacted you the most.

The only way to decide is to choose someone who impacts you in several aspects of life, is always there for you, and not only helps you in your life but lives theirs in a respectable way.

It is important to know that Coach U had a tough childhood. He was headed in the wrong direction until a family friend set him in the right one. His past inspires me because I understand his reasons for wanting to take help that was given to him and pass it along to so many people.

Coach U did not save me from the wrong direction, but he has encouraged me to continue on the right path. I admire his concern for and devotion to others, and I benefit not only from his direct help but from my own observations of his values whether he is interacting with a nervous swimmer, a struggling baseball player, or a troubled teenager. I have learned a lot from his selflessness, concern, and dedication in these situations, and I have become more aware of others' needs by being more appreciative of both their strengths and weaknesses.

During the twelve years that I have known Coach U, he has given me skills

MARTY URAND

and great advice that I will use for the rest of my life and pass on to others. He taught me to swim when I was five years old and coached me for eleven years. I am now a very experienced and strong swimmer, and I know this skill may very well save my life one day.

He was there for me both times I tore my ACL; he even sent me to a very good doctor he knew to give me a second opinion and more options on surgery. He attended some of my basketball games and offered to practice with me to help me become a better player.

Possibly most important of all, he sits down with me to have serious conversations about life and what I plan to do with mine, never ceasing to give fantastic advice and help. Over the years, I have come to admire many characteristics in him that I want to incorporate in my leadership abilities such as patience, optimism, and encouragement.

Coach U's influence on me also affects the people I interact and work with. Seeing the results he has with individuals made me want to develop the skill she uses to deal with people and incorporate them into the way I deal with others. It seems that I am always teaching people how to do things, whether teaching a friend how to properly shoot a basketball, teaching my cousin how to play a card game, or teaching a child how to swim. I have learned to be patient and understand that even though the activity seems easy to me, it is a very new experience for the person I am teaching it to.

Coach U has also taught me to consider other people's weaknesses and to be tolerant of them, and I use this tolerance while I am teaching. I have also learned to be patient when I am babysitting children. Children are very demanding and can be irritating sometimes, but staying serene and understanding works better for both my attitude as well as the child's. Even when talking to younger Girl Scouts about life, I emulate Coach U and talk to them with compassion and understanding instead of preaching or lecturing as if I were superior to them.

Coach U's example has made me better at interacting with others, more tolerant, and a better listener. Coach U has aided me in developing into the type of woman I want to be. The great role model he has been has made me more caring, more mature and a better example for others. I owe so much to him, and I hope to enhance and better others' lives and continue the chain.

MARTY URAND

**Our Junior Coaches were
the "Backbone"
for the five year dominance!**

The Spring Board swimming team staff (2008).

Top Row: Ex coach, Justin West, Jason Harn, Austin West, Nick Olson

Bottom row: Coach Cutler, Ashely Chancey, Sara Groome, Brittany Groome,
Katie Loewen, EmilyHorstmann, Jennifer Edwards, & Coach Urand

In 2005, I hung up the whistle and Jay Boy took over the coaching. It was a perfect transition for the swimmers and the community. With Jay as head coach, the funds were still an issue at Spring Board Pool, which resulted in insufficient lighting and poor water circulation at the pool. This lack of safety at night mandated that all their meets be held at the opponents' pool. However, in spite of this disadvantage, the team still went undefeated!

Way to go Jay Boy and Swordfish!

Marti & Gene get married

How in the world can the wedding "Top" the engagement party that was held in the Dominican Republic? Well it did! This time Gene pulled out all the stops as we all met in Cabo, San Lucas, Mexico.

The Johnson Family, Casey, Gene, Marti, & Alex

MARTY URAND

Gene had set up a phenomenal Villa overlooking the Sea of Cortez, for the ceremony and celebration. He brought in his sons, Casey and Alex, Gene's parents, a few close friends, and Marti had Dee and me, and her sister, Jacqui, and Jacqui's husband Chad and their children, Conner and Kylie. It was a beautiful ceremony on the beach. It was a wonderful celebration joining them together.

Danene and Ralph Johnson

We all stayed around for five days and enjoyed the company of the two families as we got to enjoy and get to know each other better. The wedding was on the beach followed by a great dinner celebration.

After we finished dinner, we assembled on the beach and were treated to a fantastic "Fire Dance".

Having the extra time together allowed us all to get to know his boys and parents better. The boys will have their teen years to find out that Marti is a loving, but **_hardnosed Aggie!_**

The Third Quarter represented my professional career in the field of Health, Physical Education, Recreation, and Dance. Upon retirement in 2005, forty-five years rounded out the third quarter of my life!

After further "Review"...

At eleven years old I didn't even know what a career was. All my thoughts were about sports and cars. And yes, I was beginning to notice the girls.

So as I think back to this photo with a 1949 Studebaker that had the "MO" of not knowing the front from the back, it could possibly have been a reflection of my life!

I am proud of my career that unfolded under the guidance of others who saw my potential, spent their time guiding me, and instilled in me the direction and ambition to become who and what I am today!

And, if by chance you are one of those who cared and took the time, I thank you from the bottom of my heart! *(urand@ymail.com)*

THE FOURTH QUARTER

Retirement

2004 - ?

Christmas of 2003

After Christmas (2003) the decision was finalized, and I decided to retire the next year in the summer of 2004. Once again, I called upon my friends to help me search for any part time positions available within the community college systems.

San Jacinto North College campus is a few miles from our home. I applied for a part time job with the department chair, Shawn Silman, and during my interview, we discovered that his wife had been an ex-student of mine when I taught at UH. It helped that his wife gave me a positive endorsement. It just confirms that when helping or thinking of others, without expecting anything from them, people often reap a variety of benefits somewhere down the line.

I was excited when I was offered the position at San Jacinto College North Campus. The San Jacinto College system has three campuses east of Houston. The South campus is south of Pasadena (Texas), and the Central campus is on the east side of Pasadena. The North campus is on the northeast side of Houston. Each campus has a men's team and a women's team. The South campus has men's soccer and women's softball. The central campus has the women's volleyball and men's basketball teams. The North campus has women's basketball, and men's baseball.

San Jacinto College, a junior college system, is usually referred to as "San Jac", and is one of the best-known JUCO's (Junior Colleges) in the Nation. They have won more championships in basketball and baseball than any other Community College System nationwide. The hall outside of my classroom illustrates it all! A baseball jersey belonging to Wayne Graham, San Jacinto National Championship baseball coach, is mounted in the hall's glassed display along with two jerseys of past San Jacinto baseball All-Americans, Andy Petit and Roger Clements. Both went on to become great professional baseball players. Over twenty major league players had played baseball at San Jacinto and they and their teams brought the school athletic program fame and prominence. Later, Coach Wayne Graham went on to coach baseball at Rice University, in Houston, Texas.

Among the San Jacinto campuses, the major sport that over time has produced the most wins and National titles are the "Ravens", the men's basketball team. Many of the major universities send their "Blue Chip" players to San Jacinto College either to improve their grades or to improve their play in the hardest Junior College basketball division in the nation, where they often play as many as forty games a year.

Throughout the years, the San Jac coaches have taken great pride, not only in training these great athletes, but also in their academics.

I was excited to have this opportunity to teach in this college environment that gives students an academic bridge, before attending a larger college and with a rich athletic setting.

I was particularly excited to have the chance to work with the athletes in the classroom as well. During 2012, the baseball team was ranked number one in the nation. The class Shawn assigned me to teach was perfect. I was to teach the one class that I had worked diligently to stop, to "sunset" when I was at the agency in Austin.

This class gives an exception for teachers to teach physical education at the elementary level without having physical education certification.

It is interesting that this teaching assignment occurred at this phase of my life and despite the past, I have come to love this class. My particular class met each Tuesday and Thursday, from 8:30-9:50 AM. Shawn arranged that on Thursdays, the campus Pre-School students would come to the gymnasium, and my students would teach them according to what we had studied in my previous class on Tuesday.

This particular class is often filled with a bunch of "cocky jocks", and I believe I can say that because I see myself in so many of them, when I was in my first college classes. Most of my students learn, as I did, that the college expects a great deal from them: whether they are on scholarship or not!

San Jacinto College, "Elementary Activities" Class of Fall 2012

The class that I teach serves as a rude awakening for any athletes who think college professors lower their expectations for the student athletes. However, sometimes it is even the opposite; some professors make it their missions to show the athletes they have to win in the classrooms, in order to have a chance to win in the field or on a court.

It may take several classes before the student athletes realize it is up to them to study and find out that most things do not come free. I believed that inaccurate theory before I had my "rude awakening" while I was in college. That was my problem when I attended my freshman year of college!

Working with the athletes was becoming more and more self-gratifying for me. They always ask about my championship ring and it serves as a tool for me to be thought of as a past college athlete who has been where they are now. At the beginning of each semester, I ask the athletes to stay after class and I give them some insight as to how other teachers might perceive them, and why their college professors just might not be thrilled having student athletes in their classes. Because of the athletes' travel schedules, keeping their grades up requires some tutoring as well as special strategies and understanding.

I explain to them that athletes do need help, but not by teachers "giving" them grades or by professors accepting their excuses, but by helping the students to become organized, to complete their assignments, and to carefully have notes to study while they are on the road. If these student athletes had these skills in the first place, many of them could have gone straight to a four-year school because they would have had qualifying grades in the first place!

I warn the athletes that for most of them, it may be their last chance to make it unless they become more conscientious about their assignments. I encourage these students to make goals to work toward the next level, whether the goal is a four-year school, an occupation, a career or beyond. Just then, one of the young men from the baseball team raised his hand and said, "Not me coach, I am here so I can get drafted!" Somehow, I didn't have an answer for that statement!

As these athletes become more realistic, it gives me hope for their futures. God only knows why I am getting this great opportunity to interact and work with these students!

Later, Rich Almstedt, who served on the cabinet as Vice President of Physical Education when I was President of TAHPERD, called me, asking if I wanted to teach an on-line class for Lone Star College in Kingwood. I was thrilled!

So much for retirement!!

Help from the Bench

In 2008, Hurricane Ike blew into my basement and left four feet of mud and water, tore my roof apart, and flooded our boat with all the rain. My son-in-law, Chad, who at the time was one of the partners of Cotton Restoration Company, came to our rescue! Dee and I were very fortunate to have Chad oversee the restoration of our storm damaged home for us.

Within hours after the storm calmed down, Chad had a crew come over to move all our valuables and furniture from downstairs and the important tools from the garage, bringing all these materials upstairs into our main living area in case of flooding and wind and rain damage. Dee and I could never have accomplished this by ourselves.

Within six months of repair work, we felt like we had a new house with all the work that Chad had his crew did for us.

The storm did not affect my car, but thinking down the road, I knew I'd like another car at some point. I had my eye on Gene's 2004 Cadillac Escalade, and I told Marti I was hoping that when Gene was ready for a new car, she would tell me so I could buy his old

Escalade. I was excited when she said he had been thinking about trading his in and was in the process of looking for another vehicle. Marti did not think he wanted another Escalade, and she wasn't sure when or if he would buy a new car.

Five months later, Marti drove Gene's 2004 Escalade over to our home and began packing up her college memorabilia, and other belongings she had stored when she had been living in her apartment. While Marti was clearing out her old stuff, I drove to teach my class at San Jac, and I told Marti I would come back and help her finish packing her stuff as soon as my class was over. When I returned I was surprised to see a second escalade in our drive with new dealer plates parked next to Gene's older 2004 escalade. I commented to Gene, "I thought you were not going to get another Cadillac?" He smiled, I'm not, and tossed me the keys saying, "This one is yours!" I was in shock! He had not traded in his Escalade, but had kept it so he could eventually give it to his son Alex.

It took me a while before I could believe it, and it sure looks wonderful under the new garage that Jacqui's husband, Chad, had built when he had extended the deck from the side of my house to enlarge our parking area. Gene and Chad have hearts of gold, and I thank them often, but I will never be able to thank them enough.

I have never been involved in anything of this magnitude and I was unsure how to deal with it. How does a person begin expressing the enormity of one's appreciation and thankfulness for son-in-laws' who have been so generous?

Both Marti and Jacqui have had good instincts about the boys they have dated, and we are proud of the high quality men they married.

One afternoon Dee and I were with our friend Steve, and I was telling him the story about Gene giving us a year old Cadillac. Steve was amazed, and I told him that it was so difficult finding the words to thank Marti and Gene and show how meaningful it all was for us. Steve is a Mormon who values his religion, and is a very giving and humanistic type of man. He spent some of his valuable time before seeing his next appointment, telling us how some people love to give gifts and that we should be more understanding of their level of giving.

Before the meeting was over, Steve mentioned that he liked my Invicta watch I was wearing. I collect Invicta watches and Steve admired mine again, telling me how great it looked. Therefore, when I left his office, I took off my watch and left it in the chair where he had been sitting.

Within ten minutes after leaving his office, Steve called me yelling, "Marty, I can't accept this watch!"

Giving is wonderful, I thought, but sometimes, just sometimes, receiving can be difficult to accept!

Back to Galveston for our annual Christmas Photo (2005)

Simon returns to Houston

On Paul Simon's second trip to perform in Houston, Deanna and I invited Charlie, Deanna's brother, Karen Fitzgerald, Anne Daily, and Barbara Cofer. This time the concert was with both Paul Simon and Art Garfunkel, and it was held at the Toyota Center where the Houston Rocket's play their home games.

My close friends were all big Simon fans and were excited to attend.

When the concert ended, we took the elevator down stairs and ran into major interference from one of Houston's finest. No matter what I said, the officer replied, "Without a backstage pass, you are not permitted!" We argued until I saw him pick up his hand transmitter to get some help. Barbara, an elementary school counselor, approached him and sort of pushed me out of the way. Anne turned me around, and we walked away as Anne and Deanna kept talking to me to get my attention off the situation. In just a matter of minutes, the police officer opened the door to the back stage entrance and waved us in. Until this day, I have no idea what Barbara said to get us through! She just flat got the job done, and I had a ball talking with Paul and Art!

Supporting my Alma Mater

Jim Board came up with a great idea to honor and pay tribute to Sam Williams, our basketball coach. Jim started a yearly raffle like no other, with each of the 300 raffle tickets being sold for $500 per ticket! The reward for the winning the Grand Prize was:

❖ Charter Jet service for 8 to Las Vegas
❖ Penthouse suite at the Bellagio Hotel & Casino
❖ Limo service to and from the hotel
❖ A night of fine dining at a Bellagio restaurant
❖ 8 tickets to the "O" Cirque du Soleil show
❖ One spa treatment per guest at the Spa Bellagio

*Jim Board presenting the first installment
of the $360,000 to the Athletic Department
at UTPA. Funds are for "The Sam
William's Basketball Scholarship."*

With the cost of each ticket being rather expensive, often several people went in together and divided the price of a raffle ticket among four couples, which made the cost for each portion of the ticket $125. One year, Dick Tate, one of Pan American College's former players, and now an attorney in the Houston area, won the raffle ticket to Vegas for four couples. He and his family were unable to attend because of a trial scheduled on the same date as the trip. Dick graciously gave two of the eight tickets to Dave Hass, another basketball player, who I coincidentally had also recruited to play at Pan Am, and the other six tickets went to Marti and Jacqui and their husbands, Dee and I. The eight of us flew to Vegas and had a dream trip we will always remember. Every time we talk about our wonderful trip, we again share the story of Dick's generosity. This was such a great gift and was certainly enjoyed by all of us. In 2012, the first *Sam Williams Scholarship* was awarded with the accumulation of all the effort, determination, and leadership of Jim Board and the many other people working toward the project.

Chris King, new AD

Chris King was in his second year as Pan American's Athletic Director. This was his first Athletic Director's position after coming from Alabama, which had been Jim Brooks' old coaching school. Chris reunited and showed appreciation for the alumni, especially the past players, and he built up a great following with many of the ex-players now attending the Pan American College basketball games.

Chris, a very personable guy, worked hard to renew our bond and brought us all back together again. In November (2011), many of the team members who had played for Coach Williams attended the dedication of the Bronc's "New" basketball floor honoring Coach Sam Williams. We had had an earlier dedication just a couple of years before, when Coach William's name was placed in a small corner of the gymnasium. We had not been too happy with that placement and had asked Mr. King for a more visible location. He certainly came through and had our coach's name placed on either side of the center circle!

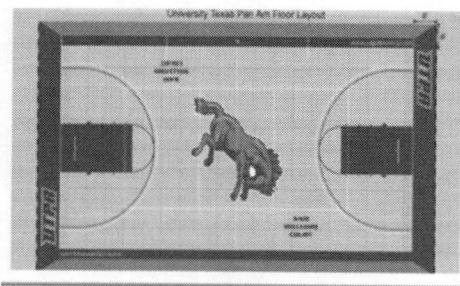

The *"Sam Williams Court"*

November 2, 2010
Paul Friddle, new coach,
Ryan Marks, and Jim Board

Coach Williams' former players supported the new coach in any way possible. Our visits to the university were never complete without going by to see coach! When we heard that "Coach" was in need of a modern TV, within a week he had a fifty inch TV set, "bought, sealed, and delivered to his home from several of his ex-players!

Howard Fuller, Fred Taylor, and Otto Moore visit with Coach Sam Williams.

MARTY URAND

Chris King had done a superb job in many areas, and one of those areas certainly affected me, as he focused on reuniting the basketball players from the past years. His effort was substantial as he traveled to Houston on many occasions, making a point to visit with ex-players, and speaking at our Houston Alumni Association meetings and events.

On many occasions, King held events that focused on former athletes to come back to campus even if it was just to meet a new coach. He has been very successful in bringing us back in the Bronc fold.

November 20, 2010
Floor Dedication for Coach Sam
Williams, 86 years of age

Pictured:

Tony De la Pena, Otto Moore, Dr. Nelsen (UTPA President) Fred Taylor, Jim McGurk, Paul Friddle, Gordon Forester, Marty Urand, and Coach Williams

Conner and Kylie

Our grandchildren, Conner and Kylie, live in a subdivision forty-five miles from us in a home with a pool. In a new sub-division, swimming was a priority for my grandchildren. I worked with them often and before I knew it, I had forty other young children wanting swimming lessons as well. The lessons continued for nine more years, and I probably taught most of the children in the Rock Creek Community during that time.

All the children know me as "Papa U", since my grandchildren refer to me by that name. In fact, the entire swim team began calling me that as well. Anne Daily had spread the name to all of the teachers in Spring Branch prior to retiring and the "Coach U" days were officially over!

During the winter months, I coached basketball at the YMCA, and my grandson, Conner played on my team. Conner is a natural athlete, he had so much practice playing on the "Sky Court" when we attended Houston Rocket games, and his skills had really improved.

The Sky Court is an area for children, and it is located on the top level of the Toyota Center. The Sky Court is available for the younger kids to shoot baskets and play basketball on a miniature "Rocket court". The only requirement is that each child needs to be under a certain height, which was checked when the children came onto the court. The "court" motivated Conner, making him play harder to try to be as good as or better than the others. Conner is a competitor and loves the challenge. He would usually play during the second and third quarters and we would return to our regular seats for the final quarter.

At six years old, Conner was taking layups on ten-foot baskets. Whatever he saw at the games or during his sessions on the Sky Court, he would practice and try duplicating them at home. Conner loves the challenge of accomplishing any skill or trick that he has seen older kids or professionals do on the court.

At the age of seven, Conner went into year-round baseball with the "Diamond Dawgs" team, and played on a second baseball team during this same season. Around this time, he pretty much narrowed his favorite sports to baseball, basketball, and football.

Jacqui, Chad and Conner after championship
game (32-12) and he scored 31 points!

Conner ~Representing the South Region baseball team for "Team USA" in North Carolina!!

Three touch downs vs Channelview,
Texas (September 2014)

Conner Weigman |*Cypress, Texas | Team USA 12U Trial Roster*

A fifth-grader at Black Elementary, Conner batted .780 with three home runs, three doubles & seven stolen bases while at the Elite 32 National Championships at ESPN/Disney World Complex, Orlando, Florida. Conner was just named to the 12 and under USA Team trial roster for 2015, after he attended the NTIS showcase at the USA Baseball Training complex in Cary, North Carolina.

Joan and Dick Weigman

On a funny note, I was standing on the sidelines with Dick Weigman, Conner's other grandfather, watching Conner streak by us for another touchdown.

Dick and I looked at each other with a great-shared pride in Conner. Before I could say a word about the run, Dick said, "You know, it just doesn't get any better than this!" I instantly replied, "Well not necessarily, if he had my last name on the back of his jersey, I would certainly feel better!" He laughed and replied, "I know how you feel. My daughter's son, Cade, provides me with the same scenario when he is in his jersey!" We both shared and enjoyed the moment of two proud grandparents!

Kylie on the balance beam   *Prodigy "Sky Team" 2014*

Kylie liked soccer and averaged several goals a game. And keeping with tradition, she took up gymnastics! It is weird to see my daughter's child doing flip-flops and walkovers all around her house, just as her mother, Jacqui, did at our house when she was younger.

On March 20, 2014, Jacqui and I took Kylie to Biron Gymnastics so I could help her achieve her back flip, which was next in the progression to move up a level in cheerleading. Beau was gracious enough to allow me to work with Kylie.

Beau Biron (Wrote on Facebook)

My old friend, former coach, and teacher extraordinaire, Marty Urand, dropped by the gym today with his daughter Jacqui (whom we both used to coach) and with his granddaughter Kylie. Kylie is learning her Back under Marty's tutelage. A wonderful surprise.

Ahhhh....The Circle of Life.

Heart of Gold

Marti's husband, Gene also loves sports and supports everything that his community and his sons get into athletically. Each year, Gene supported their local little league fundraisers by bidding on Astros events. This particular year (2010), He won his bids for all three events. And when Gene wins, we all win!

Gene and Marti with Astros
General Manager (Ed Wade)
"sky box" (2012)

On Gene's first bid, he won the right to use the Astros owner's box for Gene's birthday. Gene invited twenty of his friends, his parents, Dee and I, his boys, and Marti as his guests. Ed Wade, the Manager of the Astros came up and spent at least a half hour visiting with everyone.

To bat against Roy was Gene's second bid in a fundraiser that he also won. About two weeks later, Gene was in the cage against Oswald, and we found Roy to be a real jewel of a person. He joked, laughed, and of course took it easy on Gene, who had not swung a bat in years. However, when Gene hit the ball, he knocked the cover off. Gene is about 6'4, 230 lbs., and he bats left-handed. He was just missing hitting the right field wall on almost every swing. In addition, this was despite the fact that it was Gene's first time ever, to use a wooden bat!

Speaking about bats, Gene received two of them when he went to lunch for his third activity with Biggio and Bagwell. They both gave him an autographed bat for his super home sports collection!

Gene was not a person to be "star struck" by celebrities. He and Marti had even traveled to Phoenix several New Year's Eves to attend Charles Barkley's blowouts. As much as I would enjoy the opportunity to meet up with them when they went to Vegas, I know this is simply out of my league.

Casey, Alex and Gene were treated like royalty prior to the Astro game!

Great day as Gene' sons, Alex and Casey, mess with the Astro's Mascot

Gene on the Astros' massive centerfield screen

The Buzzer Beater!

On April 20th, 2010, on my 67th birthday, Deanna and I made plans to attend Lafayette High School's 50th Reunion in New York. We made a weeklong trip to visit my youngest sister, Enid, in PA., and then stayed with my Cousin Mark in N.J.

It was a fantastic week, especially since the NFL draft was being held at Radio City Music Hall during that time. The city was buzzing with football fanatics wearing their favorite team gear and talking about their teams' selections! Smack was everywhere! Not only was this evident in the city, but in Penn Station and on the train back to Morgan Town. Posters, conversations, and the clothing people were wearing, were all geared to the football frenzy that hit the city. Excitement was everywhere, and that is what primed us even more for my high school reunion, which was being held on Staten Island.

Traveling on the Staten Island Ferry was a treat for Deanna and me after hearing all my life that the ferry was the best "buy" in the New York, since the ferry was free! It passes right in front of the Statue of Liberty, which was another plus.

The reunion was scheduled on Staten Island because our high school, Lafayette High School, had been closed earlier in the year due to the violence within the school. It certainly was a weird feeling attending a reunion of a school that was boarded–up and shut down!

The evening before the reunion, we met Stu and Anita for dinner, which is always a treat, not only to see them, but also to have Stu's limo pull up to the hotel and pick us up. Stu is one of the few people who we make time to see whenever we visit N.Y. He is one of the most interesting, caring, and invigorating people I have known. As busy as Stu and Anita are, they have always made Deanna and me feel welcome and important. Stu serves on so many Executive Boards that we feel like we have the city in the palm of our hand when we are with them. If we go to a play, he sometimes has tickets available for us to be able to sit "front and center". Dining with them is always a joy, attending restaurants off Broadway, or one of his "favorite" places is always a dining delight where we all receive the "royal treatment". But most importantly, he is still the caring, thoughtful, friend, I remember from our youth.

I am awed by the life of Stu and Anita. Knowing they have worked hard and earned their way without losing themselves on the way, is impressive. Stu has a great head on his shoulders, and as some would say, "He is living the dream". On one of our visits, we talked about someone who had been diagnosed with cancer, and Stu said that over the last fifteen years, he had been involved with funding studies and investigating methods for finding a cure for cancer.

The study is in the approval stages with the FDA, and he is expecting some breakthrough news. Many experiments have proven positive and are giving the medical personnel, as well as Stu, confidence and hope. His hopes are that when the vaccine is approved and ready to be sold to the public, to provide the drug for those who are suffering from cancer, making it affordable to everyone.

Talk about making a difference in a person's life! Stu has assisted people for over fifty years, making significant donations to assist groups in need. Being associated with research for possible cures for cancer is astonishing to me! I think it would be like growing up with Jonas Salk, and later discovering he had been the person who found the cure for Polio! For me, being in the health field and teaching make for some amazing stories when I returned to my college classes.

On a more humorous note, while in the limo coming back to the hotel, Stu leaned over to me and whispered, "Do you remember the "Shirley evening?" We both laughed so hard that we were in tears! Whenever we visit, we have great conversations about our past. I appreciate and marvel as I listen to such a brilliant, down to earth, truly good person talking about magnanimous works, and still have time to reminisce

MARTY URAND

about the past! I can only appreciate his attitude for making life and the world better.

The day after meeting with Stu, Dee and I prepared to attend my H.S. reunion, and I certainly had a wide range of feelings about that. Thinking about the last time that I was with my classmates was not exactly a highlight of my life! I was the class clown, the kid who was often in trouble and who had been a good jock, but certainly not a good student.

Nevertheless, in some ways I was looking forward to seeing friends from that time. When we went to the reunion, and entered the Country Club, we just stood back for a few minutes, taking in the festivities. No one, of course, looked quite like I remembered them when we were in high school, and they probably felt the same about me. I had to lean in to look at the high school picture pinned on each person's blouse or jacket before I excitedly could say, "Oh, I remember you!"

A few of my classmates had not changed a bit! David (Ditto) Tawil was one. I had seen him about seven years earlier, so I was comfortable with Ditto, and I recognized Myrna and her husband, Stan, who Deanna and I had also gotten together with on that same trip.

It was Jon Ciangiulli, the City Champion Handball player, who was a great surprise to me. He looked the same and in fact, the first words out of his mouth were, "Marty, do you remember Shirley?" We once again laughed and Deanna joined in laughing.

The night turned out great for me, especially because Deanna was seeing everyone for the first time. I was happy that my old friends could meet her, and that she could have a better understanding of the people and stories I have told her about from my New York days. Hearing their New York accents, mannerisms, etc. was a hoot!

We all sat around a table listening to each other's stories and telling our own stories about the past. We mainly talked about what we had been like in high school, and how we had changed… or had not changed. In addition, we were discussing our careers, successes and some failures, and financial successes and failures as well.

It was amusing to hear what fields and opportunities my old school friends had achieved. It was sometimes surprising as I listened to them tell stories of their success. My success in education surprised everyone!

It was interesting that as far as I could see, Dee and I were the only people among the group of my old friends at the reunion who were teachers or involved in education. Moreover, it was especially shocking that I, of all people, had the most formal education within that group.

We visited with some people who I had been close with, some I had only heard about in school, and with others who I never knew had existed. Lafayette was very a very large school and students that attended in the morning never knew the athletes for the most part that attended in the afternoon. It was a very large school with many differences both academically as well as economically!

Nick Lambrino was a student in my graduating class who no one had dared to mess with. He had seemed mysterious to most of us. During the reunion, I asked him why he was absent so much from school. He said that it was mostly on Wednesdays that he had been involved in singing and acting in musicals in the City. In fact, West Side Story was one of the plays he sang and danced in most of our high school days.

What an experience that must have been! During the reunion, he sang several songs, and he still has a super voice. It was also interesting that we knew many of the guests by their nicknames, but we did not even recognize their real names.

Jon Ciangiulli was sitting on my right, Nick was on the left of Dee, and we each told stories about our memories in school. Jon blurted out to Nick, "Hey, how come I don't know you?" Jon, for some reason, did not have a picture badge, and although he looked familiar, no one remembered who he was! Nick replied, "I don't know, but everyone knew me as Nicky "Bop". When Jon heard the nickname of Nick, Jon jumped up and ran over to hug him! We all started laughing our asses off!

Dee and I stayed until the end of the night, which had not been our intention, but it had been so much fun, we could not bear to leave early. As the guests began leaving, and the wait staff was preparing to shut down, the real fun began! It was like seeing "The Goodfellas", as different scenarios happened throughout the night. One of the best looking and most popular girls when we were in high school, sat at our table. She said she was there alone, but she was eagerly waiting for her boyfriend to get out of jail. That one sentence brought me back to my high school days in a hurry!

Many of the guys pulled out their wads of money with rubber bands wrapped around their bills with credit cards on the inside of the bills, as they fought with each other to pay for an additional bottle of scotch or whatever. This occurred again when tipping came about! I did not know if the "Rubber band billfold" was a New York thing, an Italian thing, or partly mafia! But the phrase that I heard over and over was, "Hey, ya money's no good here!"

Dee took it all in, as her eyes moved around the table, absorbing the personalities and stories being told. She looked stunning that night, and caught the eye of all the guys. Jon kept saying how beautiful she was, which certainly made me feel good.

It was a great evening. I would have enjoyed visiting with Ditto a little more, but he had become a producer of "Off Broadway" shows and he worked the room because he still knew everyone. He had been class

President and certainly an outstanding politician. Ditto was loved by all, and I had always looked up to him during our school days, especially when we were Co-Captains of the basketball team.

"Ditto" was always the King of the Ball, and at the reunion, it was no different!

Jon still calls me occasionally when traffic is very slow on the Belt Parkway or he might call when he is going home after a big meal and drinks! When I left New York after the Reunion, I felt a renewed relationship with my closer friends. It was quite a visit! Having had stored up negative feelings for fifty years is traumatic to say the least! However, this high school reunion changed many of my negative thoughts, and I lightened up regarding my past.

Closing out, not "Tapping out"

I hope I have many years left in the fourth quarter of my life, and remaining "Healthy" will certainly be a key player! I believe that eating right and exercising will be the prescription for preventing the "Big Sunset" from arriving too early!

Face Book reunites Diana and Me

Hi Marty,

Diana Anglin Miller commented on Cammie Ward Moise's photo of you.

Diana wrote, "Mr. Urand, WOW, what an influence you had on me. You sparked a passion in me that basically has fueled my whole life! I did gymnastics for the University of Oklahoma...27 years ago! My husband and I own a competitive cheerleading gym in McKinney, Texas... so, just wanted to say THANK YOU!

You asked me how it all began. This is what I remember from the days at Ashford Elementary.

Because my big sister, Melinda, did gymnastics at her elementary school, Ashford Elementary, I naturally wanted to do it too when I started kindergarten. Later in life, my parents told me that they just shut their eyes and prayed, A LOT when I went to my first day of gymnastics. I was born without the lower part of my right arm. I was fitted with prosthesis at 6 months so my physical development was right on track. My parents were amazing. They were told by a close doctor friend not to sulk in sadness or denial, and not to move away from family and friends who may "enable" their decisions to do what's best for Diana. They took this advice and because of their strength, I never really knew I was different from other children.

Which brings me to Mr. Urand; I honestly don't know if my parents spoke previously with you before that first day of gymnastics with "special concerns" or just dropped me off? I also don't know if you were worried or uncomfortable with me participating. I just remember loving gymnastics!!

The Ashford Elementary gymnastics program was the beginning of my whole life. I did competitive gymnastics which was, back in the day, the USGF. I was a Class 1 gymnast, comparable to today's Level 10. I competed for the University of Oklahoma and was a part of the Big 8 Champion Team in 1986. After two years of gymnastics, I tried out for the cheerleading squad. I cheered and was captain (during the "Switzer" years) and had the opportunity to cheer at the NCAA final game, The Orange Bowl, and the NCAA final game in basketball in the same year!

I graduated with a degree in special education and taught high school English, coached gymnastics and was the cheer advisor for 6 years at Berkner High School in Richardson Texas.

Currently my husband, Jeff Miller of 20 years this November and I own Pro Spirit, Inc., a competitive all-star cheerleading gym in McKinney Texas. We have been honored through the past 16 years with such awards as "Gym Owners" of the year, the recipient of the "Chairman's Cup" an award that recognizes community service involvement and we were inducted into the Spirit Industry Hall of Fame in 2010.

Mr. Urand, you truly gave me my start. Whatever really happened on that first day of gymnastics as a kindergartener at Ashford Elementary was the key to my success.

I was encouraged, supported, and loved by my parents for giving me the opportunity just to try. Mr. Urand, you let me be a part of the gymnastics group without restrictions or even blinking an eye at the fact that

I was "different". The fact is that was true, I was different; I was the one that had the desire to take it all the way!

Maybe that is what you saw that first day when I appeared in your class...desire!

My Summer Love "Camp"

The summers always seem to present interesting adventures for me! Ever since attending Camp Cherokee during the last two years of high school, I thought of each summer as "camp!"

Jay Cutler, my assistant coach, and I took turns running day camps to try and help make ends meet for the community pool. We started a small swim team for the children, hoping to keep the community pool open.

CAMP URAND

*Camp Urand (2011) was very enjoyable
especially when the teachers were my*
Grandsons Alex and Casey Johnson

Fifty Years Later... Back to the Future!

The new Athletic Director at Pan American College, Chris King, certainly outdid himself with creating the most impressive basketball schedule ever! There were two major swings through the East that even Coach Rockwell could not have helped our team against our competition! It began with DePaul and Ohio State (ranked number 1 by UPI). The DePaul game was not too bad of a loss, but Ohio was just too much and slapped Pan American's team by 34.

The next two games that Pan American played in New York really got my attention! The first game was against Army at West Point. What a trip that would be, seeing my alma mater playing in the foothills of Bear Mountain from my Cub Scout field trip days, and then, to travel to Queens, N.Y and see UTPA play St. Johns!!!! The Red*men*--I mean the Red Storm... (Yes, even basketball has to conform to the sensitivity and political correctness of modern time).

Cherokee Jerry (Stein) offered this definition for being "politically correct."

"Political correctness is a doctrine -- fostered by a delusional, illogical minority and rapidly promoted by an unscrupulous mainstream media -- which holds forth the proposition that it is entirely possible to pick up a piece of shit by the clean end."

There was a method to this madness of Chris King scheduling such high quality teams. The average person would never have guessed the real reasons. I kind of knew, but not nearly to the degree that the schedule affected the budget until I read Coach Ryan Mark's article in ESPN Magazine. Coach Marks, who is a sharp individual, was asked to write about the trials and tribulations of recruiting and traveling on small budget.

UTPA competes in the Great West Conference and their travel expenses are enormous. Therefore, in order to make ends meet, Pan American University scheduled the big time, major schools for the guaranteed money.

Marks told me it was a real balancing act, keeping his team from getting mentally demolished as they raised in the excess of five hundred thousand dollars which helped complete their season's travel obligations.

After discussing the finances with Deanna, it was a wash. She said yes, and I said no, to combining a trip to visit New York and to go see Pan American basketball while they were playing in that area during the Christmas Holidays. So back and forth, we went looking at the pros and cons of spending that kind of money. I called Chris and told him to hold off on the tickets, we were not going!

About that time, I received an email Christmas card from Marti and Gene presenting us with an all expense trip for Deanna and me to go to the "Big East" I just sat there looking at the screen, until I realized that this meant my dream was coming true. We would be attending those basketball games that meant so much to me. I was on cloud nine and within a half hour of the exciting news, our other daughter, Jacqui called and informed me that she and the kids were crashing the party! Deanna and I were excited that our grandchildren could share in our experience, and as always feel so blessed to have such a loving and giving family. We are so proud.

With plane tickets in hand, Dee and I picked up 8 year old Conner after he had played in his All-Star football game in Texas, and the three of us were off to New York. Jacqui and Kylie, 6 years old, met us at the hotel on 43rd and Broadway the next afternoon. Dee, Conner, and I would have already attended the Army game at West Point.

Sunday morning: We drove right through Bear Mountains and reached West Point. We met up with Jerry Stein (Camp Cherokee), his wife Judy, and their son Travis. What a treat: I had not seen Jerry in fifty years! He told Conner that his grandfather, me ☺', once scored 100 points in a basketball game, and Conner couldn't believe the story.

After the Pan Am/Army game, Deanna and I discovered that the bookstore had closed for the weekend, so we headed into town and found a little old store with memorabilia from West Point. I eyed a hat lying upside down in the corner shelf with the West Point Logo on it. When I turned the hat over, the embroidered letters read, "Army Gymnastics". How ironic was that? My friend, Garland O'Quinn, had represented the USA during the Olympics.

He was a gymnast on Army's team. What a great Holiday gift that hat would be.... for sure! I wondered how long that hat had been sitting there before I came along. It felt to me like it had been waiting just for us to come along and buy it. That was another very special moment.

As far as Pan American's basketball game, we lost by three, but the game could have been had! Our Pan

American team shot very poorly from the outside, but we still almost caught them at the end.

Rockefeller Center
Dee and our (girls) 1976, and then
grandchildren in same spot- 2011

At noon, Conner, Kylie, Jacqui, Dee, and I took the "F" train to South Ferry Street and boarded a boat to see the Statue of Liberty! We entered the subway on Times Square where my dad's malt shop used to be. We took a picture in front of where Dad's store had stood, and I had visions of the big glass window on the side of the store that faced the hundreds of people who came up from the subway every minute of the day.

1976 -Marti and Jacqui   2011 – Conner and Kylie,

Once again, Marti and Gene played Santa and bought two tickets to "The Book of Mormons" waiting at the lobby desk that evening. This was currently the hottest show on Broadway! We had tried to get tickets, but the scalpers told us there were no tickets to be had. When we asked Marti how she was able to get these two tickets, she replied, "Don't ask!"

Again..... We were so grateful!

One day, while Dee, Jacqui, and Kylie went to a play, Conner and I caught the "E" train to Kew Garden Hills. It was the same train that I had caught for years commuting to the Malt Shop when I lived in Kew Garden Hills. I knew it from memory....up the stairs; hop on the Q-46 heading up Union Turnpike; get off at 172nd street, where St. Johns University is located.

This had to be the trip of all trips for me: walking through the gates of the school where I had truly wanted to play my college ball. Conner was extra quiet, sensing that I was taking everything in: from the plaque on the gate, "Established in 1806", to the large silver letters spelling out "Carnesecca Arena" over the entrance of the field house.

We found the bookstore, but it was on an almost empty campus due to the holidays. Walter Yates had called me from Texas the night before and had placed his order for a St. Johns shirt. "Trim" knows me well! He knew that I would head right to the bookstore when I hit the campus. Fortunately, the bookstore was open, and Conner found his size shirt, I got Trim's shirt, and we were set!

The game was a shocker to say the least. Pan Am held the lead throughout the game, until the final minute, that is. Then it was time for the refs to work on our Texas school, and their refs, "took" the game that was supposed to be a "blowout!" Pan American held the Red Storm to just 24 points in the first half! We were up at that point by eight and their fans in the stands were mortified!

*Coach Ryan Marks prepares the team
for the final three and a half minutes.*

During the half, the only excitement came when they held the "Ugliest sweater" contest in a tribute to Coach Lou Carnesecca. Even Coach Marks went out and bought a diamond patterned vested sweater to show his support of the evening.

Coach Marks had all the tickets for the player's parents and his friends at the "Will Call" window and we all sat in the first row behind the Pan Am team. Our crowd was very vocal as the game progressed. At each time-out, the Texas supporters introduced themselves to each other and bonded in their support for the team. Conner took it all in!

We sat next to Coach Mark's close friends from the East and we had a ball. There were two brothers sitting next to us, Mike and Mark Groothuis. How we did not know each other was beyond me! We knew so many of the same people who had crossed the paths of each of us. We were the same age with the same basketball pedigree. Mark mentioned that he graduated from *William and Mary* and I asked if he knew Jerry King, a tennis player. Mark was shocked and responded, "Holy crap, he was my fraternity brother! How did you know him? I replied, "He was the son of my camp director at Camp Cherokee."

One ironic episode after another continued until the game began again. We repeated that scenario during each time out of the game. Names such as: Tony Jackson (Tilden/St. Johns), Howie Jones, Lou Carnesecca, Barry Krammer (NYU), Ditto, Billy

Gallanti (Midwood), and finally the big one, "Clair Bee!" Both the brothers stopped taking in the action on the court and looked at me simultaneously.

They both had attended his camps when they were youngsters and had the same admiration for Bee and his books as I do! That is when our stories started coming out, and we would have needed a double overtime to finish. Another friend, Jon Ciangiulli was supposed to meet me at the game, but unfortunately, at the last minute he could not make it. Jon would have had even more names to throw around since we were all the same age, and Jon played his college ball in the "City".

I still could not believe that I was sitting in the St. John's gym! It was even a bigger thrill sitting next to my little buddy, Conner. It is hard to imagine that if I had attended St. Johns instead of Pan American, Conner would not be at that game with me or wouldn't even be my grandson for that matter!

I kept telling Conner about a kid who played for St. Johns by the name of De Angelo Harrison from Houston. He had a great game for a freshman, and he impressed Conner and me with his three point shooting.

Sure enough, as coincidence would have it, the next day Conner and I met him at the airport, on our way home to Houston.

DeAngelo Harrison (St. Johns player
from Dulles High School in Houston)
with Conner in LaGuardia Airport
catching a flight to Houston, Texas

Both Conner and I were nervous about catching the Q-46 back to Kew Gardens after the game. It was drizzling and cold, and most of all; he was worried that I would sneak him on the bus again. Conner does not believe in cutting corners! When I left the city fifty years ago, the bus fare was 15 cents and we were able to place the coins into the change meter. At the bus stop before the game, I had asked a woman how much the fare was, and to my shock, she replied, $2.50. I asked if either the bus driver or the meter itself would take bills. "Oh no," she said, you have to either have a ticket or the correct amount of quarters. I could see Conner beginning to get nervous.

The bus came and we got on, but I still didn't have enough quarters, so I placed the handful of quarters I did have into the machine and quickly moved on and pushed Conner toward a seat. The driver never said a word, and I figured that I got away with one. A young girl got on at the next stop and placed her ticket in the machine. Two blocks down the route, she asked the bus driver if she put in enough or if she still owed anything, and he immediately answered, "One dollar more". Hmm, this man was sharper than I gave him credit for. I wondered if he realized anything about my transaction. I felt like I needed to feel him out, so I asked if he would let me know when we got to St. Johns. The driver nodded, and ten minutes later, while looking straight ahead, he said, "Next Stop, St. Johns." We stood up when the bus came to the stop, and as we began to exit he said, "I hope they win tonight, and by the way, the boy is four, right?" Meaning that "four years and under" ride free! That was pretty decent of him not to embarrass me in front of my grandson! I could have withstood the jab, but Conner would have never forgiven me. Con certainly does not fit the mold of his N.Y. Granddad!

At half time of the game, I felt like I had known the brothers forever, and asked if either of them were going toward Kew Gardens because we could certainly use a lift. Thankfully, after the game, Mark drove us to catch the train back to the city. While in the car I asked

Mark where he lived, and he said that he was from "the Island" (Meaning Long Island, NY) It is practically a given that when someone says they are from the Island, your next response is, "Where on the Island?" I took it all in stride when he replied, "Elmont!" Wow! What a coincidence. Elmont is the town where the cemetery for my Dad and Jeffrey is located.

When Mark mentioned Elmont, a warm, sentimental feeling came over me. This entire trip, after fifty years, was one coincidence after another.

The next day we all had our next outing together, to go to Ellis Island. It took our breath away when Conner and Kylie turned their heads on the boat going to Ellis Island, and they were yelling and pointing at the Statue of Liberty, seeing it in person for their very first time! Conner was especially excited because he had just studied about the Statue of Liberty in his class at school. We took pictures of Conner and Kylie so they could show it to their teacher when they went back to school.

Another one of the highlights of this trip had to be when Deanna and I were standing on Broadway with Jacqui, Conner, and Kylie, in front of Radio City Music Hall waiting for the doors to open. I had bought both Kylie and Conner hot dogs from a street vendor, bringing a connection of my own memories to them! And most importantly for me... they loved the "dogs"!

Having Conner and Kylie with us on this trip to New York, and sharing so many of my personal memories with them, made everything particularly extraordinary for me. As young as they are, I believe Conner and Kylie will remember many of the experiences they had in New York, as well as some of the stories I shared with them about my life growing up in New York City, and the sights we showed them throughout "The City".

While Conner and I were at the St. Johns' game, Kylie, Jacqui and Dee were on 42ndstreet (a few hundred feet from where our old Malt Shop had stood) at the theater, watching Mary Poppins.

Kylie and Mary Poppins
enjoying New York City

Between the five of us, we did the City! Every minute we were taking in something; The NBA store, The Hershey Chocolate Factory, The M and M's store, Toys Are Us, and of course, the Official New York Yankee store!

It was time to split up as the grandkids and Jacqui headed to the airport. Dee and I then packed up, took the rental car out of storage, and made our way through the Lincoln Tunnel to visit my sister, Enid, in Doylestown, Pa.

It was great seeing Enid, her daughter, Meena, and Meena's husband, Jonathon with their two daughters, Nadia and Sonia. It was fun to reminisce and to know firsthand that all was well with Enid and her family. We all went to a great Japanese restaurant and shared stories and just enjoyed the rare opportunity of being together. It was very special visiting with my Pennsylvania family and traveling along turnpikes and interstates that I had been too young to drive on when I had lived in the East.

We left Enid and her family and drove to Philadelphia to drop off our rental car and to catch our flight back home. On the flight to Houston, all I could think of was the meaning of the "dash" (between birth and death) and the significance of this little chiseled mark between the dates of a person's life. The meaning of that dash was certainly very evident on this remarkable trip. It was so momentous, remembering each piece of the "puzzle" and more importantly appreciating the life: the dash - that represents over a half century of my life!

The Fifty year celebration of the National Championship 1963-2013

The University of Texas at Pan American selected the 2013 Homecoming as the time to celebrate important athletic events all in one night! Prior to the homecoming basketball game, the athletic department, headed by Chris King and under the watchful and caring eyes of the college President, Dr. Robert Nelsen, sponsored an event that brought the past and present together.

A tribute to Coach Sam Williams, who passed away on October 22, 2012, was a very emotional and meaningful gesture from the University to acknowledge his outstanding career. During a Pan American basketball game, Sam's picture was placed on a plaque and permanently placed on the gym wall. Coach Williams' son, David, placed his dad's championship blazer over the end chair where he had sat for seventeen years, compiling a record of 244-164.

See you tube video. http://www.youtube.com/watch?v= MisfFseFv8o

David Williams, Chris King, and
President Nelsen showing bronzed
plaque of Coach Williams.

A major sunset for our coach who was a "second father" to many of his players

UTPA Loses a Legend: Coach Sam Williams

A man considered a father figure and a true student of the game, Coach Sam Williams left a legacy unmatched for the UTPA Basketball program. Williams passed away on Oct. 22 at 88 years of age. Although the winningest coach in UTPA history, the NAIA Championship in 1963 was considered by Coach Sam his biggest achievement. He was also inducted into the Rio Grande Valley Sports Hall of Fame. UTPA Houston Chapter Alum, Marty Urand, a member of the '63 NAIA Championship team delivered a touching eulogy at a memorial service at the Kreidler Funeral Home in McAllen, TX. The Williams Family is asking that donations be made to the Sam Williams Endowed Scholarship Fund. To many, he'll always be "Coach."

At halftime, our championship team made it out to midcourt for our fifty-year recognition by students and faculty that had not even born yet! They exemplified their spirit and pride for their school as we took each step trying not to show our seventy-year-old aches and pains!

NOT RECOMMENDED FOR COLLEGE

February 17, 2013
"Oh what a night"

From left to right front row

<u>Chris King</u> - (Athletic Director), truly went out of his way to bring us in to showcase the improvements to the gym and to honor us.

<u>Big Jack</u> - was gracious during the fifty year recognition for all he achieved and accomplished for himself and the college while at Pan American College

<u>Mitchell ("Topper") Edwards</u> - came with five carloads of his family, to honor him as he was inducted into the Hall of Fame.

<u>Jim Board</u> - was all smiles as he presented the school, once again, with a check for $40k that he had collected with his fund raising activities.

Gordon Forester - our team manager, who did so much more for our team than many realize.

Second Row: From left to right in back row

Tony Dela Pena- A crowd favorite having taught biology for 37 years and graduating from UTPA.

Jim "Sweede" Harter – Was in shape and ready to go! Brought his 6'5" daughter (All-American volleyball player).

Jim McGurk – Had most of his six grandchildren in attendance along with his wife, Linda, who was a cheerleader during our historic event.

Paul ("Banty") Friddle – Left his ranch to come down and celebrate. Our Captain does not miss parties! A true leader...

Ramiro Villegas – Still tough as a boot after all these years. Never heard a bad word from him, a true friend to each of us...

Marty Urand –Proud to be along for the ride, and proud to be a part of this group of men.

Walter ("Trim") Yates – Delivered the opening blessings and introduced his cousin for induction into the Hall of Fame at the luncheon, held that same day. Trim recruited his cousin (Mitchell Edwards) who replaced him in the starting line-up!

<u>Dr. Robert Nelsen</u>,- University President — Always smiling with pride for Pan American College athletes.. *"Our best fan just happens to be our President!"*

<u>Tito Salanis</u> — The bus driver came to the event and somehow did not join us on the floor. I was sitting next to him prior to the game. His son came over and asked if there was anything that he could do for him. Tito thought for a minute and said, "I just wish I had my championship ring on, I must have left it on the dresser." His son did not wait for a second as he was off to the tiny town north of the campus, Red Gate. Before the tribute for coach began, Tito's son brought Tito's ring to him. Tito said, "I would have hated to watch the tribute to coach without my ring!"

Our Thanks to UTPA

*Our championship team, represented
by Jack and Trim, acknowledged
President Dr. Nelsen and Chris King,
the Athletic Director, for "bringing
the past to the present"*

Luke Jackson's jersey is retired
at Homecoming, 2013
"A Giant banner for a Giant of a man!"
http://www.youtube.com/watch?v=wyluVTUndhk

Over the years, many coaches had asked how our team had stayed so close together. We always stayed in contact with each other and knew about each other's highs and lows over the fifty years. With that came the proverbial question, which came first the chicken or the egg? This was referring to whether we were very close before the championship or did we become closer due to the championship.

I always felt like it was a moot point without the "Big Fella!"

MARTY URAND

The Old timers meet the new guns!

On Sunday, Coach Marks and his current team held a brunch for the two teams to meet and watch the video of the championship game of 1963. I am sure seeing the short shorts we used to wear, and the black and white footage didn't impress them too much. But the short vignettes of Luke playing for the Olympic Team and fighting Wilt Chamberlin for rebounds did!

The new 35 x 14 foot scoreboard was on fire as we watched the Philadelphia 76ers play in bigger than life figures! We sat in the gym at round tables with a mixture of teams eating barbeque and cutting up. It was a great idea by the coach, who has commented many times about the closeness of our team and how he would like to see his teams pick up these attributes.

Brunch with current team was a hit with the old and new players!

Big Jack sends a message to the current UTPA team, "Defend our House!"

With the brunch, closure was brought to the National NAIA Champions! With the hope of staying involved and financially supporting Broncs Athletics, we all left the gym for probably the final time that we will be together as a team!

So after 71 years, of which fifty-three were in Texas and eighteen in New York City, I came to the realization that basketball is not just a game but also a seed for life!

Marty Urand

urand@ymail.com

It's Over Time!!

By the time this book is published, I will be 71 years of age. With this publishing, I can honestly say that I reached an important goal in my life. I do have several other objectives or goals that I still would like to accomplish, other than staying healthy, and being with Deanna, watching our children's kids grow up!

I have now been living in Texas for fifty-three years. To think that a little game like basketball would be **the** thread throughout my entire life is hard to believe! It is especially interesting when talking with one of my dearest friends, Jack Watson. Jack shares with me his past that extends the roots of basketball to my modern outlook on the effects of a game that began with "Peach baskets!"

In an email addressed to me just after we attended the 2013 TAHPERD convention, I brought Jack a copy of the Sports Illustrated edition that focused on Kansas University. The article had a photo of Phog Allen and Wilt Chamberlain reaching up to the rim holding a basketball. The ball was touching the underside of the rim! The caption shared Coach Allen's goal of raising the basket do to the increased height of the players!

During one of our conversations regarding basketball, I asked about his earlier encounters with basketball at Kansas. He emailed me this information:

Dr. Jack Watson

About James Naismith:

I have been interested in his life ever since I met him in 1937. After high school in Canada, James Naismith attended college in Montreal, earning a B.S. in Physical Education in 1888. In 1890, he earned a diploma as a minister at Presbyterian College. He later served as a physical education instructor at McGill University, before going to the YMCA in Springfield, MA. James Naismith invented the game of basketball while in Springfield.

Dr. Naismith then went to Denver where he studied to be a medical doctor. He then moved to the University of Kansas in Lawrence, not to coach, but as a medical doctor and a chapel director.

He started a basketball program and became the coach at KU. As a coach he did not have winning teams but soon became the athletic director.

It was about 1937, when I met Dr. Naismith and Forrest C. Phog Allen. My coach in Topeka, Kansas, where I lived, took two or three of his players to Lawrence to see the Kansas Relays, a big track and field carnival at the time. We were standing right down by the track while we waited for our events to begin. There were few people around when we saw two men, Dr. Naismith and Phog Allen, coming toward us on the track. They stopped and visited a few minutes, we shook hands, and they moved on.

Phog Allen had played on Naismith's teams and he became a premier coach among college coaches in the United States. Dr. Naismith died in 1939, and was buried in Lawrence. Meeting both of them was quite exciting, especially when I learned Naismith had actually invented the game of basketball.

*****

Dr. Jack Watson is a wealth of knowledge at the age of ninety, and he still has a keen memory. His twinkling blue eyes through his bifocals spiced each of his reflective stories!

MARTY URAND

"Chalk Talk" by Karen Fitzgerald
My life through my good
friend Karen's eyes

By most odds, this story would never have been told because my life would have been so much different. Thinking back on my growing up days in New York, the odds were stacked against me. Take a kid like me, who moves frequently with his family from home to home and school to school. Add the fact that reading didn't come easily to me and that I often struggled in school in the academic areas, and it makes one wonder . . . what is it about me and my influences that helped create such a wonderful ending to this life full of both good and bad experiences?

Was it tenacity, strength, personality, ambition, stubbornness, or was it my stick-to-it attitude, luck and other influences, or what? How is it that many others raised in the same circumstances did not succeed where I did? What would my life have been like if I still lived in Brooklyn and experienced a middle-class more street-like existence there? I probably would have married a neighborhood girl, hung out with my high school athletic friends, played on local sports teams, and worked at a blue-collar job, which is fine. But would I have grown and achieved and received so many benefits as I have here, in Texas. I probably would have raised average kids and lived an average life, which is fine for some, but I always knew I wanted more, especially once I went to Texas and began college, and realized how many avenues were available.

Looking back to 1961, my life changed drastically back in 1961 when I made the *huge* decision to go play basketball at a small college in Texas. What an opportunity I had been given! People believed in me! They respected me, valued me, and knew that I could contribute my many talents to the world. Many young men would have turned down that offer to leave New York, the only place I had lived, and go far, far away to the Rio Grande Valley in Texas. You know I knew that the opportunity had many scary "if's" and "whatever's" tagging along with it. However, my strength, my optimism, and my sense of adventure, led me to choose the path less taken by others. Never one to have *moss grow beneath my feet,* I leaped into a life of the unknown, leaving family and friends behind. I must have known that my close relationship with my father, mother, and sisters would never be the same. You never really can go home again once you leave the state for college and/or a new life! And this was my opportunity to create a totally new life where no one knew me, no one understood the struggles that I had been through, and where hopefully everyone could like me for my friendly personality, my ambition, and my funny jokes.

MARTY URAND

Yes, this is my incredible story of life between the "dashes"... the story of my life to date. I like to think of it as a story about the fine line between being a leader and being chased ... by education. How grateful I am for those loving, compassionate people who really cared about me along the way. I also am thankful to my parents and family who allowed me to go to Texas. How nice it was to have their support rather than to run away to Texas without it.

America is a land of many opportunities, and I have taken advantage of many of these opportunities. Over the years, I always believed in myself. That is key to my story. I was never a quitter and always liked to take the high road when others chose not to do so. From my parents I learned love, humor, life experiences, and ambition, among other important lessons.

The other significant adults in my life taught me the value of hard work and perseverance. These were the school custodians, the NYPD, a college professor, a world famous singer, and my coaches, where I learned to always work to become better, to believe in myself and the strengths that I have to offer this world. How fortunate I have been. Without the village of family and friends, who always supported me, where would I be today? I'd probably be sitting out on my stoop in Brooklyn in my t-shirt, and sippin' a tall one. "God only knows!" I am a lucky, lucky man. And life is good down here in Texas!

The Final Shot Chart

BIOGRAPHICAL DATA
MARTIN A. URAND

Present Position:
- Adjunct Faculty at San Jacinto College (8 years)
- Adjunct Faculty Lonestar College-Kingwood (6 years)

Years in Present Position: 10 years

Years in Profession: 50 years

Academic Preparation:

B.S., Pan American University, 1965.

M.Ed., Sam Houston State University, 1967.

Post Graduate, University of Houston, 1980

Previous Experience:

❖ Edinburg High School - Physical Education Teacher (1965-66)
❖ Sam Houston State – Assistant Basketball Coach Teaching Assistant (1966-67)
❖ Pan American University Associate Professor – Assist. Basketball Coach (67-74)

- ❖ University of Houston -Teaching Assistant – (1974-76)
- ❖ Houston ISD -Elementary Physical Education Teacher – (1976-80)
- ❖ Katy ISD - Elementary Physical Education Teacher – (1980-84)
- ❖ Spring Branch ISD Director of Health and Physical Ed. (1984-94)
- ❖ Texas Education Agency – Program Director for Health & Physical Education, - (1994-99)
- ❖ Southwest Texas State University –Adjunct Professor (1995-97) (San Marcus, Texas)
- ❖ Spring Branch ISD – Director of Health and Physical Education - (1999-04)
- ❖ University of Houston –Adjunct Professor (2000-06)
- ❖ Houston Baptist University – Adjunct Professor (2005-08)

Professional Activities:

- ❖ Chairperson for Elementary Physical Education Section TAHPERD, 1978
- ❖ Chairperson for Gymnastic Section of TAHPERD, 1982
- ❖ Chairperson for Professional Education Section of TAHPERD, 1985
- ❖ State TAHPERD PEPI Coordinator, 1981, and 1982
- ❖ Originated the PEPI Games – TAHPERD -1984
- ❖ Region IV Repetitive - (TAHPERD), 1986, Foundation Scholarship Committee – TAHPERD, 1988
- ❖ TAHPERD Board of Directors - 1986

- ❖ Committee on Teacher Evaluation –TAHPERD, 1981
- ❖ Chairperson for the American Heart Association School, Task Force (Houston Affiliate), 1985
- ❖ Chairperson for the American Cancer Society – Coordinated School Health, 2002
- ❖ Vice President of TAHPERD (Physical Education Division) 1990
- ❖ Member of the United States Olympic Committee (Educational), 1984
- ❖ Executive Director for the Governor's Commission on Fitness, 1993.
- ❖ Board Member American Cancer Society, 2000
- ❖ President-Elect, TAHPERD 2001
- ❖ President, TAHPERD, 2002
- ❖ Past President, TAHPERD 2003
- ❖ University of Texas at Pan American Alumni Board member (Vice President)

Grants/Projects

- ❖ Spring Branch ISD – PEP Grant – (2001-02) $1.2Million
- ❖ Spring Branch ISD – Bicycle Grant – (2001 – 2004) $3,500
- ❖ Spring Branch ISD – Memorial Herman Hospital (2000-04) $37,000
- ❖ Spring Branch ISD – Elementary Gymnasiums (2001-08) $20.4Million
- ❖ TAHPERD Convention – Pulse Heart Rate Monitors (2002) $15,000
- ❖ Spring Branch ISD – Wellness Centers /Bally's Fitness Center $62,000

Professional Achievements

- ❖ Texas Education Agency Demonstration School – Ashford Elementary, 1977AAHPERD National convention, Houston -School Tour Program, 1976
- ❖ Texas Education Agency Demonstration School – West Memorial Elem., 1980
- ❖ TAHPERD State Pepi Award, 1976
- ❖ TAHPERD Honor Award, 1990
- ❖ The "Marty Urand" New Teacher of the Year Award, Spring Branch ISD, 2008
- ❖ Adjunct teacher of the year, 2013, Lonestar College - Kingwood

Publications and Presentations: (Books)

- ❖ *"The Three Domains of Physical Education"*, Mel Finkenburg, and Urand, Self-Published, Houston, 1976
- ❖ *"Not Recommended for College"*, Xilibrus Publishing Company, 2015
- ❖ "Health is in your Hands" – McGraw-Hill Publishing Co., 2006 Ancillary material for Physical Education Adoption, (2006).

Publications: (Articles)

- ❖ TTAS, TAHPERD Journal, winter, 1988.
- ❖ Building Confidence through Play", Kindergarten Teachers of Texas Journal, 1989.

- ❖ "Education through The Physical", Kindergarten Teachers of Texas Journal, 1988.
- ❖ "The Fitness Contest": Generating Data, Great Activities Publishing Co., 1988
- ❖ TAHPERD Journal, TEA Corner, Yearly column 1996-1999.

Presentations: (Visual/Video)

- ❖ The All-American Health Fitness Class. Inter-Act
- ❖ Television, A monthly telecast to 56 school districts in Region IV, 1987-1990
- ❖ TI-IN Network, "Coaches Corner", Broadcast to 36 States. Three broadcasts over two years, 1989-1990
- ❖ TI-IN Network, "Health Related Fitness", 1987

Presentations:(Video Releases)

- ❖ "The Young and The Breathless", Channel 13, 1987.
- ❖ "A Changing Attitude toward Physical Education", NBC, Television National distribution Network 1990.

MARTY URAND

Presentations: (Over 250 presentations, nationally)

- ❖ 80 School districts in Texas
- ❖ 20 Educational Service Centers in Texas
- ❖ 9 States(FL., WY, RI, LA, OK, NY, NM, Mass, & TX)
- ❖ 3 Keynote Speeches (AAHPERD)
- ❖ 44 Colleges and Universities in Texas
- ❖ 6 Colleges and Universities outside of Texas
- ❖ 3 National Student Conferences

Date	Year	Elem	Secondary	District
December	1965	✓		TAHPERD Convention
December	1966	✓		TAHPERD Convention
December	1967			TAHPERD Convention
July	1984	✓	✓	TAHPERD Summer Conf. Houston
August	1985	✓	✓	Ft. Myers ISD, FLA.
August	1985	✓	✓	Florida State Conf. -
December	1985	✓	✓	TAHPERD Convention
July	1985	✓	✓	TAHPERD Summer Conf.
December	1986	✓	✓	TAHPERD Convention
		✓	✓	
October	1990			State Board of Education
January	1991	Principals		TEA Winter Conference
April	1990			State Board of Education
October	1992	✓		TEA State Convention
January	1992	Principals		TEA Winter Conference
February	1992	Principals/Teachers		Texas Secondary Demo Program
November	1993	✓		American Cancer Society
October	1993			TEA State Convention
November	1993	Tx. Sec. Demo Program		Aldine ISD

January	1993	Tx. Sec. Demo Program			San Antonio ISD
September	1997	✓		✓	Irving ISD
December	1998	✓		✓	TAHPERD Convention
January	1997	✓		✓	Pasadena ISD
January	1999			✓	San Antonio ISD
January	1999	✓		✓	American Cancer Society
March	1999	Students			Univ. of Texas – Pan American
September	1999	✓		✓	Cypress Fairbanks (HOPE)
August	1999	✓		✓	McAllen ISD
August	1999	✓		✓	Pharr San Juan Alamo ISD
		✓		✓	
September	2000	✓		✓	Del Rio ISD
September	2000	Students			Youth Summit Conf., ACS /UH
January	2000				ESC 19 (El Paso)
January	2000	Students			Yeslita ISD Yeslita ISD
September	2001	✓		✓	Plano ISD
September	2001	Students			University of Texas – El Paso
October	2001	Students			OAHPERD Student Conf. Okla. City
October	2001	Community			Rotary Club –Spring Branch
November	2001	Students			Stephen F. Austin University
December	2001	✓		✓	TAHPERD Convention
December	2001	Community			Rotary Club – Pasadena, TX
January	2001	✓		✓	ESC 1 (Edinburg)
January	2001	✓		✓	Victoria ESC 3
January	2001	✓		✓	San Antonio ISD
January	2001	✓		✓	University Texas Pan American
February	2001	Students			University of Texas Arlington
February	2001	✓		✓	ESC 10 (Dallas)
February	2001				Brownsville ISD

Month	Year			Location
March	2001	Students		East Texas State – Commerce
April	2001	✓		Dallas ISD
May	2001	Students		Lamar University
June	2001	Students		Texas Christian University
August	2001	✓	✓	ESC 15- San Angelo
August	2001		✓	Brownsville ISD
January	2002	✓	✓	ESC 19 – El Paso
January	2002	✓	✓	Ft. Worth ISD
January	2002	Students		Texas Wesleyan University
February	2002	✓	✓	ESC 10 – Dallas
June	2002	✓		Irving ISD
November	2002	Students		LAHPERD Student Conf. – LA
October	2002	Students		Texas Christian University
June	2003	✓	✓	McAllen ISD
October	2003	✓	✓	Oklahoma HPERD Convention
October	2003	✓	✓	Lubbock ISD
January	2003	✓	✓	Houston ISD – Winter Conference
February	2003	Students		Lamar University
August	2004	✓	✓	Brownsville ISD
August	2004	✓	✓	Pearland ISD
September	2004	✓	✓	Texas A&M Commerce
September	2004	✓	✓	Dallas ISD
September	2004	✓	✓	Metroplex
September	2004	✓		Pasadena ISD
September	2004	✓		Sinclair Elementary, HISD
September	2004	✓		Goose Creek ISD
October	2004	✓	✓	Corpus Christi
October	2004		✓	Beaumont ISD (Secondary)
November	2004	✓	✓	Silsbee ISD
December	2004	✓	✓	TAHPERD Convention

Month	Year			Location
February	2004	✓	✓	Spring ISD
February	2004	✓	✓	Houston ISD
September	2004	✓	✓	Texas A&M Commerce
September	2004	✓	✓	Dallas ISD
September	2004	✓		Pasadena ISD
September	2004	✓		Goose Creek ISD
October	2004	✓	✓	Corpus Christi
October	2004		✓	Beaumont ISD (Secondary)
November	2004	✓	✓	Silsbee ISD
November	2004	✓	✓	Alief ISD
April	2005	✓	✓	Providence, RI
June	2005	✓	✓	ESC 10 (Dallas)
June	2005	✓	✓	ESC 11 (Ft. Worth)
August	2005		✓	Brownsville ISD
January	2005	✓	✓	ESC 4 (Houston)
January	2005	✓		Wichita Falls
January	2005	✓	✓	ESC 10 (Dallas)
January	2005	✓	✓	Laredo ISD
January	2005	✓	✓	Edinburg ISD
January	2005	✓	✓	Brazosport ISD
February	2005	✓	✓	Houston ISD
February	2003	✓	✓	Wyoming AHPERD
January	2005	✓	✓	Edinburg ISD
January	2005	✓	✓	North Forest ISD
February	2005	✓	✓	Houston ISD
April	2005	✓	✓	Providence, RI
June	2005	✓	✓	ESC 10 (Dallas)
June	2005	✓	✓	ESC 11 (Ft. Worth)
January	2006	✓	✓	ESC 4 (Houston)
January	2006	✓	✓	Pearland
March	2006	✓	✓	Providence, RI
April	2006	✓	✓	Providence, RI
June	2006	✓	✓	Providence, RI
August	2006	✓	✓	Alvin ISD
August	2006		✓	Lamar CISD

Month	Year			Location
August	2006		✓	San Benito ISD
August	2006	✓	✓	Providence, RI
January	2007	✓	✓	Angleton ISD
January	2007	✓	✓	ESC 19 (El Paso)
January	2007		✓	Lamar CISD
September	2008	✓		Ft. Bend ISD
September	2009		✓	Ft. Bend ISD
			✓	
June	2011	Students		University of Houston
November	2011	Faculty		Kingwood College - Kingwood

Athletic Career:

Basketball Player:

❖ Lafayette High School,(2 Years) Brooklyn, New York Co-Captain, 1960
❖ Pan American College, (4 years) Edinburg, Texas

- Most Improved player, 1962
- All-Tournament, Edinburg, Texas, 1963
- All-Tournament, Quincy, Illinois, 1964
- Co-Captain, 1964
- N.A.I.A National Championship-1963
- N.A.I.A. Runner-Up—1964
- Hall of Fame (Team) at UTPA, 2007

Baseball Player:

- Little League—Queens, New York
- High School—St. Francis De Chantel Church, Brooklyn, N.Y.
- University of Texas at Pan American—1961-63

Basketball Coaching:

- Edinburg High School, JV, 19-1
- East-West High School Basketball, (East Coach) N.Y.C., 1967
- Sam Houston State University—Graduate Assistant, 1967
- University of Texas at Pan American, Assistant, 1967-1972
- YMCA, 2009 and 2010
- AAU, Assistant coach, Runner-up team at Nationals in San Antonio, Texas, 2014

Gymnastic Coaching:

- Ashford Elementary, Dual workout with Russian Team (Astrodome, 1975)
- Owner and Head Coach of Katy Kips Gymnastic Club, Katy, Tx, 1980-1993
- State Team Championship (9-11, 12-13, and 15 and over) Dallas, 1982
- State Team Championship (9-11, 12-13 and Overall) San Antonio, 1983
- State Team Championship, (Overall) Corpus Christi, 1985
- Greater Houston Gymnastic Association City Championship, (1982, 1983, 1984, 1987, 1988, 1989, 1990)

Swimming Coach—(Summer League)

- Memorial Parkway, (Head Coach)1979-1981
- Cimarron Parkway, 1981—(Head Coach) 1985, 1982, 1983 *Championship* 1983, 1982, 1983
- Williamsburg Settlement, (Head Coach) 1986-1988
- Royal Oaks, 1995—(Head Coach)1998
- Spring Board, 2000-2005, (Head Coach) *Championship* 2000, 2001, 2005
- Swimming Lessons, Cypress Fairbanks, 2004-2014

Other Sports:

- Intramural Racquetball singles Championship, University of Houston, 1979

Other highlights

Lonestar College – Kingwood
Teaching Excellence Award
January 13, 2013

Adjunct instructors:

Douglass Maraffa, Claudine Simpson, Martin Urand, and Gwen McCormic received the Adjunct Excellence Award during in-service.

Kid Fit—May 5, 2011
"Under Construction"

My life has been devoted to touching the
lives of children,
and in the process, my life
has been touched!

"Another generation that
will fall in love with Coach U"
(Brandi Lani, Ashford Elementary School, 1975)

Swim Graduation (August 2014)
"We were sunk without you!"

Thanks
Briana Tesch and Dawn Lito
(Parents of your youngest swimmers)

2-15-12

Good Morning Marty,

Congratulations. You have been nominated for both the *Brace Award* and the Scholar Award, however you can only apply for one Award. I ask that you please look over the Awards and let me know which one that you would like to apply for, by 2-20-12.

Thank you,
Congratulations again!

Becky

I truly thank God for not surrounding my life with professionals who could have over-looked my potential, my worth, and my love for children.

Promoting Healthy Lifestyles

Dedicated

To those people who have empowered me through their wisdom, education, and sorrow!

Coach Sam Williams
Basketball Coach
1924 - 2012

Jeffrey Scott Urand
1956 – 1960

It is often hard to distinguish between the hard knocks in life and those of opportunity.

—Frederick Phillips

Dedicated To
University of Texas
UTPA

(previously known as Pan Amercan College)

This school, changed my life forever, and it has certainly been a blessing for my family and me. Finding the words to describe an ending down such a rocky road will always be a mystery to me.

But somewhere between gratefulness and power in its purest form, is where UTPA will be in my heart until my "Sunset.

Marty Urand 2014

In Appreciation

I would like to thank those who have assisted me in editing during the seven years of my procrastination on this book as I second guessed what I wanted my grandchildren, wife, daughters, and the so many other children who I have taught know about me:

- ❖ My wife Deanna-Hours of editing
- ❖ Dr. Joel Bloom – Lifelong friend, wrote the "Back cover"
- ❖ My friend Karen Fitzgerald (including her "Chalktalk" addition)
- ❖ My daughters Marti and Jacqui
- ❖ My brother In-law, Charlie Powell
- ❖ My sister in-law, Jackie Nicolls
- ❖ My friend, Jack Shanks
- ❖ My friend, Jerry "Cherokee" Stein (Wrote an addition to camp)
- ❖ Dr. Jack Watson Career segments

It was just a little bittie piss ant game of basketball! (1961-2014)

The Urand Family

From Left to right :*Deanna Urand, Casey Johnson, Conner Weigman, Gaven Frasso, Drew Frasso, Jenna Steele, Kylie Weigman, Sonja Hendrexson, Dominic Frasso, Hanna Frasso, Nadia Hendrixson, Enid Dershon, Kyle Frasso, Billy Whitmire, and Marty Urand,*

Bottom:*Ilene Frasso.*

Missing: *Jacqui & Chad Weigman, Danielle Steele, Marti Johnson, Alex & Gene Johnson, Meena and Jonathan Hendrixson, Chris & Sara Frasso.*

The game of basketball was the avenue that paved my way to Texas from New York City. As a result, thirteen lives blossomed and filled the hearts of my sisters, daughters and me.

The sorrow of my brother's death fifty-four years ago still seems like it was just yesterday. Somehow, the laughter and joy that resonates in each of our family's homes would not be possible without the memory of Jeffrey Scott!

Married forty-nine years, and all it took was understanding from a wonderful woman with a heart as big as TEXAS!

MARTY URAND

"It has been said, 'time heals all wounds.' I do not agree. The wounds remain. In time, the mind, protecting its sanity, covers them with scar tissue and the pain lessens. But it is never gone."
— Rose Kennedy

The "Dash"

1943   -

In My Life

*My path during my seventy-one year
adventure has been filled with
wonderful people!*

*Many of whom, will never accept the
fact that they molded my
life!*

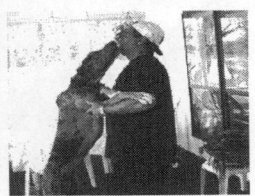

Abbie (2000-2014)

Conner robs another HR

Casey at Rockets game   Gene & Marti "Kentucky Derby"

Alex, Marti, and Gene Johnson

Marti behind the scenes

Beautiful Kylie

Marti, Casy, Alex, & Gene Johnson

Chad and Jacqui Weigman

Kylie, Alex, & Conner

Conner searching for a hole

UNIVERSITY OF TEXAS AT PAN AMERICAN

UTPA Athletics Announces Pan American Athletic Club

Houston Alumni

tos

ıl Trejo

Mel, Trim, and T

Gordon, Banty, daughter, and Tony

Conner and Otto

JB, Chris King (AD), Me

TEXAS ASSOCIATION OF HEALTH, PHYSICAL EDUCATION, RECREATION, AND DANCE

PRESIDENTS 2013

Tips from Marcella before the General Assembly   Presenting Dr. Jack Watson with the Honor Award

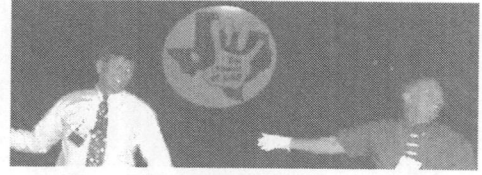

Rich Almstedt leading the audience in "Fits like a hand in a glove"

S P R I N G   B R A N C H   I S D

Elem. Track meet, Gavin, Beth, AD, Jon & Rod

Happiness was attending our State Convention!!

Sara Ruffing

E.C. "Pop" Snapp

Assessment "A+"

We Treasure What We Measure!

Tom Hubble and Dr. Joel Bloom

Dave Roberts AHA Award

Dr. Jack Christie and Karen Fitzpatrick

Our fun loving group of award winning teachers!

AAHPERD Convention in Philly, PA

Dawn Lawrenz

My Replacement Rebecca Fuchs

Cherrie Ziese and Cathy Warren

Karen

Northbook Middle Staff
Rod

Kathy

Frank Beard (Drummer ZZ Top) & Debbie Moore

Judy K. and Margaret

Retirement party, Maryanne, Anne Daily, Karen Fitzgerald
Helen Wehring, and Barbara Cofer

Beth, Jody, and Kro

Me, and Connie

Sylvia, Scott, Lisa, Me, Maureen, and Joy

Linda, Maureen, Kay, & Joan
Tom, Terry, Sam

Kathie and Janet

Sally and Jackie

Phillip, Joyce, and Pat Schraub

T E X A S

The Tourneur Family & Mom

Jackie Goad and daughter Barbara Cofer

The Pruitt/Tacconelly Family

Katy Kips team in San Antonio (1982)

Debbie, Suzanne, Siena, Me, & Peggy

Garland, Ginny, Dee & Me

NEW YORK @ Heart

Jon Cianguilli, Larry Yellen and wife

Son and Dad Spencer, & Jaci

Cousin Mark, Me, and Cousin Ira

Cousin Delly, Ruthie, Jacqui & Con, Ky

The Family meets my bride (1965)

P O W E L L S

Jackie, Nell, & Deanna

Lt. Colonel C. Powell & wife Nell

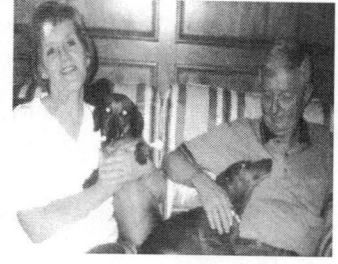

The Powells, Nicolls, Smiths, & Urands

Jackie and Tim Nicolls

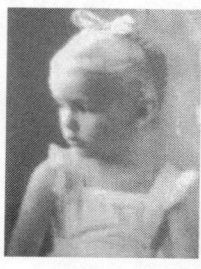

Mike (Tim), Priscilla, Jackie, & Mariah

Dee at 4 years old   Charles & Dee

Amy Nicolls

Troy and Tim (Mike's sons)

Charlie and Deanna (Wedding Jan. 2015)

SISTER ILENE FRASSO

Oh Dave...

Ilene with Jenna

Dave, Ilene, Me, & Enid

Chris, Dominick, & Sara Frasso

Jenna, Danielle, and William Steele

The Frasso Family

Chis & Dominic

SISTER ENID DERSHIN

Enid Dershon

Enid, Delly, Daughter Meena & Nadia

Enid & Meena 80's

Sonia

The Hendrixson Family

Nadia

Grandpa Andy, Nadia & Sonia

Nadia, Meena, & Sonia

Enid & Granddaughters